Ownership Section: ⬡DDC

Name:
....

Title:
....

Address:
....

List all prizes, medals, awards: List all shortcomings, felonies, etc:
....
....
....
....

Expectations Checklist:
This book should/might/better:

☐ Blow me away.   ☐ Be really orange.   ☐ Remind me that life is
☐ Change my life.   ☐ Defy expectations.   weird as shit and we are
☐ Rearrange my career.   ☐ Collect dust on a shelf.   staggeringly insignificant
☐ Make me happy.   ☐ Be loaded with logos.   in our tiny speck within
☐ Make me sad.   ☐ Get kinda weird.   the theoretically infinite
☐ Make me freak out.   ☐ Raise blood pressure.   universe at large. Really.

(Please check all that apply.)

Signature Zone:

DDC Representative:	Year No.
	....

Recipient Analysis:

☐ A buddy from way back.   ☐ Keep up the good fight.   ☐ Fidgeting needlessly.
☐ Our new friend.   ☐ Good to see you.   ☐ Really eyeballing me.
☐ Big smile.   ☐ Thanks for buying this.   ☐ Work release.
☐ Sweating profusely.   ☐ Big ol' golden buzz.   ☐ The break in our wind.
☐ Wild eyes.   ☐ No chance in hell.   ☐ Owes the DDC loot.
☐ Challenging face.   ☐ Young, wild & radical.   ☐ Glad you are still alive.

(Please check all that apply.)

DO NOT LOSE THIS BOOK.

When disposing of this book, please do so in dramatic fashion. Whipping against a brick wall is a good
start to loosen the binding up. Launch it off a cliff. Burn it. Back over it a couple times. Let it soak
in a bathtub overnight and take the pulp and make your own goddamn book. Digest it. Throw into air
and place face directly underneath, and hold tight until impact. Long-lasting results. Fun for all.

Draplin Design Co., North America   Publishing Div.

DDC

Draplin
Design Co.

Pretty Much
Everything

Aaron James
Draplin

File Under:
So Here's The Deal

001

Draplin Design Co.

Pretty Much Everything

Aaron James Draplin

Abrams, New York

Table of Contents

DDC

Draplin
Design Co.

Pretty Much
Everything

Aaron James
Draplin

File Under:
Start Your Engines

002
003

Didn't Think It Would Come to This

I didn't get into this stuff with the goal of making a book. I just wanted to make a life in art. And typing this, it hits me—*I did it.*

Early Influences

My cousin Tom Draplin is the first person I looked up to in the art world. He had the cool sketchbooks and colored pencils and was a natural artist. I remember seeing bits of drawings and illustration from his time at Parsons in New York City. Tom was also the first person who inspired me to hit the road. Tom made it out of Detroit to the big leagues of art school, and that was always something I'd think about when weighing my options as graduation from high school neared.

I first learned about Charles S. Anderson at Northwestern Michigan College, from a French Paper poster promotion floating around the design studio. It was in a big pile of paper promos being kicked around, and somehow it ended up in my little cubicle. I studied that thing ferociously. His work was an incredible mix of type, illustration and wit. Which led me to the mighty CSA Archive in Minneapolis. I was hooked right away. There was an appreciation for the past, and yet it all felt fresh, considered and respectful. Chuck will always be my design hero, and I'm proud to consider him a friend and mentor. We've slayed some pretty serious pork chops over dinner in Minneapolis!

In the fall of 1997, I did my very first East Coast road trip. Starting from my parents' home in Michigan, I went all the way to Portland, Maine. Then to Boston, New York, Philly, and all the way down to the doorstep of House Industries in Wilmington, Delaware. I loved their beautiful design, detailed typography and sense of humor. I knocked on the door and a confused Andy Cruz answered. "My name's Aaron Draplin. I'm here to buy some fonts." He was a bit startled but let me in. They gave me the full tour and loaded me up with so much cool shit. They didn't have to accommodate my nerdy curiosity that afternoon, but still made time for me. And in turn made a lifetime fan with that little moment of spontaneous hospitality.

A Company, But Not A Company

When I got going in the mid-'90s, the design world was at the height of the post-post-postmodern design craze, with the wild forms, damaged text and provocative boundary pushing. All the companies sounded technological, dizzying and cold. I liked the idea of using my name in my "thing." And yet, you'd meet a couple turds who were a "company" and they'd act the part. With all the pomp, plural-speak and lofty aspirations. And I set out to poke fun at that shit, and it stuck. Speaking in third person, and yet, the whole time, it's just little ol' me. That was funny to me when I had nothing, and still is, with a shop filled with equipment and treasures. I guess it was a reaction to designers who took themselves a little too seriously. So why not blow it out of the water, right? So I did. The "we" and "us" of the Draplin Design Co. was just me. This whole time. Secret's out! I call my shop a "shop." Just like my dad did. Not a "studio." Not a "space." Not a "multidisciplinary, form-challenging, content-resuscitating, image-recontextualizing, language-defetishizing firm/studio/collective/fart chamber" a couple wheezebag Yale grad student pricks are starting. Anything but that bullshit.

Blue Collar? In Spirit, at Least

I always squirm when interviewers or fans ask me about the "blue collar" quality of my work and way of doing business. Let's get something very, very straight: This is a white collar profession. And, can be embarrassingly pretentious. Could I apply some of the simple, hardworking values I'd been around growing up to this stuff? Hell yes. Art school teaches you to elevate. Sometimes, a little too high. I was careful to learn as much as I could, and still be able to shoot the shit with the guys at the scrap metal yard. It's a badge of honor that I got myself out of the economic ruts I'd find myself in. I've had a factory job pushing thousand pound tool and die molds around. I've trimmed trees with roughnecks. I've washed dishes for five months at a stretch in Alaska. I used design to get me out of that shit—plain and simple. Design is a trade to me. Artist? I guess? Tradesman? Closer. Hard worker? Always, always, always.

Took it on the Chin Just Enough Times

There were some stinging moments along the way. I've had my heart broken a handful of times. Be it snowboard graphics that fell through, gigs applied for and handed to folks who didn't give a shit or a logo job promised and then complete silence. I've had things taken away. At the start, middle and end of jobs. And I'll never forget that feeling. It taught me to buckle down, savor the jobs I had and never, ever half-ass this stuff.

Six, Seven, Eight Trick Pony?

In twenty years, I've seen some pretty fun tricks come and go. When I started, it was all that post-post-post-modern bullshit. Then some kind of techno thing. Then it was being ironic. Then it was "snipped corner" thing. Then fuckin' antlers. Then everyone became a Supply Co. of some sort.

Don't forget the Great Ampersand Epidemic of the early 2010s! I get a lot of flak for "retro stylings" in my work. I like things that work. Things that are time-tested. Free of superfluous elements. The grid. I like simplicity. Straightforward solutions. I've tried to develop consistent styles to work in, but pride myself on being able to deliver what's approporate for the client. And that always isn't Futura Bold dipped in Pantone Orange 021.

Busy Being Busy

Man, I've been busy. This stuff still doesn't feel like a "job?" I like being in the shop. It's where I am the most comfortable and can maintain a big 'ol golden buzz of productivity. At my pace. And I've used all the hours, weeks, months and years to fight hard to make something out of this stuff. But I know that has a flipside and I missed some special things around me. Allow me to take this opportunity to apologize to my Mom, sisters and Leigh for always being busy, frazzled and all-consumed with this shit. But shit, I had to go for it.

Did it as Creatively as Possible

I'm proud of the effort I've put into my career. I can proudly say that I gave my all to this stuff. The whole fuckin' time. It's a sickness, sort of. I just won't let myself phone something in. I'm always afraid it'll be some lazy little decision that is the lynch pin that get pulled, and then we go whirling off the rails. I've worked my ass off in graphic design. And took advantage of the creative space it allows. I did things as creatively as I could. With humor, a little wit and was always careful not to take myself too seriously. What a privilege to operate within such a cool trade.

My Proudest Paragraphs to Date

I tried to build a life in design my own way. Can you make a career out of something on your own terms? I think you can. And yet, I still fear this stuff. That was pounded into me from a young age: No matter how good things seem to be, it's up to you to keep it all going. I'm always freaked when I take my eye off the ball. Which is irrational. My little thing has momentum, and I know it'll keep chugging along. But then again, a little part of me feels so insanely entitled to write that out, and will never take my teeny nugget of success for granted.

I made this stuff my life. When something is your hobby first, the "work" part never feels the same. I love making this stuff. And I'm hoping that'll never change. I've been lucky to pull off a killer little life in design. Let this goddamn book be proof! Facts are stubborn things.

DDC

Draplin
Design Co.

Pretty Much
Everything

Aaron James
Draplin

File Under:
Beating The Odds

004
005

Questionable Words From Questionable People

Thomas Draplin, Artist & Influential Cousin
It is an impressive thing to trust in yourself, what you love, the people who love you and to follow where your heart leads you, passionately. Aaron is that example of staying true to who you are. I find his honest, practical, down-to-earth creativity infectious. The hard-working generous, little shit done good, and I'm proud. Its been amazing to see the sparks of joy that kid had with a simple magic marker and how it has lead to a truly amazing life and career. I'm inspired.

Eric Campbell, Graphic Designer
The English language prefix pro- is one I have always admired. It means "forward." It also means "for." As in, one that stands for something. And it happens to be the perfect prefix to describe Aaron James Draplin. When we were young skateboarders and snowboarders coming up, we lived by the word "progression." We were always pushing forward, trying hard to first land, and then master, new tricks. Aaron was always on board for progression. In high school, he created, branded and profited from selling the "Draplid," an embroidered knit hat that cleverly featured the root of his last name—an emerging self-promoter. As we grew up, we became professionals in our respective fields, putting "forth" our knowledge and advanced skills to the public. And certainly no one disputes this man's proficiency. But the pro that may best describe Aaron was palpable at a recent gallery exhibit, as I stood ogling at the staggering amount of his work hung before me. The guy is prolific! Probably to a greater degree than anyone currently in the graphic arts. Need proof, just thumb through this book. As a lifelong friend and fellow designer, it's been surreal seeing Aaron's meteoric rise. You could chalk it up to his talent, charm, humor and his firm handshake. But, most of all, it is Aaron's straight-up hard work that has propelled him to cosmic success. He's a hard-working, good human, and that's something we can all stand for.

Cameron Barrett, Blog Pioneer
I've known Aaron since we were both teenagers and attending the local vocational school. When the Internet blew up in the late '90s, I dragged him kicking and screaming onto it, where, as with anything Aaron does, he mastered it. I am Aaron's voice of reason, his online muse, his brother from another mother. I taught him that backups are sacred, replying to e-mail is important and to always bet on the underdog. The best part about Aaron is that he is a friend to everyone, no matter the sordid past, vices, gambling problems, messed-up family or whatever poisons ail you. If you let him, Aaron will love you, give you guidance and nudge you in the direction you need to go. If the graphic design industry had a superhero, Aaron would be it, amazing powers and all.

Mark Phillips, Master Junker
Aaron Draplin is the cog that keeps the modern vector graphic machine cranking out lean, mean quality. Fueled by Coca-Cola and a spite for garbage strip-mall signage, Aaron pays homage to the kind of traditionalism that holds the weight of an anvil. As of this printing, Aaron has been bumped by Sinbad on Marc Maron's *WTF* podcast.

Jay Floyd, Graphic Designer
I met Aaron in 1994 in Bend, Oregon. He was driving the wrong way down a one-way street. I called him an idiot, he told me to fuck off. We've been friends ever since. In those Bend days, he bought a Power Computing Mac clone and kicked its ass relentlessly. Without any formal education at the time, he churned out graphic after graphic—always simple, always powerful, always unapologetic. Since then, I've scratched my head wondering how he's bamboozled the masses into listening to his stories, buying his trinkets and useless junk—and going nuts over his miniature books of paper. Well, all you gotta do is meet the man to understand any of it. He's larger than life, insanely talented and full of piss and vinegar, but most important, he's the real deal and I've always been proud to call the son of a bitch a friend.

Chris Coyle, Red Fang Tour Manager
When I think of Aaron James Draplin, two words come to mind: "bold" and "thick." Not only do they describe the work coming off the Factory Floor, but also the man himself. Aaron doesn't enter a room and go unnoticed. Equal parts no bullshit and complete bullshitter, he has never wavered from who he is—a man of mid-'80s Midwestern roots, where your word and a solid handshake meant something. There is no half-assed with Draplin. If he commits to you, he'll be there until the job is done, and the finished product will make you feel like you just won the lottery (the kind of lottery where the check is delivered by a bear of a man wearing nothing but boxer shorts and a blown-out Flaming Lips T-shirt).

Arlie John Carstens, Writer & Musician
Today, most people are just trying to figure out how to exist in their own skin—how to move, how to dress, what to eat, how to love. With all the ads and cultural signifiers whirling around, deciphering what anything is really about is sometimes awfully hard. The thing about Aaron Draplin is this—he's a kid from Michigan who used to wash dishes on trains in Alaska. He's in awe of the human experience. He marvels at the improbability of our beautiful, complicated existence. He drives around, picks through the ephemera, thinks about life and gets excited about the things that others just can't or won't allow themselves to see. His work reminds us that we all come from somewhere. More importantly he's living proof that we can help each other get somewhere further down the line. Whether laying out work or giving his talks, Draplin understands that visual communication is not just typesets and vector art on a digital screen or advertisements designed to sell products. Rather, it's an attempt to convey a feeling, to breach isolation, to communicate ideas and give expression to the chemistry of common life.

Fred Green, Social Worker & Artist
I knew Aaron when he was making his first T-shirts, stickers and logos. And despite our frantic wrestling and drinking sessions trying to prove our emerging manhood, I knew back then that not only would my friend be successful but that he would grow into greatness and influence generations. That being said, I'm still ready to kick his ass any and everyday. Salute, brother.

Andy Cruz, House Industries
With a middle finger that rivals the strength of his work ethic, Aaron has Zip-Stripped both the pretentious layer and the glossy corporate finish off of graphic design and exposed the genuine beauty of commercial art. But let's not go into aesthetics. The most impressive thing I've seen Draplin design is his quality of life.

Charles S. Anderson, CSA Design
I don't actually recall hiring Aaron. His buddy P.J. was an intern for us at the time and I think he just showed up with him one day and started working. Over the decades we've had many interns work with us to help build the CSA Images archive. Many of them viewed scanning images as nothing more than mindless grunt work. Aaron was different. He immediately grasped that the printed paper scraps he was scanning represented a cross section of the most amazing images from the history of graphic design, illustration and type, and that for every image selected a thousand had been rejected. Aaron also began to understand our approach to design and realized that instead of always beginning the process with a blank slate, he could also gain inspiration from the past and build on the shoulders of designers who've gone before. As evidenced by this book, Aaron went on to become an immensely talented designer. In addition to his considerable design skills is his God-given gift for storytelling, which has made him one of the most dynamic, entertaining, humorous and humble speakers the graphic design profession has ever known. Some have mistakenly viewed Aaron's gregarious, larger-than-life personality as some sort of fabricated character, or an invented persona. Having known Aaron from the very start of his career, I can attest that he's the genuine article, and I'm glad to call him a colleague and a friend. I have no doubt that Aaron's dad is very proud of everything he's achieved, and is watching over him right now, smiling down from heaven.

Ryan "Ryno" Simonson, SS/CF
A lot of people tell stories about going on vacation to places like Paris or Cozumel. I'm sure they're really cute. Whatever. I prefer to end up in places like Erwin, Tennessee. You know what they did in Erwin, Tennessee, in 1916? They lynched a fucking elephant with a crane. And they still brag about it. Why were me and Draplin in Erwin, Tennessee? Because it was there, and we ran into it. Just like the pink, apocalyptic roadside shrine in Mississippi; the greasy diner in Kermit, West Virginia, where that pack of rednecks stared us down from the back booth while we nervously ate lunch; the landfill outside of Castle Danger where we slept under the stars and woke up with chunks of old clay pigeons poking us in the back; and the creepy crucifix out in the desert, where that 1,200-pound longhorn tried to ram the car. The good stuff, and the fucked-up stuff and the dirty stuff that gets under your fingernails is out there. Most people avoid it altogether, never getting off the interstate or leaving their resort to find it. Aaron Draplin's the kind of guy who goes looking for the dirt and the rust. He's the guy who trades in the swivel chair for a bucket seat and the mouse for a steering wheel and gets at it. And that's why he's a better designer, and way cooler than most of the assholes who are reading this. Hell, that's why you're reading this.

P.J. "Hoss" Chmiel, Freehand Artist
Aaron is a rare combination: the earnestness of a Mark Borchardt, the work ethic of a John Henry, the no-frills authenticity of an old Carhartt, the wit of an Andrew Dice Clay, the artistic chops of a Bob Ross, the quiet humility of a Freddie Blassie, the generosity of a doting grandmother, the charisma of a tent revival preacher, the physical presence of a Randall "Tex" Cobb and the business acumen of an Earl Scheib. We met at MCAD, both skate rat designers from Michigan who worshipped Charles S. Anderson. We did scanner time together at CSA, and Draplin was the only intern who could talk as much as Chuck—and with as much passion. He set his sights high and has worked like a fucking madman, seventy-plus hours a week since the 1990s, to earn his place standing shoulder to shoulder with his design heroes.

Pat Bridges, Creative Director, *Snowboarder*
Aaron James Draplin is a man of ideals. There is an underlying practicality to everything he is drawn to, as well as everything he does, with the exception of gambling on roulette. I met Draplin at a time when we were both outsiders. We instantly bonded over the Replacements. Draplin isn't a graphic artist, he is a graphic designer. The difference being that Draplin creates visual tools with purpose. While some of Aaron's efforts have been in the name of the greater good—the emblem for Recovery.gov for example—other projects take on less weighty duties, like conveying the emotion of an album. Thick lines distinguish Draplin's efforts from his design peers. Whether it is a layout, icon or logo, Aaron will infuse it with thick lines. Why? Because, like Aaron himself, thick lines convey conviction, are practical, lack ambiguity and get the job done efficiently. Aaron James Draplin, a thick line of a human being.

Evan Rose, World Champion Snurfer
"Wait until you meet this guy." That line came furiously and frequently from the mouths of many compadres before I had the opportunity to meet Draplin. When the introduction came to be, he surely lived up to the forewarning—as Draplin is the type of guy you expect to meet when a good friend looks at you and says, "Wait until you meet this guy." Furthermore, if it helps, the friend who introduced me to Draplin was also introduced to me years before with the line "Wait until you meet this guy." So, if you're a "this guy" type of guy, then you surely understand the essence of what I'm trying to say.

Jeff Baker, Photographer & Publisher
Aaron used to always remind me that "he has more creativity in his pinkie finger than I do in my whole body." Well, that might be true, but what Aaron has never realized is that, all these years that he's been comparing me to his little stump, he should have been comparing me to something different—his heart.

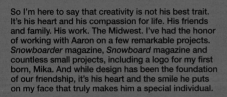

So I'm here to say that creativity is not his best trait. It's his heart and his compassion for life. His friends and family. His work. The Midwest. I've had the honor of working with Aaron on a few remarkable projects. *Snowboarder* magazine, *Snowboard* magazine and countless small projects, including a logo for my first born, Mika. And while design has been the foundation of our friendship, it's his heart and the smile he puts on my face that truly makes him a special individual.

Mike "Chief" Nusenow, Surf Donkey

I was introduced to Aaron while I was working at *Snowboarder* magazine. Our editor, Mark Sullivan, knew Aaron and thought he would be a great art director for us. It was an incredible experience to work alongside him, and the talent he brought to the magazine was significant. Roughly twenty years later, I have learned that design is Aaron's addiction. He is an amazing designer and he will never stop. It defines who Aaron is, and I know he is 100 percent thankful for that. He loves the life that design has given him. He has worked incredibly hard for what he has accomplished and downright deserves this book. Don't let the fame get to you, wahoo.

Jared Eberhardt, Director & Photographer

What can I say about Draplin that he hasn't already told you and your graduating class/local graphic design club/executive creative director? First off, congratulations to you for buying this book. You have great taste, and, of course, thank you to Aaron for making this pinnacle of thoughtful beauty. I can't see it because it hasn't actually been printed yet, but I can say with confidence that you bought the best orange book of this century, and it's an honor to be included in this place in the book that you are reading me from. Likely this section was 6-point Futura until I wrote that; now it's surely been changed to 5.99-point Helvetica Neue just to be contrary. And that's what it's been like working with him on and off for the last nearly twenty years. The process is always somewhere between a celebrity roast and a Lincoln–Douglass debate, the difference being that, after the humiliation of having your project brief/ musical taste/fashion sense scrutinized, you are left holding a gorgeous logo/layout/artifact. Aaron, for all his grandstanding, is too humble to say it, but if I were to sum up his philosophy I'd say it's something like this: A good designer gives you what you asked for but makes it better. A great designer gives you what you need, fuck what you asked for. If Draplin cares about you, you'll get the latter, even if it means a bloodbath. After all this time, I have to say, he's always been right. Looking forward to the next one!

Larry Nuñez, Writer & Stuntman

Aaron Draplin went from a snowboarder from Michigan with artistic tendencies in his teens to a college-educated artist who loathed snowboarding in his twenties. If that's not ironic, I don't know what is. Nevertheless, he found whatever love of it that was left in him to take a job designing a snowboard magazine in Southern California with a bunch of guys who say "dude" all the time (something else he hates). Then he left for the Northwest, where he still designed stuff for a heap of snowboard brands and ended up making another snowboard magazine with the same group of dudes! Doesn't this guy learn anything? Well, eventually he wised up . . . and now he travels around the country telling hundreds of punk-ass design kids not to do what he did. Or is it to do what he did? Shit, I can't keep track. Anyway, he did most of it without pants on. Which I'm sure he considers the most important thing.

John "Goo" Phemister, Wilderness

Having sat next to this guy for more than a decade, I can attest he's the real deal. I've watched him make as I like to say, "something from nothing" countless times, and it's been amazing to see. He's got oodles of talent, gumption and genuine character and he knows how to put it all together and make it work. Of course this includes a lot of "hot air" in the process, but that's part of the deal with Draplin.

David Nakamoto, Wilderness/Multifresh

Riverboat Gambler. Boaster. All-around asshole. Cardboard hoarder. Second-most-proficient Quark user in Portland. One of my best friends ever.

Brad Scheuffele, Coal Headwear

Back in 2003, I was one of Draplin's few side projects, something he took on outside of his regular 9 to 5. "Normal" for us was working through the night, hurling insults back and forth until the sun came up—the kicker being that it never felt like work; it was always just two buddies talking about our formative years of skateboarding and snowboarding. Concepts were never pitched; our collaboration was intuitive, natural and organic. DDC has remained an integral component of Coal's aesthetic for over a decade, partly because I view Aaron's design work the same way I do style: You can't buy it and it's impossible to be taught; you either have it or you don't. Aaron has it.

Martino Fumagalli, Union Binding Co.

When I think of Aaron bring me back to all the MAGIC happen on his basement, pants off, vision and creativity and all the power in a simple Field Notes little book. Idea, sketches… Boom! Magic take life in our product and complete everything. Thanks for all hard work and passion.

Jim Coudal, Coudal Partners & Field Notes

I met Aaron through a mutual love of a properly kerned headline, practical no-nonsense American design and the importance of a good story, well-told. As we came to know each other we conspired on a number of small projects and found that working together was easy and rewarding. We took a chance and decided to start a business called Field Notes, and building that has been just about the most fun I ever had in my career. That's due, in no small part, to Aaron's design talent, endless passion, and fierce loyalty. I can say that I'm a better businessman for having him as a partner. And, more important, I'm a better person for having him as a friend.

Willy Vlautin, Musician & Author

Aaron's saved my ass so many times I feel like I've always known him. I think he took on Richmond Fontaine as a favor, like feeding the homeless. I'm lucky as hell that he did. He helps direct my book covers, designs the record covers and posters. Hell, now we even sell good amounts of merch 'cause the shirts he designs look so damn cool. He's a crazed genius who just pulled over and picked up a struggling band, gave us all a haircut and a cool-looking set of clothes and did his part to keep us stumbling along.

Dale Allen Dixon, Master Junker

Here are three things that 95 percent of designers don't have that Aaron does: (1) Work Ethic: He sits in front of his goddamn computer twelve hours a day, and if he is not in front of that he is doodling in his notebook. It's done wonders for his health and social skills. (2) Passion: He has been into design since he was a child. He sees things that most designers don't realize are even there. (3) Salesmanship: His father was amazing at it and he is, too. It's his best quality—the art of bullshitting. So set down your Apple products and unfollow your blogs and go get a real job. Draplin's got you beat, and there are too many of you.

Kate Bingaman-Burt, Educator & Designer

One of the prouder titles that I have worn is being the chief operator of the Mississippi Field Notes Distribution Warehouse (aka: He sent me a big box of Field Notes way back in 2006 or so and told me to hand them out to my Mississippi State students). That sweet, sweet generosity continued when I moved to Portland in 2008 and conned him into talking to one of my classes at Portland State for the first of MANY times. Pretty sure he hadn't started doing ANY talks yet, but he was super game to hang out and throw out Field Notes and pencils and freaking coin purses and amazing advice to my ten students like a crazed Rip Taylor throwing out confetti. They went nuts and haven't stopped being nuts about him since. ME TOO.

Vin LaVecchia, Instrument

Aaron Draplin is 100 percent unique in his field and as a human. He's deeply talented and deeply conflicted. He believes in what he's doing wholeheartedly, but he wonders if the rest of us are all just doing it wrong. Aaron is 100 percent honest in every way. He's opened himself up and given up a large portion of his large life to expose people to his unique ways. To reach out and teach people about what really matters. To call bullshit on everything "they" tell you, and to give every kid a dose of design reality. Great design can be done without pants on. Great design can be done at all hours of the day. Great design can be done at three-hundred-plus pounds. Great design can be done in less than twenty minutes (if you're good enough). This book needs to be made to memorialize a moment in design culture when a complete rebel outsider upended the establishment and showed what an everyday dude can do with a computer, a passion for junking and solid Midwestern values.

Eric Hillerns, Graphic Designer

Like Draplin himself, this thing is 100% Prime. Generously marbled. Full of flavor. Equal parts tender and firm in the areas that count. Aged dry. And because it's no secret that the best cuts begin with the finest stock, the writer and subject here—Aaron, no less—owes his own choice grade to those from which he was reared: the lithe and lovely Miss Lauren and the immortal old bull himself, Big Jim. So I'd reckon it best you sit your ass on down. Grab a steely knife, a rubber bib and let it feed your appetite. You won't soon forget the abundant mouthfeel.

Mike Davis, Burlesque North America

In September 2008, I was standing in front of the World's Largest Collection of Giant Shoes in Seattle's Pike Place Market when I saw a mysterious 503 number show up on my phone. I answered and was greeted by the unmistakable voice of the graphic designer whose work I'd been admiring for years. He told me he wanted to send me some images of some First Day of Issue envelopes so I could share them on my design blog. It was a small gesture, but spoke volumes about one of the hardest-working and most generous people in our community. Aaron is successful because he genuinely cares about design. He's eager to learn, eager to create and eager to share. He loves what he does, and that love shows through in every single vector point and pixel that leaves his desk. Graphic designer laureate, this guy.

Leigh McKolay, Educator & Shipper

As Aaron's girlfriend for eight years now, I kind of wound up running the fulfillment part of DDC out of necessity. Aaron works A LOT. That's what he does. He was/is very, very busy, and needed help as the order numbers grew and grew. The big reveal of a career in commercial art is that there is an end product—and if there was some equation where we could plug in hours spent, number of icons, logos, identities and pieces of art created, "n" would equal "a book." The incredible amount of work that Aaron's produced really could fill SEVERAL books. I assume that is how the story will unfold.

Mike Whitehead, Finex

I had just mortgaged everything to found a new company and needed a real graphic designer willing to roll the dice on me. Problem was, I didn't know one any more than I know a good tattoo-removal guy. Word on the street was that DDC was solid, and how busy could they be? Wrong. No reply. So I did what any potential client would do. I posed as an inmate seeking graphic design help for our prison newsletter. Boom! My phone rings from a guy named wanting to know who the fuck I am. The rest is history. Finex is now a national brand carried in hundreds of stores around the country. I don't have to tell you that Aaron is good, but I can tell you a few things about why he is good. He is good because he works a lot. He is proof that if you do what you love, you do it a lot and have a decent shot at mastery. Now multiply that focus by his talent. He is good because he really listens to his clients. He never told me what my brand should be. He only asked a thousand questions and pointed out the inconsistencies in what I was trying to say. But most important, Aaron is good because he is a good guy, and that is inseparable from his body of work. We don't choose our families, but if you are lucky enough to choose who you work with, Aaron Draplin is a damn good choice.

Growing Up

"A beautiful small town upbringing."

DDC

Draplin
Design Co.

Pretty Much
Everything

Aaron James
Draplin

File Under:
8097 Brooks Street

008
009

With my little sister Sarah Barah Pumpkin Pie, Central Lake, MI. 1978.

Humble Beginnings in Detroit, Growing Up in Central Lake and Then Plotting My Escape from Traverse City

I was born to Jim and Lauren Draplin on October 15, 1973, at Grace Hospital in the northwest section of Detroit. Mom says I was "eight pounds, three ounces" and that the labor took "twenty-six and a half hours, and it was worth it." The story goes, Dad was in the process of rebuilding a '54 Chevy. "He bought a second one for parts. And it just so happened to coincide with your birth. And I had some complications. I was in the hospital for nine days. That gave him the opportunity to strip the second car of parts. Hence the joke 'I gave birth to you and Dad gave birth to a '54 Chevy.'"

Always the stickler for details, I asked Mom where I was conceived, and she gave me a sideways glance and had this to say: "Are you serious? Okay then. That would've been on the way back from California. I think it was somewhere in New Mexico or Amarillo, Texas." Just the facts, people. About that trip, Mom offered this little tidbit: "We were driving through a big canyon, took a wrong turn and what I thought was lightning turned out to be a big meteor. It lit the sky up like it was day. I had never, ever seen something like that. It was beautiful. Your dad was like, 'Holy shit!'" Cosmic beginnings!

Living in Detroit

Mom was a homemaker after I was born, and, before I came along, a secretary at Chrysler in Southfield. Dad was an electrician at Great Lakes Steel downriver in River Rouge. I can still remember picking Dad up after his shift. There was a big metal walkway with a set of stairs that emptied out into the parking lot. And Mom and I would wait there for him and I'd go crazy when I saw him. "You would be so excited. I can't believe you remember him coming down those stairs," said Mom.

Mom's side of the family was led by Gramma Leo in Wixom, with all my aunts and uncles close by—Unca Pat, Unca Mike, Aunt Mary, Unca Terry and Unca Kevin. My dad's mom, Gramma Josie, lived in Dearborn, with Uncle Tom and Auntie Barbara in Southfield and Uncle Bob and Auntie Chris in Westland. I remember a couple elaborate camping trips to Tobermory, Ontario, with Dad, Uncle Tom and his boys. And how cold the water was. Let's just say your "hardware" would basically retreat inside toward warmth. There was a lot of talk about great adventures while fishing for surbots on

Farkus Lake. All of which I'd come to learn was entirely fictional, of course.

Leaving Detroit

From Mom: "Ultimately, we didn't want you kids shoveled onto buses to go to school in Detroit suburbs. Things were changing so fast in Detroit and we wouldn't be able to send you to schools in our neighborhood. Plus, there was one time when we were coming from dinner at Gramma Josie's . . . Sarah was a baby, the two of you were in your car seats, and when we turned onto Tireman, someone shot a BB gun at our Pinto, shattering the back window. It scared the hell out of us. That's when we really started to talk about leaving. Then, through one of your dad's random painting side jobs, he met Archie Noorian. He said that Dad was a 'natural salesman' and offered him a job selling industrial tooling to tool shops. Dad took the job and started going more and more north, up toward Gaylord and Traverse City. We loved to vacation up there, and started looking for a place to rent in Traverse City, but couldn't find anything. My cousin Bonnie lived in Central Lake. We found a house there for a good price, which was just forty-five minutes from Traverse City." This is where my memory starts, more or less. Our little house on the corner, just a block from Main Street in Central Lake. Population: 1,000.

Grade School

I look back at my childhood with a thankful pause—I had it really good growing up. I had a dad and a mom who loved my siblings and me and built us a great home life. I grew up with my little sister Sarah, who was born in 1975. My baby sister Leah, came along in 1983.

Central Lake was the kind of little town small enough that you could ride your BMX bike from end to end in about fifteen minutes. But to a ten-year-old, the town felt enormous! From my house down to C-Foods? One or two small blocks. Down to the bait shop? Six to seven small blocks. Big distances! Hell, the middle and high school was less than a block away from our house on Brooks Street. Just two blocks to the grade school. I had thirty kids in my class, all the way from that first day in kindergarten in 1978, until I left in the spring of 1987.

Favorite things from my youth: Lego, Adventure People, *Stars Wars* action

figures, G.I. Joes, drawing, riding bikes, playing "guns" in the woods, Saturday morning cartoons, Hot Wheels cars, working at my little workbench while Dad was working at his big workbench, *Saturday Night Live, The Flintstones, The Brady Bunch, Diff'rent Strokes,* Bigfoot lore, hanging out with my older cousin Patrick, playing baseball in the summers, playing football in the fall.

I have so many great memories growing up in Central Lake: Christmas mornings with my little sisters; snowmobiling; family road trips to Florida; swimming in Torch Lake and Lake Michigan; driving down to Detroit for holiday get-togethers; summer rental cottages on Intermediate Lake; the time Ronnie and I were cleaning out reeds near the sandbar and got leeches on our legs and balls; Mom's basket-weaving and the smell of the reeds soaking in water; cutting wood on the eighty acres in Alden with Dad, Gary and Ronnie; playing Little League baseball and making the all-star team a couple years with Ronnie and Brent; kicking Kalkaska's ass that one time; sandlot football games; traveling with the football and basketball teams as a manager; making snow forts with Dad in our big backyard; climbing the big tree between our house and the Youngedykes'; getting stung in the eye by a couple of nasty hornets while Dad was up on a ladder painting; the anticipation of our annual Fourth of July festivals and fireworks. It was your basic all-American small-town kind of youth.

For the archaeologists: Somewhere near my grade school is a stack of Playboy magazines, buried away since about 1981. Near where the creek went under the road, up to where you were dropped off for school. Some kid stole them from his dad and that's all I've got on the matter.

Middle School

Middle school for me was probably as awkward as anyone else's experience. I tried my hand at a little bit of basketball, which didn't pan out so well. Still hopeful to play football in high school, I had all but phased sports out of my life. I did a stint with some school government but didn't have the taste for seventh-grade politics. Anne Westerlund and Linda Richardson pushed me into as many art classes as Central Lake offered.

Like any rural town, cool stuff would trickle

Mart photoshoot with Dad. 1974.

1976.

veet part, man. 1985.

BMX bandit. 1983.

in here and there. I was a kid of the early '80s, with MTV leading the charge. Like all Midwestern kids, we were intoxicated with "California culture." Ocean Pacific shorts, Panama Jack hats and Swatch watches. *BMX Plus!* was the magazine I studied from cover to cover. Its comic, "Radical Rick," was my favorite! The bike brand logos, number plates and stickers: these were my first introductions to—for lack of a better term—"action sports." I'd just call it "the cool stuff." In my seventh-grade year, I got a Haro FST freestyle bike and started reading *Freestylin'* magazine. The magazines were my connection to everything. From BMX to freestyle bikes, and then my very first skateboard in 1986. There was a certain danger to all this stuff, and you could tell the art, language and moves were from the hands of the kids who were inventing the stuff along the way. That was different from organized sports. You weren't gonna find the cool shit on ABC's *Wide World of Sports*, you know? Years later, I got to meet Mark "Lew" Lewman, one of the original editors of *Freestylin'*. It's one of those cool moments where you meet a hero and realize you are one of them.

I had a close call in 1986, almost dying in an accident with my high school buddy Tim Mox in his shitty little Chevy Citation. I broke a couple ribs, cracked my pelvis and had stitches in my chin and elbow. I remember putting my seat belt on that morning after jumping into Tim's car. That little belt saved my life, and I think about that each time I forget to snap that belt a block away from the house or shop. Wear your seat belts, you scrubs!

We moved to Traverse City in April 1987. Moving is always hard on a kid. I left the comfort and friends of our small town, and didn't quite appreciate what Mom and Dad saw for us in Traverse City. They knew it held better opportunities, and within a year I started to see what they saw. They took some flack from my sisters and me for that big move, but I'm so thankful for their foresight. That little leap opened us up to the world that much more.

High School

I started ninth grade at St. Francis High School. Complete with dress codes and the whole dogmatic nine yards. As much as Mom and Dad hoped St. Francis was the premium option for Traverse City, I quickly found out it was more or less just another small school but with a couple nuns hammering on you to learn the sacraments. St. Francis was the last stop in town for the bad kids from the public school, too, so we had a couple of those incorrigibles. I kept to myself. I loved my pizza job at Crusted Creations, was into drawing and skateboarding and discovered heavy metal and punk rock. In one last

attempt at organized sports, I tried out for the junior varsity football team, excited to finally play the sport I loved as a kid. I made it through the "conditioning phase," where you run until you puke, and got on the team. I was small for a ninth-grader, just thirteen and a late bloomer. I made it through the season, just barely. Dad wouldn't let me quit. I remember being so relieved when that shit was done.

I was at St. Francis my ninth- and tenth-grade years and made the leap to Traverse City Senior High in 1989. I went from sixty kids in my class to seven hundred. Now I could blend in and not be singled out for bringing my skateboard to school. I remember that being something risky at St. Francis. Meathead jocks fucking with me as I walked down the hall.

Public school offered a place I could hide out. I fell in with kids I knew from summers skateboarding around Traverse City. I had an army jacket with a hole in the pocket for the headphones cord to snake down into my Walkman. I always had that thing on, blasting the Dead Kennedys, Fugazi, Black Flag and Metallica.

I chose punk rock. And that was daring. It wasn't about the music or the T-shirt graphics as much as it was about the ability to think for yourself, being free from the conventional teenage pitfalls, and ultimately to make your own life exactly what you wanted it to be. It was punk to me to be completely drug-free. All the kids were messing around with the latest shit and getting in trouble. I remember a cop pulling me over while I was delivering pizza, with my long hair and all. He starts in, fully grilling me. And then was floored when I looked him in the eye and called him on his bluff. "Search the car, man. You aren't gonna find anything. These pizzas are getting cold." I was confident and in complete control of my little world. He paused, a bit stunned, gave me back my license and told me to finish my delivery.

Skateboard graphics were everything to me. Jim Phillips and his Santa Cruz decks were my very favorite. I learned how to ink stuff, emulating his style, re-creating Jason Jessee and Jeff Grosso graphics in my sketchbooks. That transferred into zines, grip tape art and homemade skate- and snowboard videos. I wore holes in my favorite Slime Balls T-shirt the summer of 1989.

The Circle Jerks were my first punk rock show! Slammed up against the stage at St. Andrew's Hall screaming, "Living, just living!" with Keith Morris? The coolest. When people ask me where I grew up, I like to say, "I come from a big Butthole Surfers community." Friends were experimenting with all sorts of substances.

I remember the tray of drugs laid out on a friend's knees in the backseat of the car while racing downstate to see the Butthole Surfers at the Latin Quarter. Names withheld, of course. I didn't have a sip or toke of anything until my first year in college. Drugs were too scary. Plus, kids downing bottles of Robitussin for a buzz? That was always a little too desperate for me.

I graduated from high school in 1991. On our graduation night, a group of us were high atop Wayne Hill, overlooking the city as the sun came up. Talking about what we wanted to do. Half of the group was heading off to state schools; the other half had no plan. I was in the latter. I knew it was something to do with art. The placement tests that summer pointed me toward visual communications at Northwestern Michigan College. Right out of high school, we heard stories of kids moving to Colorado to snowboard all winter. Temptation! And I almost took the bait. My friend Rod Snell had it all lined up, and we were breaking down rent and season-pass prices, so excited. But I also had Mom and Dad dangling community college in front of me. "Just go for two years and get an associates degree, and then go west," they pleaded. I couldn't pass it up. I decided to stay.

Getting My Associates Degree

I was seventeen when I started at Northwestern Michigan College in the fall of 1991. Grunge had just exploded. I remember how great Nirvana's "Drain You" sounded at full blast in my hunk-of-shit two-door Buick Skyhawk on the way to school. My two years there went pretty quick. It was this all-inclusive introduction to the graphic arts world. I learned how to draw naked people, take and develop pictures, draw in painstaking perspective, paint, hand-lettering words, style of Roman architecture, write a paper and use computer drawing programs to draw things in vector form. This is where it started.

I came in just on the precipice of where the paste-up world dropped off and the newfangled computer world exploded. I missed that fabled cutoff by about a year. And I loved doing it the old way with the trimmed, waxed paragraphs, Rubylith and keylines and shit. There was something technical and almost architectural about all of it. But that was the old way. Computers were taking over with waves of skilled paste-up and typesetting folks suddenly obsolete. It was heartbreaking, and all these years later I understand what a weird time for design that must've been for those folks.

Once I had my associates degree complete, we started saving our cash to head out west. I was nineteen years old and ready for our big adventure.

Young artists winners announced

TRAVERSE CITY — Northwestern Michigan Artists and Craftsmen honored the winners and contributors in the Ninth Annual Young People's Art Show April 28. NMAC sponsors the activity each year to help promote growth and awareness of arts and crafts in the Grand Traverse region.

In the 15 to 18 age category, first place ($25) went to Aaron Draplin, 15, from Traverse City for "Skate Boyz," an original cartoon in colored pencil. Second place ($15) winner was Alexia Warburg, 14, from Leland for her watercolor "Fishtown Leland." Janet Ottgen, 16, from Mancelona took third place ($15) for her painting "Guess Who."

In the 10 to 14 age category, Jeannine Hinds, 13, from Traverse City won first place for her acrylic painting "Duck Stamp." Christine Plucker, 14, from Williamsburg received second place for her pottery bowl. Third place went to Herbert Lentz, 11, from Ellsworth for his painting "Field of Flowers."

There were several honorable mentions in both age categories.

You will travel to many places.

High School

Emulating the incomparable Jim Phillips' groundbreaking Santa Cruz skateboard graphics. 1988.

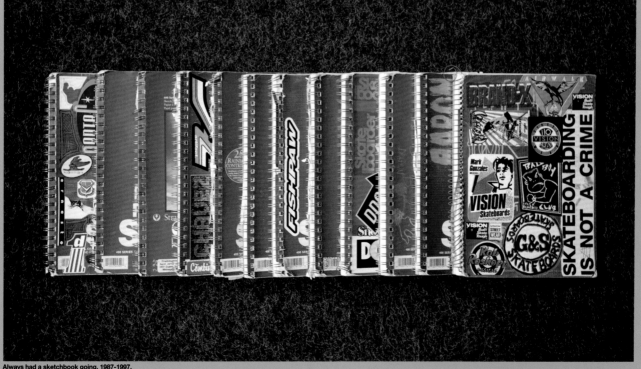

Always had a sketchbook going. 1987-1997.

DrapZine. 1990.

Heading down to the Hash Bash with Rick Harker, Jay Moncel and Trevor Beardsley. I-75. 1991.

Mom thought I was faking. 1987.

St. Francis Junior Varsity #65. 1987.

Carving at Eat Concrete, Omaha, Nebraska. 1990.

NMC graduation party. 1993.

TBA Career Tech Center jitters. 1989.

Rare shot with Brian Johnsen, just before the morning bell. 1990.

Bry Aleshire presenting his handiwork at Crusted Creations. 1990.

Leaving the Nest

"Move somewhere wild."

◻◻◻

Draplin
Design Co.

Pretty Much
Everything

Aaron James
Draplin

File Under:
Wide Open West

016
017

There were a couple young girls in a Saab that kept
passing Chad, Darrin, and me in our rented Ryder truck
that day in Colorado. And the final time they passed
us, I snapped a shot. This was early October, 1994.
A long day down the Rockies from Summit County
into Utah and through Moab. We were making good
time. The world seemed so big those first couple runs
out west, on our own. Still does, really.

Moving Out West

I still consider "moving out west" as one of my finest achievements. Growing up a snowboarder, I heard the stories of friends moving out to Colorado to get to the mountains and the good snow. The first wave of my buddies went in 1991. I wanted to go so bad, but took Mom and Dad's advice and jumped into Northwestern Michigan College. I would be pursuing an associates degree in visual communications. I'd still be living at home, doing pizza jobs in the fall, a tree-trimming job in the summer and ski-lift operator jobs at Mount Holiday over the winter. The two years went by quick and I earned my degree. We were ready to go. I can still feel the excitement we had, all these years later.

When it was time to finally go in the summer of 1993, I was just nineteen years old. Just a pup. And the world exploded for us. In my little Creative Mornings talk I did in 2012, I told the youngsters in the crowd to "move somewhere wild" while they still could. I did it and am so thankful we made the leap.

Bend, Oregon, was our target. Our high school buddy Derek Denoyer had made the jump from a winter in Colorado out to Oregon. His reports back to us were what sealed the deal. So many of our buddies had gone to Colorado. By the time it was our turn, it didn't have the same magic. Oregon sounded mysterious! And far away. The anticipation during the summer of 1993 was insane. Bry and I worked at a family restaurant called Sweitzer's. I was a fry cook and Bry a busboy. We saved every single cent that summer.

I'll never forget leaving that morning. It was August 10, 1993. Bry and I had packed my '84 Buick Skyhawk a couple days before in anticipation. Of course, Dad took one look at our half-assed job, had me empty the thing and repacked it.

We gained another sizable chunk of space after Dad's refinement of the packing job. That man knew how to pack a rig.

When it was time to go, everything got quiet. I remember my littlest sister Leah, crying first, and then Mom, and then Dad and how he completely lost it. I'll never forget how hard Dad hugged me. I didn't want to let go. That's one of the saddest, and yet greatest, moments of my life: Mom and Dad letting me go. So painful, but absolutely beautiful. Thank you.

I think that's important for every rat kid from the Midwest. And everywhere. As hard as that was, I had to do it. This was the classic "leaving the nest" moment. I remember crying at the intersection where Barnes Road meets Silver Lake Road, and kind of not wanting to go; cars lining up behind me, impatient. We had worked that whole summer, pined over the possibilities of our new lives out west, and here was that big moment, and I was seizing up. I pulled off Barnes and down the big hill of Silver Lake, and it was surreal—both sad and one of the most exciting moments of my life. Down the hill to grab Bry at his house on Pine Street and off to the West!

I'll remember that road trip with Bry my whole life. Every place we camped, lurked, ate…each state falling away as we made our way out west. The sky seemed so big. And it was.

We went all the way to Bend, Oregon, and locked into a lease for a shit apartment in a place that we'd learn the locals called "Felony Flats." That first winter offered up so much for us. We learned how to pay our bills, be frugal, thumb rides up to the hill and, most important, go without. We'd buy our season passes, guaranteeing us access to the mountain and that's all that mattered.

The priority was to snowboard every day with all our buddies. We all had pizza jobs at night, to cover our minimal rent and expenses. I lived this life for five winters, snowboarding one-hundred-plus days a year in Oregon and all over the West, along with big roadtrips across America every fall and jaunts down to Las Vegas to lurk at the annual snowboarding trade show. The last couple years, we started to explore outside of Oregon. Big road trips with buddies, snowboarding at Jackson Hole, Targhee Pass, Mount Baker, Snowbird and Telluride. We'd go up to Portland every two to three weeks to see bands and hang in the city, then ride Mount Hood Meadows on the way back. La Luna was our place. Saw the Lemonheads, Sebadoh, Monster Magnet, Paw, the Jesus Lizard, Pavement, Hole, the Meat Puppets, Grant Lee Buffalo, Gwar, Built to Spill, Thirty Ought Six, the Jon Spencer Blues Explosion, the Red House Painters, Boss Hog, the Reverend Horton Heat and a little Portland band called Richmond Fontaine, who were opening for Mike Watt.

To youngsters reading this: Save your money and hit the road. While you still can. There's just something magical about splitting when you are young. The world, it's so much bigger. The bands, they sound that much better. You aren't cynical yet, and everything is new. I'm so thankful to the skateboard/snowboard culture that propelled us west, out of Traverse City. Some never leave, and we were lucky to be able to.

It's the older brothers who did it. Gary Aleshire inspired Hale to go. Hale inspired Shumsky, Miner, Tad, Bug, Murrah and Waller to go. Those animals inspired Derek to go, who planted the seed in Bry and me. And Eric, Johnny and Chad got roped in, too. That's how this stuff works. Thanks, fellas. We did it when it mattered.

The morning we left. Last bits of advice, minutes before everyone lost it. August 10, 1993.

Bry writing his first letter back to Tracey, somewhere in South Dakota. August 11, 1993.

Draplin
Design Co.

Pretty Much
Everything

Aaron James
Draplin

File Under:
Wild West Winters

018
019

Early morning method air across the street from Cinder Cone. Mt. Bachelor, OR. 1996.

Jay, Rod, Aaron, Chris, Chad and J.P. 1995.

Robby Hottois blasting! Mt. Baker, WA. 1995.

Cow's Face, Mt. Bachelor. 1995.

Hiking with the Solid Snowboards team. 1995.

With Chad Smith and John White. 1994.

With Derek Denoyer and Robby Hottois. 1994.

Hitting jumps on Cinder Cone. 1996.

Taking a break in the Mt. Bachelor lodge with Chris Fink and Chad Smith. 1996.

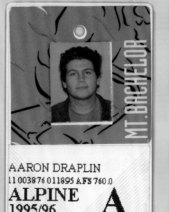

AARON DRAPLIN
11 003876 011895 AFS 760.0
ALPINE A
1995/96

Mt. Bachelor season pass. Winter 1995/1996.

Couch surfing in some shithole town. 1994.

With Darrin and Chad Smith, heading west. 1994.

Reveling in the Analog

Those first couple winters out west, every bit of my output was analog. I'd draw on all the letter envelopes I sent back home. I always had a sketchbook going and would draw the environment around me from the backseat on road trips.

That spring, I took a painting class at Central Oregon Community College. "Cock on a Rock" is what the kids called the place. I was priming myself for what I thought would be a triumphant return back to the Midwest to continue my education. That didn't happen.

We had our ways of getting computer access and e-mail. I remember a buddy, one Frankie Bilello, was taking classes at COCC and either dropped out or just sort of wasn't going to class. We'd use this e-mail and passwords to get to get access. Some of my first e-mails were sent from Frankie's address. "Francesco Bilello!" The lab we'd barge also had drawing programs on the computer. PageMaker and FreeHand. I'd use PageMaker to make little business cards for myself and then would use Berol Prismacolor markers to color them in. I'd make fifty cards or so and would hand them out around town. I remember how precious the time in that lab was.

I had to be careful not to draw attention but still get all the stuff done.

Computers were so expensive. There was no way I'd be able to afford one on the meager living I made in Bend. I was a snowboard scrub, working a pizza job and had a couple freelance illustration gigs here and there.

I did my first snowboard graphic for Solid Snowboards in the fall of 1993, from a tip from Matt Hale, a high school buddy and pro rider on the Solid team. That was the first real taste with this stuff. And maybe I could make a living at it.

Various illustrations from my stack of sketchbooks. Pencil and India ink. 1993-1999.

DDC

Draplin
Design Co.

Pretty Much
Everything

Aaron James
Draplin

File Under:
Pencil, Ink & Paint

020
021

Five By Ten zine. Winter 1994–1995.

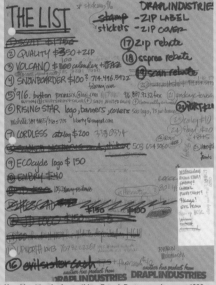

How I kept track of everything. French Paper sample scrap. 1996.

Spark plug illustration. 1995.

Jeff Wastell graphic for Solid. 1994.

Unsent envelope illustration. 1994.

Untitled. Acrylic on canvas. 1994.

My favorite painting from that one painting class at COCC. 1994.

Was really into spark plugs in the mid-'90s! Acrylic on canvas. 1995.

Unfinished paint collage. Acrylic on canvas. 1994.

Solid Snowboards Jeff Wastell pro model. 1994.

My Summer as a Carny

We were coming off our first winter out west. I came back to Michigan in early May. My buddy Chad Smith finally made it back from Bend a couple weeks later, and, like me, was seeking gainful employment. After a long winter of making pizzas, little did we know we'd be "doing I-talian" again all summer long.

Mom and Dad ran into some old friends from Central Lake: Ray and Rose. Ray was a barrel-chested, fast-talkin' rabble-rouser; sorta famous for tearin' the hell out of that little town and making all the concerned fathers' shit lists. Rose straightened Ray out, and they were slowly growing their amusement business.

They had a couple food carts and rented out some space in a small, mid-Michgan-based traveling carnival. They were looking for a couple of nice young bucks to man their pizza wagon across the way from their lemonade/corn dog wagon.

I spoke with Ray and we agreed on $250 cash per weekend. That sounded really good the first time I heard it, thinking, *$250 bucks for Friday, Saturday and Sunday.* Under the table, too. Michigan-wide adventures. Carny chicks. Not bad, and I'd get a truck to drive for the summer. I accepted, and got Chad hired on, too.

The first couple gigs were in the Detroit area. So that meant we had to drive down the night before with the wagon in tow. That added an extra day to the "three-day weekend." There was a lot of jockeying of equipment, moving from event to event. Ray and Rose had a fifth wheel they slept in, so they'd drive down separately, with Rose towing the lemonade wagon and Ray towing their summer home on wheels. It took a couple days just to get all the gear to the site and up-n-running. The final piece to show up was the fifth wheel Chad and I slept in. It was hot and musty, the bathroom smelled of piss and the shower more or less peed lukewarm water on you. But these were "luxury accommodations," considering the shady and sheisty sleeping quarters offered up for the ragtag roster of carnies. We'll get to them in a couple paragraphs.

Our day in the wagon consisted of waking up at about nine A.M. to prep the dough, sauce and toppings. Thawing the goods was a crucial step. We'd make sure the soda pop was flowing like a river, too. The crowds would show up around ten A.M., with the first couple slices hittin' the gums at about eleven. Chad and I would stagger the slow time, offering relief to each other every hour. There would be a dinner rush around seven P.M., lasting a couple hours into the night, with the lights going down around midnight.

In no time, we were six weeks into the season and humming along. Man, we hit some ugly little towns. Clare, Irons (home of the annual, Michigan-famous Flea Roast and Ox Market festival), Ironwood, Iron Mountain and the Coleman Junefest were some of the colorful destinations. Our downtime on the road was spent reading, drawing, junkin' in between ports and sweating the nights out in the fifth wheel. Things weren't so bad, and hell, if anything, the constant traveling was dirty, kinda reckless and fun.

The carnival's family hierarchy is broken down systematically. At the top of the food chain you have the owners. They own the equipment, book the shows and cut the checks. The main guy had this perpetual look of disgust and exhaustion on his face and his wife had big blond hair and lots of gold dangling off her buxom chest. Oh yeah, and a couple of spoiled, shit-ass little kids running around getting into everything. Moving right along, the next step down is the food court. The court vendors rent space from the owners. If they are lucky, they'll build a little empire of elephant ears and corn dogs and have a whole row of wagons set up at any given event. Ray and Rose were responsible people, with a nice house in some little town somewhere, a couple big trucks and lots of determination to succeed. For all I knew, they took the winters off, due to the riches from their summer. Chad and I—somewhat reluctantly— were a part of the food court caste.

But our hearts, well, they were pumping carny blood.

The carnies. Oh man, what a wild lot. Rough around the edges, oddly enigmatic, stereotypically undereducated, dirty, colorful, loyal, sunburnt, simple, repressed and "kinda lost" are descriptions that come to mind. It's been over twenty years since that fateful summer, so the names are fuzzy, but the faces and their hearty personalities are ingrained in me forever.

There was this older lady named Alice, who'd lie like a rug. One day she'd claim to have six kids, the next day, seven. Her husband, "Bob," was this hefty bruiser some twenty years her junior with no front teeth, deep-set eyes, a dangling smoke and a big smile to share with everyone. He'd just nod along with her lies.

There was a guy with green, rotting teeth who'd get a big "Dew" from us each morning. After some time he and I got to know each other. He'd ask me about living out west. I'd ask him about living in Saginaw. One time I asked him if he ever planned to fix his teeth. With a toothy grin and a poetic delivery he said, "Hurts too much to brush 'em, so I'm just waitin' for 'em to fall out! *Ta-ha-haaaaa!*" And that was that.

Carny life is a tough go. First of all, they don't get paid shit and are expected to work long, long hours. Set the shit up, run it all day, tear it down and travel to the next gig. And that's their summer. Each night after this crew shut the fair down, they were allowed a "draw" on their earnings. Now, if I remember correctly, the cash was dispersed in an envelope, carefully recorded and doled out to the eager workers. Their money often went to smokes, trashy food and beer. And, man, the whole draw thing was one more way for the owners to keep the carnies under their thumb and eating out of their hands. Because when payday would hit, well, they would be taxed for the whole amount and would have tiny paychecks. Plus, they had to rent their sleeping quarters. The deck was stacked against them in every way. The work, the hours, the safety issues, the food options offered…nothing was in their favor.

So I took matters into my own hands. After seeing how much the wagon made, and how fast it made it, I started to "give back" to the people who I felt were taken advantage of. The carnies had to pay for the food, which, considering how they were treated overall, was complete bullshit. So, say a guy would come up to get his daily fifty-ouncer of Mountain Dew. It was three bucks. He'd give me a five-dollar bill, I'd give him the wink and then give him seven dollars in change. And so on. I took it upon myself to give these guys a break, and in the process, won them over.

Now if anyone messed with Chad or me, the carnies would come to our rescue. I remember some drunk frat fucks messing with us somewhere in Michigan's Upper Peninsula and having one of the carnies come over to police the wagon's canopy area. Backup. Brothers. And it's not like Ray and Rose lost very much from my benevolence that summer. Maybe a couple hundred bucks, which I'd gladly pay back. It put smiles on the carnies' faces, and maybe, just maybe, made 'em feel like someone gave a shit about their plight.

The highlight of the weekend was "going AWOL" long enough to hit a thrift store or a local restaurant. That, and when friends would visit. I can only wonder how we looked inside that cockpit.

Now, things were rolling along just fine, and some ten weeks into it, a meltdown changed everything.

It was a late night in Norway, on the west end of the Upper Peninsula. We were busy right up until closing, and, being hungry after a long day, we shut the rig down and left without cleaning up, in order to get into town before all the restaurants closed. So we go and eat, hitting a Subway or something. (I remember that felt "premium" after spending a whole summer around corn dogs and shit.) When we rolled back into the site—to do our nightly cleanup and then hit the sack—we noticed the wagon's back door was open and the light was on, with some movement inside.

We walked up to find Rose feverishly cleaning up. "Rose, we'll get that," I said. "We just wanted to go into town to grab something before everything closed." She didn't reply, visibly miffed, scrubbing away.

And that's when Ray showed up and went nuts. Accusing us of "making Rose clean up after us"—which was bullshit; we always cleaned the place up, like we were supposed to—and of "not caring anymore." He was getting close on the latter, as our paycheck stayed the same with the days on the job being more and more each weekend. For instance, he never told us about the fairs that were Thursday to Sunday, which meant driving out on Wednesday night and back on Monday morning, in turn becoming six days all together. But we still made it and honored our pact.

I remember him specifically bringing up an incident about the panty hose. At the end of the night, we were "trained" to put a panty hose on the release drain, and then release the waste water into the grass or dirt, catching all the crud in the panty hose, and then remove it and cap the drain back up. This was against the law, as we were supposed to drain the waste water into a state-sanctioned receptacle. So this one night, we forgot to remove the

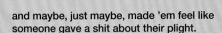

panty hose. We crashed out, and as we were walking up to the wagon the next morning, we were greeted by an official from the Michigan State Health Department. Well, Ray got a big fine for that one, and was pretty bummed at us. Thanks for the good training, boss.

Then he started to talk about how "he oughta fire us," when I interrupted him and said, "Nah, you won't have to do that. I quit." Or something to that effect. And, man, it stopped him in his tracks. He went double nuts at that point. I think I said something about how pathetic his "career" was as a fucking corn dog

huckster. I just remember Chad cautioning me as I unloaded a summer's worth of disgust on the guy. And I let it all out.

We worked hard for him and Rose and never lost a sale or turned people away. We made them a ton of loot and were always on time. And this one time we broke protocol in the name of getting somewhat of a square meal and he loses it and freaks out on us.

So I quit on the spot, and, man, it felt good. I had saved all my summer loot, so my western nest egg was secure. Then they asked Chad what he was gonna do. I remember him saying, "Nah, I'm outta here. I'm not gonna listen to you talk shit about Aaron for the rest of the summer." My brother had my back. I remember being outside the owners' fifth wheel and hearing that little snake-tongued wife say something along the lines of "I wouldn't give them a thing. Get 'em out of here, then" as Ray sought guidance on how to handle our leaving. And that was it. We were free.

It was two A.M., in the middle of the U.P., and we were done. Ray paid us for the weekend and gave us a hundred bucks for Greyhound tickets back to Traverse City. Then he recruited this guy with spotty hearing and one eye with Coke-bottle glasses to drive us off the premises and to the next little town, where we'd wait the night out until the next bus came through.

Once we were on the road, we bought the guy some smokes or a big Dew or something and he drove us all the way to Escanaba, down on the Lake Michigan coast. He dropped us off at a twenty-four-hour Laundromat, where we caught up on laundry and watched the sun rise.

Luckily, Mom and Dad came to our rescue the next morning, and drove us back down to Traverse City.

Two weeks later, after an amazing Ryder truck road trip back to Bend, we were settling into our second winter in Oregon.

Four Summers up in Alaska

A group of my buddies and I went to a party right where the Old Mission Peninsula started, and it was a bit of an older crowd. I got to bullshitting with this tall, wild-eyed adventurer-looking guy with long curly blond hair and breath that smelled like stale beer. This was a year before we'd ultimately split, and I told him of our tentative plans. I remember him telling me this: "You need to go to Alaska. The land is wild, the women are wild and you can make a fortune." The conviction in his voice was something I'll never forget. I took his advice and never forgot those words. Fast-forward five winters, and it's weird how prophetic that guy was.

I was living in Bend, and my friend Jackie Boiseneau told me about a group of people coming down from Anchorage to interview for summer positions on a sightseeing train that went from Anchorage to Fairbanks and back, serving food to golden-oldie travelers. She put my name in, I pedaled out to the Shilo Inn on Highway 97, north of Bend a bit, and had my interview. It went well enough, and we discussed a dishwashing job that was up for grabs.

A month later, I got the big call. As much as I wanted to do another summer at High Cascade Snowboard Camp in Government Camp, you just couldn't make any loot up there. I ended the summer of 1995 with just a couple hundred bucks. That wasn't gonna cut it. I heard the tales from Jackie of being able to make a load up there, and I had to give it a go.

Up to Alaska
Here's why I went: It was the only way I'd be able to get a computer. I had worked at the Nickel Ads and had access to machines, but that job was long gone. Sneaking into the community college wasn't gonna cut it, either. So I went up there with one focus: to make enough loot to buy my very own machine. And I did just that.

Even with all that midnight sun, those were some dark days up in Alaska. And that train ate you alive. The thing took off super early and there were strict policies for what time things got going. All the workers watched over one another to get to the train on time.

The shifts weren't all that bad. It certainly wasn't rocket science. Dishes come in. Dishes get washed. Dishes get put away. Repeat one thousand times over the course of a summer. But there was an art to it. I quickly devised a system to efficiently sort and wash the stuff as it came in. It's easier to do a whole rack of plates. Like-minded shapes, you know? Whereas my colleague Tyler Fanning applied a "go apeshit and wash whatever comes in as it comes in" policy, I was scientific in my approach, quickly getting the numb-nut servers to adhere. It made sense for them, too. And when servers would just shuck stuff into the pit? I had ways of getting my revenge.

The dishwashers are at the very bottom of the kitchen food chain and always get the shitty end of the sprayer nozzle. I was the last one to leave the kitchen. I'd clean my pit and shut it all down when some fuckhead server would throw one last coffee cup in, screwing the whole thing up. So here's what I would do: I'd pour a little splash of milk in each of the servers' reach-in coolers, which meant, during final inspections, they'd have to pull everything out again, clean the milk up and put it all back in. Any of you guys remember that? I sure do.

It's the cooks who stayed with me until the end each night, helping until the last dish was done. I'll forever love those guys. A team effort to the end. That meant the world to me. When Tyler and I became cooks in 1998, we did the same for our dishwashers each night.

I need to thank Manager Tom for allowing me to wear my Walkman when washing. Sure, it was against Princess Tours policy, but once we left the yard, we were on our own. Some managers would scoff at this, but Manager Tom leveled with me. "Wear them, man. No sweat. Just get the job done and we're good," he told me as he put in another chew. He had his vices. I had mine. Those mixtapes saved my ass every shift. Thanks for being cool, man.

The summers were beautiful up there. The temperatures never really broke seventy-five degrees, which was great weather for riding bikes and skateboards around town. I'd hit Mammoth Records, the bookstore downtown, and go catch a movie at the theater where Northern Lights hit Route 1. I'd rent time on machines at Kinko's to design stuff, storing work on Zip disks. This is how I survived my summers up there.

I always had this sinking feeling that I was whiling away my youth in pursuit of Alaskan greenbacks. I mean, I was, but this was the only way I'd be able to get a machine that first summer. By my second summer, I started lugging the machine back up there with me so I could work. I would make T-shirts for the train workers as a way to supplement my summer savings. I remember making four trips on my bike to that screen printer to get all the shirts back to the house.

And for the record, Fred Green, I hated the job up there more than you. Now it's in print, bud. Two left shoes.

Back Down to the Lower 48
I got back down to Bend with my $9,700. And dropped the whole wad on my very first design rig: a Power Computing PowerTower Pro 180 MHz computer, a Power Computing monitor, a color scanner, a Hewlett-Packard laser printer and the Adobe Illustrator student edition. Everything else was pirated.

I remember putting in the order for the computer with a local reseller in Bend. I had already ordered the monitor, scanner and printer. He called and told me that he was on his way to deliver the computer. I had worked five months washing dishes for this moment and was so excited for the delivery. The guy pulls up in some shitty four-door Dodge Sadness. I was watching through the blinds. He parked, jumped out and opened the car's back door to grab the computer. There was my machine, just sort of lying on the seat back there. I was fuckin' horrified.

I remember setting it all up that night, so proud, so excited and so ready. That's when my new life in design started. Now I had all the tools at my disposal.

In no time, I had more than enough work to keep me going. One job from Lance Violette at Scott Snowboards was enough to float me all winter long. He gave me my first shot, and a taste of what was out there. I did product icons for an upcoming Scott catalog.

I ended up doing four summers up there. Surprisingly. After that first summer, I swore I'd never go back. But of course, one gravelly-voiced, sagelike cook named Chris Rosemond had these words for me: "Alaska is in you now. You can leave it, but it'll never leave you." Something poetic like that, and I remember rolling my eyes, counting down the hours until I'd get to hop that flight back to the Lower 48. But on some level, he was right.

I still get a little fidgety in late April each year, thinking about heading back up to the train. What a beautiful, pristine place Alaska is.

Leaner, meaner and counting down the days to go home. 1996.

Dishpit sketch...   ...and then inked. 1996.

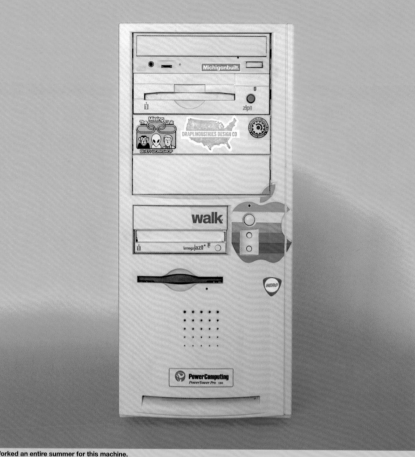

Worked an entire summer for this machine.

Butter tray postcard illustration. 1996.

Found this rock in Anchorage's mud flats, and tuned it up. 1996.

Summer On The Rail kitchen zine. 1997.

Strawberry jam packaging postcard illustration. 1996.

"Fruits of the Forest" pie packaging postcard illustration. Rare Dinosaur Jr.-inspired use of the color purple. 1996.

Digital Explosion

Minneapolis College of Art & Design

In the fall of 1997, I headed back home to explore the Midwest and hit a number of art schools. I checked out Kendall in Grand Rapids, the University of Michigan in Ann Arbor, MIAD in Milwaukee and MCAD in Minneapolis. I got a mixed bag of advice from the assorted admissions people. The woman at the U of M told me, point-blank, "We offer more of a cerebral approach to graphic design." That was a fun one. The guy from Kendall looked over my stuff and shook his head. "Man," he said, "you gotta go up the food chain a bit." He pointed me to MIAD. The woman who gave me the flustered tour there was mean and uninterested in my myriad of questions. That sealed the deal on that one. When I got all the way up to MCAD, they were really welcoming. The work the kids were doing looked complex, wild and a bit foreboding. The catalog alone was a nightmare of coded forms, adhering to the latest post-post-post-modern graphic design tricks. But that felt exciting and provocative. MCAD was my choice, and I started the admissions process.

That following spring of 1998, with all my work submitted for admission and scholarships, I got the first letter detailing my acceptance to MCAD! I remember how scary it all was, not knowing if I would make the cut. You see, the stuff I showed, that was from my time in Bend; self-taught, more or less. Reckless with big spirit, but still no idea of where I stood in the contemporary ranks of art school.

My last snowboard trip was to Telluride, Colorado. Chad Smith and I caught a free ride with friends from Bend, all of whom were competing at a snowboard contest there. I was up on the hill and remember some screaming nightmare mom, with a fur coat and everything, yelling at her kid to get to snowboard practice. That's the moment I knew I was done with snowboarding. I was so disgusted, I didn't even strap in for the final ride down the hill. That wasn't the snowboarding I knew and loved. I skated down to the bottom, walked up into Telluride's downtown, and checked my e-mail at some overpriced Internet café. That session, I got the e-mail telling me I was awarded the Wanda Gag scholarship, along with some Wisconsin kid named Mike Gaughan. $36,000 for four years! In my case, it would be $9,000 a year for the two years I would be attending. That made it possible for me. I remember telling the crew I got accepted…so proud, freaked out and excited. I was going to art school! Officially. Just had to get through a summer up in Alaska, and then I'd head down to Minneapolis to start school in the fall. School was a great experience for me

on so many levels. First, it allowed me to shed the shrinking, claustrophobic snowboard world. Both its somewhat incestuous and predictable artwork and its limited language and trajectories. That world is pretty big when you are nineteen, but I started looking for the next thing outside of it. I'd go up to Portland and hit Powell's Books to flip through *How* magazine and *Communication Arts*. Couldn't even afford the things, but they gave me a taste of what was going on outside of our little mountain town.

Second, school opened my eyes to the contemporary design world. The issues, trends and possibilities. I remember being blown away by the Walker Art Center in Minneapolis. And hell, I didn't understand but a third of the stuff. I was more interested in their materials and catalog designs than the stuff on the walls. As challenging as the work was, the elite quality of the design was aspirational.

Third, school helped me to realize and develop what I had already cultivated inside of me. And the opportunity to act on it. My little life in Bend was great and all, but I quickly knew there was a ceiling to what I could pull off there. Moving to Minneapolis removed all the barriers.

The main thing I learned at MCAD was how to attack a project. Thinking, analysis, taking notes, making sketches, executions and then refinement. From my first graphic design class up to those final couple projects, process was something that got drilled into you. I needed it.

My favorite teacher was a guy named Jerry Allan. I had him for one class, Foundation: 3D. A required class, kids were sleeping and phoning it in. His infectious positivity really made me look at the process of making things in a new way. In a couple projects, Jerry taught us not only how to look at a single sheet of paper in a new light, but most important, how to design our lives. With good thinking, anything was possible! And, man, that guy had the coolest boots!

I'll forever be indebted to Kali Nikitas and her commanding knowledge of type. First she taught us the power and privilege of the computer as a tool—by cutting out each letter and word from laser prints and reassembling them into sentences. Or how to re-create a ligature with french curves, rulers and ink. Classic production techniques; frustrating as hell, but ever so crucial. It quickly taught you how to savor each little letterform, and just how important each piece was. Kali taught me a hit list of typographic tips that I use

each day in my work. This was precisely why I went back to school.

The coolest part about my time in Minneapolis was my internship with Charles S. Anderson Design. My MCAD buddy P. J. Chmiel worked there and vouched for me. Todd Piper-Hauswirth looked over my work and gave me the gig for $2.20 an hour! I scanned in thousands of Eastern Bloc matchbox labels. I'd get a big "batch scan" going and then go explore the archives, peek into Todd's and Chuck's cubicles or head down a floor to bug Aaron Dimmel in the photo studio. I'd go home each Friday with a big headache, exhausted by how much cool stuff I was seeing. Never cracked open Illustrator once at CSA!

I've gotten into a little hot water with interviews and speaking fiascos talking about college. Even though I was self-taught for the most part, I knew school would be great for me. I thought I had to do it, to attain accreditation. So how *do* I feel about school versus self-teaching? I get that question all the time, and try to answer it consistently like this: Go to school if you can! Learn as much as you can! Invest in yourself and hold them to it.

But on the other hand, the idea of some kid coming out of school with $80,000 in debt and their heart not completely into it? Highway robbery. I remember meeting this kid from a pricey art school. He approached and deadpanned me with one question: "How am I going to pay off my school loan from this place?" He was in deep. And I went into this long, convoluted answer about how to attack it, how to rearrange priorities to get a good jump on paying the thing down with design. And he looked surprised and said, "Design? I have a degree in fiber arts." And it just sort of broke my heart. Design is a commercial thing, and there's ways to make loot *and* pay off the loans. I did it. But to get out from underneath everything with fine arts? I didn't know what to tell him. I still feel bad for that kid. He was so cynical and lost.

My two years getting my bachelors of science in graphic design went too quick. I learned so many tactile things at MCAD: welding, building things out of wood, controlling metal, sandblasting, screen printing, publication design with Jan Jancourt, bookbinding with Jody Williams and the power of the graphic novel with Frenchy Lunning. And most important, I learned I had what it took to make a life with design. I still miss my fruitful time in Minneapolis and kinda wish I never left.

Draplin
Design Co.

Pretty Much
Everything

Aaron James
Draplin

File Under:
Making The Grade

028
029

Process sketches for "Grizzly Habitat" pictograph project. 1998.

"D'Stries" T-shirt. 1998.

Hierarchy studies. Typography I class. 1998.

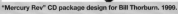

"Amtrak Card" from Typography II class. 1999.

"Mercury Rev" CD package design for Bill Thorburn. 1999.

"Open Road" road trip publication for Andrew Blauvelt. 1999.

Grumpy's Bar & Grill redesign. 1999.

3' x 4-1/2' process posters and final piece for 3D Foundations with Jerry Allan. 1998.

Minneapolis College of Art & Design

Washington Street Bridge. 1999.

Slide guitar player's hands. 1999.

Self portrait. 1999.

Arlie and Gabe from Juno. 1999.

Juno, raging. 1999.

Uncle Kevin loading in his gear. 1999.

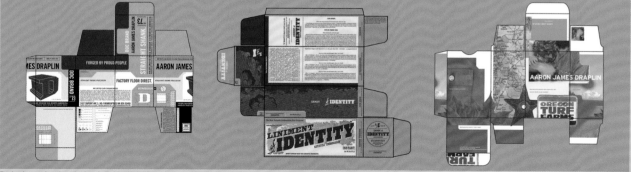

Packaging explorations for Laurie DeMartino's "Graphic Design III" class. 1999.

Draplin
Design Co.

Pretty Much
Everything

Aaron James
Draplin

File Under:
Making The Grade

030
031

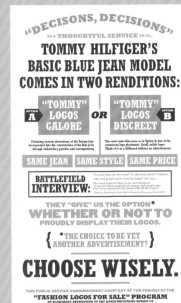

Senior projects posters. 2000.

"Famous Child Star Alcoholics," 2-color screen print. 1999.

"Kurt" school-wide propaganda campaign. 2000.

"Chico Shuda" book cover design. 1999.

"The Record Show," 2-color screen print. 2000.

"Nashville Pussy at First Avenue," 7-color screen print. 1999.

Gocco relocation postcard. 1998.

Gocco graduation announcement. 2000.

Self portrait, acrylic inks on masonite. 1998.

Gainful Employment
"First jobs. Making a living with design."

DDC

Draplin
Design Co.

Pretty Much
Everything

Aaron James
Draplin

File Under:
Ready To Punch In

032
033

Shitfaced at the World Quarterpipe Championships.
Top of the quarterpipe. Waterville Valley, NH. 2001.

My First Job out of College

In early 2000, I was in my winter semester at MCAD when I get this call from Mark Sullivan, representing *Snowboarder* magazine. I knew his name. He was from *East Infection*, a scrappy snowboard magazine from Vermont. I had met those guys briefly at High Cascade Snowboard Camp in the summer of 1995. The first time was up on the glacier, with "camp cop" Jason Lily kicking those hooligans out of the half-pipe. And later that afternoon down in Government Camp, where Pat Bridges gave me a copy of their mag. And I remember thinking, *These are the derelicts we kicked out earlier today?* I want to hang with these guys! There was an art director position opening up at *Snowboarder*. Duties included doing all the design for the mag, as well the events, clothing and website. The whole mess. Mark was Editor, Pat was Assistant Editor.

It would mean moving down to Southern California, and I remember how unsettling that was. I was so excited to stay and work in Minneapolis after MCAD wrapped up. I even had an internship lined up at Bill Thorburn's wing of Carmichael Lynch right downtown. Things were looking up for the upcoming summer. But of course, I was intrigued enough to put together a portfolio to send down to Mark and the guys. If anything, to see what they'd say. *Snowboarder* had been my favorite snowboard mag growing up. That was the only mag that showed guys I rode with from the Northwest.

Its competitor *Transworld Snowboarding* was the leading magazine in the industry and ruled the roost. A year prior, I had gotten a call from my old Bend buddy Dave Sypniewski. He was working at *TWSnow*, and told me about a design position that was opening up, and how

I'd have to move down to Oceanside. As cool as it sounded, my heart just wasn't into that mag. I politely opted out.

Something was different about the *Snowboarder* offer. You got the sense of what they were up against, and their frisky underdog quality. They were shaking things up, which sounded fun as hell. I took the job, finished up the school year, finagled a externship through MCAD, loaded up a Ryder truck and moved it all down to Hellhole, Southern California.

My first morning down there, I remember feeling like I had made a mistake. It was everything I loved about a place: congested, hot and expensive! Great. I instantly wanted to hightail it back to Minneapolis. But Dad had taught me to stick to my guns. I told them I'd do two cycles of the mag, and was determined to slay each and every issue.

With the new team assembled, it was an opportunity to reset the mag, shedding the cliché writing styles, photography, and design. I loved the all-for-one clubhouse feel. We all worked toward a common goal—getting the issue done.

Covers were always tricky. We had some intense cover battles, internally with our team, and then with the top brass. That's the one spot the higher-ups would weigh in on; all the analytics and cover tricks would be sort of forced on us. I remember taking the time to hear out our boss, Norb Garrett. And the guys were freaking out that I was consorting with the enemy! I knew there was a way to make both sides comfortable. In the end, we weren't gonna win some bullshit battle when possible sales were on the line. Aesthetics? Right out the window when

it came to moving product. And that was okay, I did my best to fulfill both sides' wishes. Design school taught me how to listen, weigh the options, and then show solutions to solve the problem. And that's what you'll see below in our cover battles.

Snowboarder is where I met Evan Rose. "Broke the mold" doesn't really work with this animal. Wild, with eccentric tastes, an eye for bric-a-brac, and one of the funniest people I've ever met. He'd call to me, I'd look down from our roost into his cubicle, and he'd be completely nude—"About to put my wet suit on"—just waiting for people to walk in. Funny as hell to watch. That's who I hung with down there. Pat, Evan and I. Three piles of shit, completely out of our element on that beach.

And the perks? As much gear as I needed! Care packages from Eddie Lee and Gravis. Promo CDs from music labels! Summers were intense, but there would be a lull after Christmas where all the writers and photographers would hit the road, scrambling to amass content for the coming year. I got to travel to New Zealand, British Columbia, Wolf Creek, Mount Bohemia and even Cabo Wabo for an editorial conference.

Here's what I'm most proud of about my time at *Snowboarder*: These guys were my brothers and it was up to us to make it work. And we did, and our numbers reflected it. From Pat's brilliant captions and stories, to Jeff Baker's diplomatic photo brokering, to Mark's editorial calls, to Mike "Chief" Nusenow's closed-door deals. It was from our hands. We were responsible for all the output. I'm still so proud of our output those twenty-two months on that damned beach.

September 2000.

October 2000.

November 2000.

December 2000.

January 2001.

February 2001.

March 2001.

September 2001.

October 2001.

November 2001.

December 2001.

January 2002.

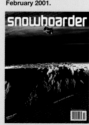

February 2002.

March 2002.

DDC

Draplin
Design Co.

Pretty Much
Everything

Aaron James
Draplin

File Under:
Band of Brothers

034
035

JUXTAPOZ
JUXTAPOZ
JUXTAPOZ

JUXTAPOZ

BLOTTER ACID
R. CRUMB

RICK GRIFFIN

GRAFFITI
DAN CLOWES

VAUGHN & MARK TODD
HR GIGER
DEREK HESS
PUNK MAGAZINE
CAMILLE ROSE GARCIA
TATTOO ART
JON SWIHART
BEASTIE BOYS
TOM SACHS
HOT RODS

STANLEY MOUSE
N. K. GIGER
MARK MOTHERSBAUGH
VALENTIN POPOV

#29 NOV/DEC 2000
#31 MAR/APR 2001
#32 MAY/JUN 2001

MARK RYDEN
KURT WENNER
MARK DANCEY & STEVE CERIO
HUNGRY DOG
LINDA BARK MARIE
ROCK
ROLL

RVW8 THE FIZZ
JAMES TRELL

#36 JAN/FEB 2002

CHARLIE WHITE
CHARLES LONG

WING CHU
RON ENGLISH

01
03
04
05
06
07
07
08
08

VOLUME 13
VOLUME 13
VOLUME 13
VOLUME 13

2001-2002 SNOWBOARDER MAGAZINE BUYER'S GUIDE

SNOWBOARDER MAGAZINE BUYER'S GUIDE

SNOWBOARDER MAGAZINE SUPERPARK 4

SNOWBOARDER MAGAZINE THE SOUL OF SNOWBOARDING

SNOWBOARDER THE EUROPE ISSUE

SNOWBOARDER GUEST EDITOR TODD RICHARDS

SNOWBOARDER 2001 PHOTO ANNUAL

SNOWBOARDER RIDER OF THE YEAR

SNOWBOARDER RIDER OF THE YEAR

SNOWBOARDER THE SUMMER ISSUE

SNOWBOARDER THE SUMMER ISSUE

SNOWBOARDER 2002 BUYER'S GUIDE

SNOWBOARDER GUEST EDITOR MIKEY LEBLANC

SNOWBOARDER SUPERPARK 5

SNOWBOARDER BRITISH COLUMBIA ISSUE

SNOWBOARDER SNOWPOURRI

SNOWBOARDER 2002 PHOTO ANNUAL

SNOWBOARDER RIDER OF THE YEAR

emap usa
emap usa
emap usa
emap usa
emap usa
emap usa
emap usa

14/01
14/02
14/03
14/04
14/05
14/06
14/07

SNOWBOARD
SNOWBOARD
SNOWBOARD
SNOWBOARD
SNOWBOARD

Products, Places & Personalities
Products, Places & Personalities
PRODUCTS PLACES PERSONALITIES
PRODUCTS PLACES PERSONALITIES

Have Fun With Your Friends.

Ride Everything. Ride Everything.

Snowboarding from a New Point of View.

Fall 2004 — Premiere Issue

Winter 2004 — Issue Two

Spring 2005 — Issue Three

CHOOSE YOUR OWN LINE.
FOR THE FUN OF IT.
TAKE CHANCES

VOLUME 02/ISSUE 01
VOLUME 02/ISSUE 02
VOLUME 02/ISSUE 03

Snowboarder Magazine

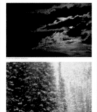

Assorted *Snowboarder* magazine spreads. 2000–2002.

DDC

Draplin
Design Co.

Pretty Much
Everything

Aaron James
Draplin

File Under:
Beach Living, Man

036
037

Promotional T-shirt design for *Snowboarder's* trade show giveaways. 2000.

Driven To Ride giveaway T-shirt for the 2001 motorhome tour. 2001.

Cinco Design Office

It was April 2002, chugging right along at *Snowboarder* magazine. I get a call from John "Goo" Phemister and he's looking for new design hires for his Portland firm, Cinco Design. These are the guys who do Nixon and Gravis! He asks if I know any kids to go after, and I reply, "Yeah. Me!" Southern California just wasn't gonna cut it. I was close to finishing my two cycles of the mag. This was my shot to get the hell out of there.

I send some work up, and a week later I fly to Portland to interview, see their shop and meet the crew. And of course, their shop is cool as hell. Super mellow, progressive and doing incredible work. They launched Nixon and Gravis, two well-respected action sport brands. This is where I got rescued back to Oregon, so relieved to work in a cool design shop, making good loot and living in Portland, a town I was comfortable in.

Cinco was my first studio job. Complete with account managers, time sheets, proper pay structures, modern furniture, counterculture art and people excited to be there. And I got my first title. I was a "Senior Designer" all of the sudden!

I learned so many things at Cinco. How to set up a multipage document, allowing for detailed PDF presentations. How to design a watch! From the dial typography to the body design to the strap materials. How to handle a client on a phone call. That clients can be friends—which makes me think of my buddy Matt Capozzi. We worked closely together on Gravis stuff, then Nixon stuff. How to refine, refine and refine, down to the perfect logo, watch dial, or ad comp. Kirk James's process and determination to do good work all the time is something I'll carry with me the rest of my life. Nothing was phoned in from that guy. I'll forever be impressed by his abilities.

And, man, I learned how to play Ping-Pong. Sure, Ben Munson ruled the roost, but I did beat the guy ONE time. And that thrashing is still echoing around Southeast Portland. I had nine serves and would just yell out, "Which one you want? Pick one through nine!" No one was impressed.

But it also scared me. We'd burn up the whole day playing Ping-Pong, then hammer for a couple hours and fire off comps at 4:59 P.M. I always felt bad about that. I remember a client yelling at us on the phone, and swearing to myself that no amount of loot was worth that shit. Or working long, confused hours and the stuff not seeing the light of day. But this is how every joint is, right? I had heard from too many people that another world existed outside of agency life. And it started to bug me, seeing so many examples of friends around Portland making a living on their own terms. The brands I was starting with friends were taking off. Coal Headwear was going and *Snowboard* mag was on the horizon. Those were substantial commitments.

I did two full years at Cinco. My freelance opportunities were starting to compete with my day job. I could make more loot off the clock on my own time. That's when it tipped. I put my month notice in, started shopping for a house and made plans to go out on my own. That would've been April 2004 when I made the leap.

Gravis advertising campaign. Art direction by Kirk James. Design by Aaron James Draplin and Chris Soli. Account management by Dean Gross. 2002-2003.

DDC

Draplin
Design Co.

Pretty Much
Everything

Aaron James
Draplin

File Under:
Just Make It Look III

038
039

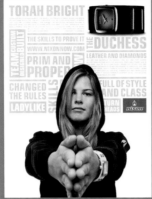

Nixon advertising campaign. Art direction by Kirk James. Design by Aaron James Draplin and Chris Soli. Account management by Dean Gross. 2002-2003.

The Dork Metal. Art direction by Kirk James. Design by Aaron James Draplin. 2003.

The Dork. Art direction by Kirk James. Design by Aaron James Draplin. 2003.

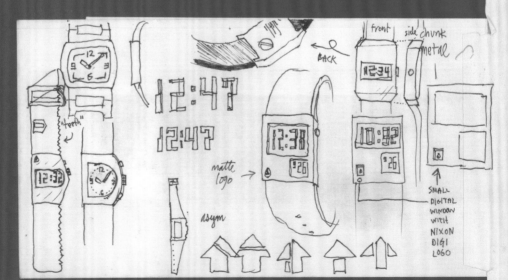

My initial idea for the Dork was sketched on a puke bag, on the way back from Encinitas, all fired up after a big Nixon product meeting.

Independence

"Going out on my own."

Tricking out the basement to our precise specs. Pants optional.

Getting Ahead By Any Means Necessary

I've always been one to take the slow, safe road when it comes to finances. From pizza jobs that covered rent out west, to that first summer in Alaska saving for a computer, and finally, pinching all my pennies while at *Snowboarder* magazine, desperately trying to pay down credit card debt amassed at MCAD. I just couldn't get ahead at the mag. Being close to $10,000 in the hole and not seeing any light at the end of the tunnel, and having to deal with all that sun? No wonder I only made it twenty-two months down there. That place just ate all the money up. Nothing was left over at the end of the month. When I got up to Cinco, I made enough loot to get ahead a little bit. In about a year, I paid off that damn credit card I'd been dragging along since my MCAD years. This was my first step to really getting free.

It was scary going out fully on my own. For a number of reasons. First off, I was leaving the security of Cinco and their steady stream of solid projects, insurance, profit sharing and account managers to track our movements. That stuff was nice, but it was a bit claustrophobic. I played along as well as I could but got a whiff of being able to do this stuff on my own, free of the conventional professional pitfalls.

I had to give it a shot. Could I make a living from my basement? All signs pointed to a big, meaty "Yes!" Overhead? That was my house. Business expenses? Every cent I made went to arming myself with the right equipment. And all of it from a simple, frugal perspective.

Going out on my own, I started to see stuff start to change right away. I had more time to focus. I could work until the wee hours or take the day off to rest. And I took every single job that came down the pipe. Everything added up. I was just hoping to hit something close to what Cinco was throwing down.

And I did. The first year I was on my own? I tripled my previous wage. No one told me this could or would happen. I'm still blown away by that little figure. I did a budget for myself, stuck to it and made time for each job. Once I got past the hurdle of having enough work on my own, I started to focus on chipping away at the bigger problems: loans, loans and loans.

Equipment

I always tried to be smart about equipment. Invest in the best gear as possible, and be frugal wherever you can. I always tried to buy the best computers I could afford, careful to be able to cover each transaction. I put as little loot as I could on credit cards. Basically, the rule is this: Don't buy something you can't afford. As simple as that. If you have to throw it on a credit card? Fine. But damn, pay that thing off right away.

School Loans

I left school in 2000 close to $27,000 in debt. And I faithfully paid each month for eight years. A couple years into that, I doubled my monthly payment to chip away at the balance quicker. Each month, I'd fill out the check, put it in the envelope, affix the stamp and send it off, fretting its delivery and subsequent reflection on my balance. I remember freaking out at the possibility that my envelope would get lost in the mail and it'd be some kind of "ding" on my account and credit. It made it each time.

Proud of having been able to make the payments, some eight years after leaving MCAD, I called to check the balance. The girl on the other end chirped a tinny "Oh, it's at twenty-thousand-something-or-other dollars." That seemed a bit high. All these years making the payments, and then doubling the payment the last four years, and I'd only chipped off a mere $7,000? It didn't seem right. The loan officer explained it to me with the principal, interest, and the whole deal. A bleak outlook. And yet, that whole time, I thought I was getting ahead.

So that day, I emptied my whole bank account and paid that loan all the way off. Flustered, the loan officer offered to reduce the rate, refinance and whatever the hell else. So slimy. Whatever it took to keep you held down. I paid it off that afternoon and got a little taller with that bullshit off my back. Now, I understand very clearly that I got off pretty easy with school. I was lucky to get an incredible scholarship and be able to pay back the loans quickly. But still, that took hard work and sticking to a tight budget.

Adventures in Homeowning

When I bought my little house in 2004, I remember feeling lucky for the privilege. That's one of the big things in life, you know? And I always build them up into these mythic, ominous creatures. I worked my ass off for the down payment and spent a ton of time finding the right place around Portland. Simple enough. Once I finally locked in, I remember being so freaked out at "thirty years of payments" and how much the bank would make. And how powerless we all were in the face of odds like that. I paid that loan each month faithfully, and yet still had money left over. Seven years into the loan, I drained the savings and paid my house off. And each year since then, I've saved close to $10,000 in what would have been good ol' interest. Screw that.

First it was paying off my school loans. Then it was the house. My Volvo? I paid cash for that Swedish meatball. Hell, I even paid off my appendix! I don't write this shit to brag, I write it because I'm so proud I did it by working with my friends, on things I love.

Frugal Living

Mike Watt called it doing things "econo." Watt booked his own tours, carried his own gear up to the stage and sold shirts from a garbage bag at the end of the show. That had a profound effect on me. He was a punk rock hero, renowned in the ranks. To see him being human with every aspect of his work made it hit home that much harder. Mike Watt made it okay to go out on my own.

On the facing page you'll see my beloved Cabela's "Bargain Cave" windbreaker. That's my security blanket. It's been around the world a number of times. I've rolled the odometer on that thing! It's been mended by my little sister Leah a couple times now. And if my memory serves me correctly, I paid a whopping $16 for it in Owatonna, Minnesota. Back in 2008 or something.

Here's the thing: I don't need five windbreakers. I need one. And I'll use that thing until it dies. There's something to be said about being frugal, and, hell, not really knowing any better. America is weird when it comes to how we consume things. Closets full of unused bullshit. And I'd reckon I'm as guilty as the next guy.

I remember reading some quip about how the writer was "the most freest I'd ever been when I could fit all my contents into one backpack." That's stuck with me all these years. I know, I know, if you've ever been to the shop you are rolling your eyes, but shit, paper and ephemera are a different thing. The important part is that I try to be cognizant of how I spend each penny. And sure, it's a bit obsessive, but I know that it's these small steps that have gotten me to where I am today.

I haven't had a cent of debt since around 2008. And that took a lot of work. I still believe that making the jump to freelance is what rescued me from a life of pinching pennies and jobs that pay you precisely as little as they can.

This fuckin' thing needs to be washed. Or burned.

Coal Headwear

Who says you can't work with your friends? Coal was the first large-scale project that took off when I first went out on my own in 2004. It all started the year before.

I met Brad Scheuffele in a couple ways. First, he was hogging up all the good windblown berms for an exclusive photo session up above Rainbow Chair at Mount Bachelor. My scrub buddies and I were grumbling something along the lines of "Who the hell is Brad Shoe-fell?" And then a couple months later we see him in an ad for Burton snowboards! That was BIG. Who was this guy?

Second time I meet the guy is at one of the infamous Cinco Design parties in Portland and he was just wrapping up a couple years working on M3 snowboards. Higher-ups had pulled the plug on the company, right when the thing was taking off. I remember how shook up he was, to have the thing snubbed just as they were getting traction. He was so dedicated and that impressed me.

Brad was looking for his next thing and we talked quickly about a headwear company he was working up with friends in Seattle. Our mutual buddy John "Goo" Phemister was busy getting Holden Outerwear going with our mutual friends Scotty Zergebel and Mikey LeBlanc. And I think they recommended me when Goo was already snatched up.

A couple months later I got going on a wordmark for the Coal Headwear company, and once that was locked down, we made our debut catalog featuring the first sixteen beanies. Brad and I hammered out the details from my shitty apartment in Portland, in the spring of 2003.

Before we knew it, the thing exploded and we were busy making extensive advertising campaigns, apparel graphics, trim details, catalogs, banner ads, hangtags and point-of-purchase messaging. Complete with a sales force, reps, management, team riders and support staff. From a basement to a real company in a couple years.

From the very get-go, Coal was a chance to quiet things down a bit, design-wise. In the competitive world of snowboarding action imagery, we'd be charting some new territory by allowing the photography to guide the brand. Simple, honest photos of the product and team out in the world. Just people standing there, with a casual focus on the headwear. By removing ourselves from the action photography pissing matches, we freed ourselves up. Eventually, we'd use action photography, and when we did, it was our perspective and not from the latest movie or clique.

Subtle, subtle moves. When explaining Coal to people, I talk about how it always felt warm to me. An odd "fuzz" to everything. Both in the look and feel, and in the voice of the brand.

We learned pretty quickly to stay away from big marketing speak sorts of directions. Just keep it conversational. Brad would be stuck on something and I'd ask him to explain it to me. He'd calm down, tell me what he was thinking, and I'd say, "Hey, just put that in there." I'd rather have it from his voice directly, instead of fumbling around trying to polish it into something we aren't.

I'm so proud of the Coal photography direction. Models can be kinda weird.

With the pursed lips and distant looks. The people wearing the headwear in the catalogs? Those were our friends, team riders and warehouse punks. That's why the stuff always felt comfortable. We'd go out and do quick, casual shoots around Portland. And the proof was in the pages. Our photographers were always our friends, too. Andy Wright, Embry Rucker and Mark Welsh. They're from the same world. That's important, as there's nothing more damaging than elevating a brand above the people who'll be using it. We'll leave that shit for the fashion brands. I've been told the close, friendly relationship we enjoyed between the people who make the Coal, shoot it, organize it, sell it and ultimately ship it is a rare thing. Wouldn't have it any other way! That's something I am very thankful for.

A decade later, Coal is an innovative company with hundreds of designs offered each season, sold in stores all over the world, building an ever-expanding ambassador team who promotes the gear. And, my favorite of all, it's beautiful proof of watching a buddy with a great sense of design, photography and organizational skills who's willing to work the long hours make something big out of something small.

Even though Brad wanted to wring my neck 3,406 times, I am forever thankful for that initial trust in my abilities to help him get Coal off the ground. I did a decade with Coal. Very, very proud of that. Thanks, Brad. Love you, bud. And hell, I'm still using that Aeron chair. You literally "save my ass" each day in the shop.

And sorry about the snoring that one time in Austria.

Where it all started for Coal Headwear. Spring 2003.

Catalog designs from a decade on the clock for Coal Headwear. 2003-2013.

Coal Headwear Advertising

coal — MIKEY LEBLANC WEARING THE "GRANDMA"

Robbie Sell in the Frena

coal

Jessica Dalpiaz in the Stella

coal

coal

Justin Hebbel in the Frena and Dylan scarf

coal

DDC

Draplin
Design Co.

Pretty Much
Everything

Aaron James
Draplin

File Under:
Mellow Movement

046
047

Jessica Dalpiaz in the Nels.

coal

coal
Jon Kooley in the Theo.

Jon Kooley   Priscilla Levac   Robbie Sell   Laura Hadar   Justin Hebbel   Mikey Leblanc

coal

coal

Jon Kooley in the FLT.

Desiree Melancon in the Cameron   coal

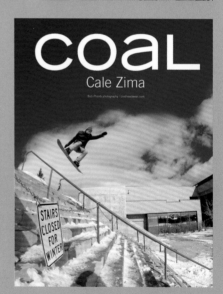

coal
Cale Zima

coal

coal

coal
Laura Hadar

Coal Logo Vault

Coal was my first client where I was completely immersed. I did it all for them. When Brad needed something, he'd call and I'd get at it. Well, I'd hem, haw, lie, cheat, steal and then cry about how busy I was to him. Somewhere in there, I'd make the logo for the badge or patch he was on my case about. After a decade, what a pile of stuff. Stuff comes and goes, and when you dig into the vaults, you are reminded of all the little instances I made Brad's life worth living.

DDC

Draplin
Design Co.

Pretty Much
Everything

Aaron James
Draplin

File Under:
Exacting Details

048
049

Trim details from a decade of Coal Headwear design, 2003–2013.

Starting a Snowboarding Magazine

They told us we couldn't do it. That's the first thing I remember about getting *Snowboard* mag going. "They" being the powers that be in the snowboard publishing industry. They said there was no room for our mag. Man, did we prove those shortsighted turds wrong.

Wait, that's the second thing I remember. *Snowboard* mag started with a call from my old buddies Mark Sullivan and Jeff Baker at *Snowboarder* magazine in San Juan Capistrano. I remember being instantly a bit miffed at getting that call. "You guys again? You already ruined my life once!" But of course, I had to hear them out, seduced by the excitement in their voices.

They were going to make their own snowboarding magazine. With beautiful photography, product-centric layouts and a simple, clean design. And I was the guy who they wanted to do the design part. All these years later, as much as I mess with these guys about "ruining my life in California" and all that, you have to know: I couldn't say yes quick enough. The spirit of starting something new with your buddies was what got me. I trusted these guys with my life. Not only did we work closely together down there, we hung out. We traveled together. Of course I wanted in, you animals!

So we assembled our crackpot team of incorrigibles in Portland and made our first issue. And fuck if it didn't turn out INCREDIBLE. The voice was spot-on—confident, feisty and positive. We'd all been through the cynical cycles of the shred world. This felt new, and so did the designing of it. I built a simple system that could handle whatever the boys lobbed at me. The cleaner, the better. I remember Baker explaining how we "wouldn't be messing with the photos" and I loved him for it. Keep it clean and let it breathe.

Starting from the ground up came with the incredible opportunity to shed all the tricks, clichés and styles going on in the snowboarding magazine world. I looked back at the simplest of grids, which allowed the photos to be free and unfettered and the words to be legible, within a system that allowed us to pound out pages. To assemble the team was no easy feat. Mark was coming from Idaho. Jeff and Gary Hansen were coming up from San Clemente. Mike Basher was coming over from Denver. Jason "J2" Rasmus would somehow make it over from Salt Lake City. Larry Nuñez, Dave England and I lived in town. To get us all in one spot, we had to focus and capitalize on the time together. Submissions would come in from the mountains. Nate Deschenes and Tawnya Shultz would send in reports

from Mammoth Lakes, California. We'd have seven to eight days to build the mag, with files released to the printer the twenty-fifth hour of that final night. The process was pretty diplomatic. It's interesting when you strip the office dynamics out of stuff. This was about making something we were proud of. The debates were always about making good decisions, or picking the best shot for the cover. Cover battles would go into the wee hours, with factions forming and *12 Angry Men*–esque deliberations.

Some three thousand pages later, we pulled off seven years of the magazine, at least enough to get everyone paid back. For the most part.

Why this is a triumph is simply this: We did it. We put it all on the line, and the first couple issues got the confidence of the brands that would ultimately be the success of the mag. Magazines rely on advertising. One by one, all the big companies got on board. I'll never forget the initial advertising buys, and owe a debt of gratitude to those who believed in us from the beginning. Thank you.

Snowboard mag is still going strong. We sold it to the Freeskier group in Boulder in 2011 and the mag just hit its eleventh season.

Mark Sullivan, Jason "J2" Rasmus and Dave England "helping along" my initial logo ideas. June 2004.

We almost went with an alpine boar enthusiast magazine.

Above: Spines and how they change from
season to season of the mag. 2004-2010.

Selecting the image for the cover was always a battle.
It'd start the night before the files were due, with debates
and arguments raging into the night. Somehow, we'd all
agree on the very perfect shot. 2004-2010.

Snowboard Magazine Spreads

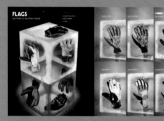

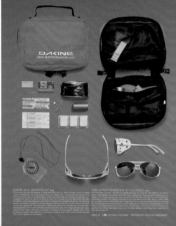

DDC

Draplin
Design Co.

Pretty Much
Everything

Aaron James
Draplin

File Under:
Guided By Grids

052
053

Snowboard Magazine Spreads

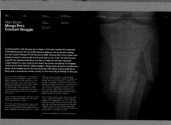

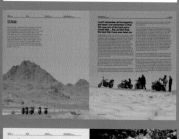

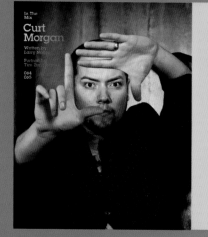

DDC

Draplin
Design Co.

Pretty Much
Everything

Aaron James
Draplin

File Under:
Guided By Guzman

054
055

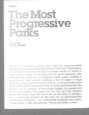

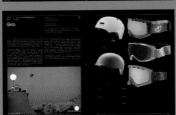

Union Binding Co.

Brad from Coal Headwear said something about how I'd be getting a call "from George about starting a binding company" from the other side of the office at C3 Worldwide. I liked the sound of that. I didn't know any Georges. It turned out that George Kleckner was an old-school snowboarder who walked the walk back in the day. A great rider in his own right, he knew the culture and how to build a team from his time at Drake bindings. This was in the fall of 2004. He got me up to speed about company founder Martino Fumagalli in Italy and his history of making bindings, went over the basic marketing initiatives with me and walked me through the logo explorations up to that point. We worked out a list of projects and got down to work.

The Design of Union
The first thing I made was the logo. To this day, that's still one of my favorites. Designed within a square, strong and bold enough to be molded into plastic, pressed into leather and embroidered at small sizes. I built the logo with the binding's needs in mind. It HAD to be successful on the product first. All the print and Web stuff would be cake after that.

Whereas its older brother Coal Headwear was warm and casual with realistic lifestyle photography, from the get-go we knew that Union would be a straight-forward, plainspoken design approach. Unapologetic. Confident. Bold, industrial typography; dramatic product photos; enduring colorways with simple messaging across the board. It's one thing to write a blurb about the strength of a binding chassis. It's another thing to simply put the word "STRONGER" next to it. Efficient and effective. I'm most proud of the catalog and advertising designs.

The catalog would be the first thing we'd make, and if you had your shit together, that would inform the advertising campaign, packaging and soft goods for the following season. The product design was Martino's department. He'd been designing snowboard bindings for fifteen years, and yet, at the beginning of Union, he completely trusted our feedback and design contributions. Martino designed the basic chassis based on strength, durability and minimal styling. Then, as a team, we'd fight it out and pick the colors, designing all the finishing details into another yearly collection.

Exotic Travel
That first time George and I flew to Milan was incredible. My first time to Europe! And you know, you get off the plane, whip up to Colico and Martino puts you to work. Under bright fluorescent lights. Exotic travel! Exotic lands! Luxurious accommodations! Actually, I will say, the house we stayed in was pretty damn nice, on a mountain, overlooking the breathtaking Lake Como. I'm still blown away by the quality of the littlest things in Europe. Be it a roof, a windowsill or a stairway. Things are built better and are built to last for generations. America builds stuff to last fifteen years. Martino Fumagalli builds stuff to last 1,500 years. The next time you are in Colico, look at the guy's roof and you'll know what the hell I'm talking about.

You get off the plane, get settled into their offices and the jet lag grabs ahold of you. Before you know it, your head is slumped and you are drooling on your supper. George spoke about "drinking through the time difference," but I don't remember him utilizing that technique all that effectively. We were notorious for getting in trouble for leaving the lights on,

due to Italy buying their power from Libya. You know, big dumb Americans, wasting this and that. Sorry, Italy, we're used to a different utilities landscape.

Making Friends in Italy
On one of my last visits to Colico to work, George and I had early flights back to the States out of Milan. Martino set up a ride for us with one of his employees. The guy woke us up early and we were on the windy road back down to Milan. I remember it raining super hard, and I also remember how fast that fucker was driving. We were sliding and gliding, at however many kilometers per hour, and George and I were packed in the backseat, holding on for dear life, sort of nervously laughing. So, I broke the ice a bit and ask the guy to slow it down a notch. In between puffs of cigarette smoke, he rattled something back to us in Italian, and who knows what the hell the guy was saying. He didn't speak a lick of English. He was jolly and nice, but we weren't getting through to him. So we sped along, and me, being ever the international gentleman, started in on him. "We hate your face!" He laughed and chirped something back to us in Italian. And we laughed in the backseat, and so it went. Somehow, we made it to the Milan airport, unloaded our shit, and as we were saying our good-byes, shaking hands and shit, I said, "You ever come to Portland, I'll kill you. And I hate your family. And I hate your face." And whatever other spirited shit I had to say that morning. He laughed, we hugged it out and made our way in to check in. A day later, I heard from Martino: "Why'd you tell Matteo you were going to kill his face?"

Union is still progressing, and has grown into the industry's leading binding brand.

DDC

Draplin
Design Co.

Pretty Much
Everything

Aaron James
Draplin

File Under:
So Good Up There

056
057

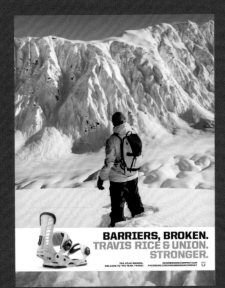

Union Binding Co. Catalog Spreads

2005
2006

2006
2007

2007
2008

2008
2009

DDC

Draplin
Design Co

Pretty Much
Everything

Aaron James
Draplin

File Under
Food Court Gangsters

058
059

**2009
2010**

**2010
2011**

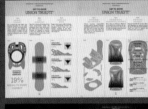

**2011
2012**

**2012
2013**

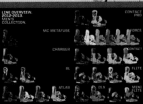

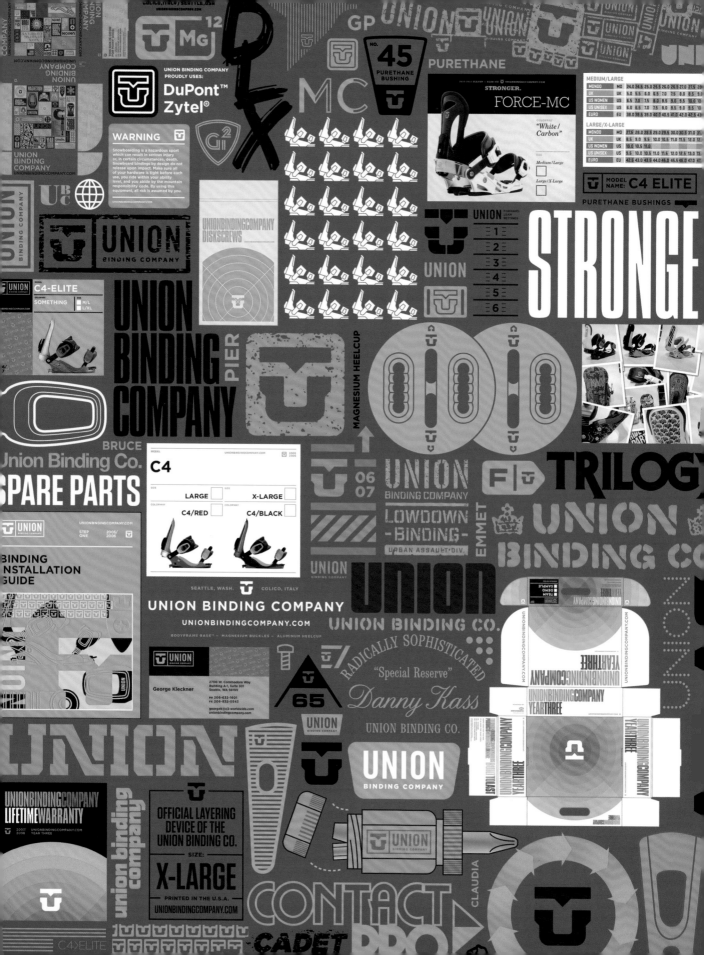

Grenade Gloves

My little experience with Grenade Gloves started when I met Danny Kass at the *Snowboarder* magazine offices. There was a large group of "Grenerds" down from Mammoth Lakes, loitering. And I remember Pat pointing out Danny and saying, "That kid, he's the next big thing in snowboarding." This was in 2002, just before I headed up to Portland. And Pat was right. In no time, this crew of ragtag scrubs would blow up in all the magazines, videos and contests.

Danny's older brother Matt was the brains behind the brand. A former pro snowboarder himself, he schemed up Grenade and its military theme and knew the right people to get those first crucial couple of glove samples going. And he had the charisma to sell it to an ever-cynical snowboard industry and their retail outlets.

My involvement started with a couple T-shirt graphics for Matt. He'd throw me an idea, I'd bust it out and that would be that. Next thing you knew, some scrub would be wearing it in some magazine spread. There was no red tape at Grenade.

If Matt dug it, he'd show it to the team. If they were on board, it would be injected into the line. And then it would explode.

I'd help Tim Karpinski and Seth Neefus with catalogs and photo shoots and try to keep things on track graphically. I had a couple years on them and would watch over the mess, while we'd all tag-team the thing. Page marathons!

That was my favorite part about Grenade. We'd have a quick discussion, laugh up a game plan and then execute. No back-and-forth bullshit. And they'd be thankful for the stuff. Matt Kass is one of the first guys to really thank me for the time I did on a job. And this was at a time when people were sort of rolling their eyes at Grenade.

Like action sports, the snowboard industry is fickle. One year it's this, the next year it's that. Styles, names and technologies come and go, and when Grenade hit, you heard the nay-saying from the bigger companies. And sure, maybe their stuff wasn't the same quality, and established brands loved to shit-talk them. But here's

the deal: Kids loved Grenade and the stuff had soul. Matt could sell sand to a camel, and the industry loved his enthusiasm and apeshit energy. And, the gang owned the company. No board of directors or bloated parent companies.

At one point Grenade was up to six million dollars in sales. Blew my mind. The line was growing, the stores carrying the stuff were lined up and things were taking off more and more each time I'd check in.

In the end, Grenade imploded. People left, people came on board and I'll never forget sitting across the table from one of the scariest people I've ever dealt with. That's when I jumped out.

I'll be forever proud of my work with those dirtbags. That's my favorite snowboarding brand I got to work on, because it embodied a youthful "don't give a fuck" attitude, didn't take itself too seriously and made cool shit for wild kids. That's the way this shit should always be. It sure was, for a hot couple years with Grenade Gloves. Viva la Grenade!

Logo iterations, working towards the final mark for Grenade Optics. 2007.

  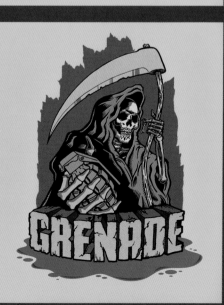

Process sketch, inking it and then coloring it up for hand-off. Grenade Reaper T-shirt. 2003.

DDC

Draplin
Design Co.

Pretty Much
Everything

Aaron James
Draplin

File Under:
We Must Exploit

062
063

"Grenade Handling Basics" T-shirt. 2002.

"Unkle Buck" T-shirt. 2005.

"Anthrax Stack" T-shirt. 2007.

"Gren-Ade is it!" T-shirt. 2007.

"Freedom Fighter" T-shirt. 2006.

"Handle Carefully" T-shirt. 2007.

"Comin' In Hot" T-shirt. 2005.

"Grenade Icon" T-shirt. 2007.

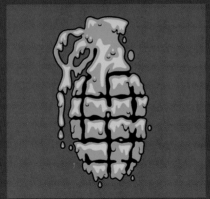

"Grenade Gore Metal" T-shirt. 2007.

"Slime Grenade" T-shirt. 2007.

"Gone Fishin'" T-shirt. 2005.

Grenade Gloves Catalogs/Assorted Grenerdery

**2005
2006**

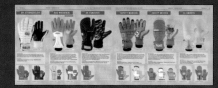

**2006
2007**

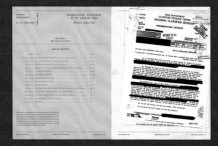
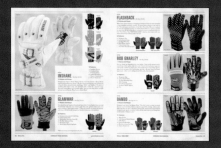

**2007
2008**

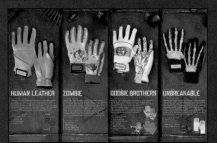

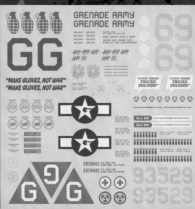

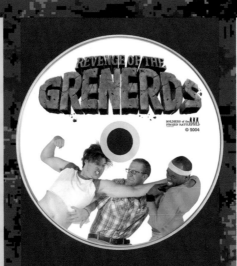
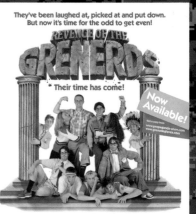

Designing Snowboard Graphics

One of the greatest moments in my snowboarding career was the first time I saw a board I designed whip by! It was the spring of 1994 and we were up at Mt. Baker when a kid whipped by on the Solid "Jeff Wastell" pro model I had done earlier that fall. I skated up to him in the lift line to get a closer look—there was my art underneath his feet! That was my first taste of the magic of this stuff. Seeing your work out in the world! And on a snowboard? That much better.

I still have a buzz from that first board. Thank you to my buddies Neil Rankin, Matt Hale, Jeff Wastell and Kurt Wastell.

Working on a snowboard project was cool for a bunch of reasons: The subject matter was agreeable, you got some free boards and it was for the "un-sport" of snowboarding. That was the coolest part. It was for us, by us. Who knows how many boards I gave away in the mid-aughts; to all my buddies who didn't have access

to the snowboard industry. I think that's the proudest part of all of this: being able to hook up friends with the fruits of my labor.

Design-wise, I loved how the art would translate to the topsheet, base and sidewall. It's one thing to see your art in a magazine, reproduced to the size of a dime. It's another thing to see a whole line in a snowboard shop, with kids checking each one out. The type was big, and the stuff was built to last a handful of winters.

Custom Series.
Burton Snowboards. 2003.

Answer 156cm.
Salomon Snowboards. 2010.

⬡ DDC

Draplin
Design Co.

Pretty Much
Everything

Aaron James
Draplin

File Under:
Fiberglass Frenzy

066
067

And when the loot was good, it was cool beyond words. I owe a debt of gratitude to Lance Violette, Jared Eberhardt, Mike "Styk" Styskal and Mark "Fank" Fankhauser. These guys gave me a shot when I was a scrub. In the spring of 2001, Lance was watching over all the boards for Burton in Burlington, Vermont. That single job helped me pay off a big chunk of the credit card debt I had built up while in school at MCAD. And then in the summer of 2004, Styk and Fank from

Ride Snowboards gave me a couple big gigs. Those two snowboard series from Ride are what secured things for me as I got out on my own two wobbly feet. Secured rent for two years. I'm forever thankful, you scrubs. And, with a little sadness: I never really got to enjoy the boards up on the hill like I should have. By the time I was consistently working on boards and bindings, I was sorta done with snowboarding. I had just moved on to new things—a new life in graphic design,

mainly. I'm still a little chapped I didn't get to ride a whole winter on Union bindings, too. We worked so hard on those things. I took one run on a pair in the summer of 2007, so proud to have them on my board.

Snowboarding used to be my whole winter, and I understood the power of saving all year to get a new board. I did get to ride my Solid that winter of 1994, which was cool as hell. (You can see that board back on page 023.)

Altered Genetics 158cm.
Gnu Snowboards. 2008.

Flash 163cm.
Forum Snowboards. 2006.

Outra Vez 164.5cm.
Compatriot Snowboards. 2010.

Designing Snowboards Graphics

Decade Series.
Ride Snowboards. 2006.

Antic Series.
Ride Snowboards. 2009.

Antic Series.
Ride Snowboards. 2010.

DDC

Draplin
Design Co.

Pretty Much
Everything

Aaron James
Draplin

File Under:
Fiberglass Frenzy

068
069

Recon Series.
Forum Snowboards. 2005.

Stomper Series.
Forum Snowboards. 2007.

Travis Rice Pro Model.
LibTech Snowboards. 2007.

"Making time for the stuff there's no time for."

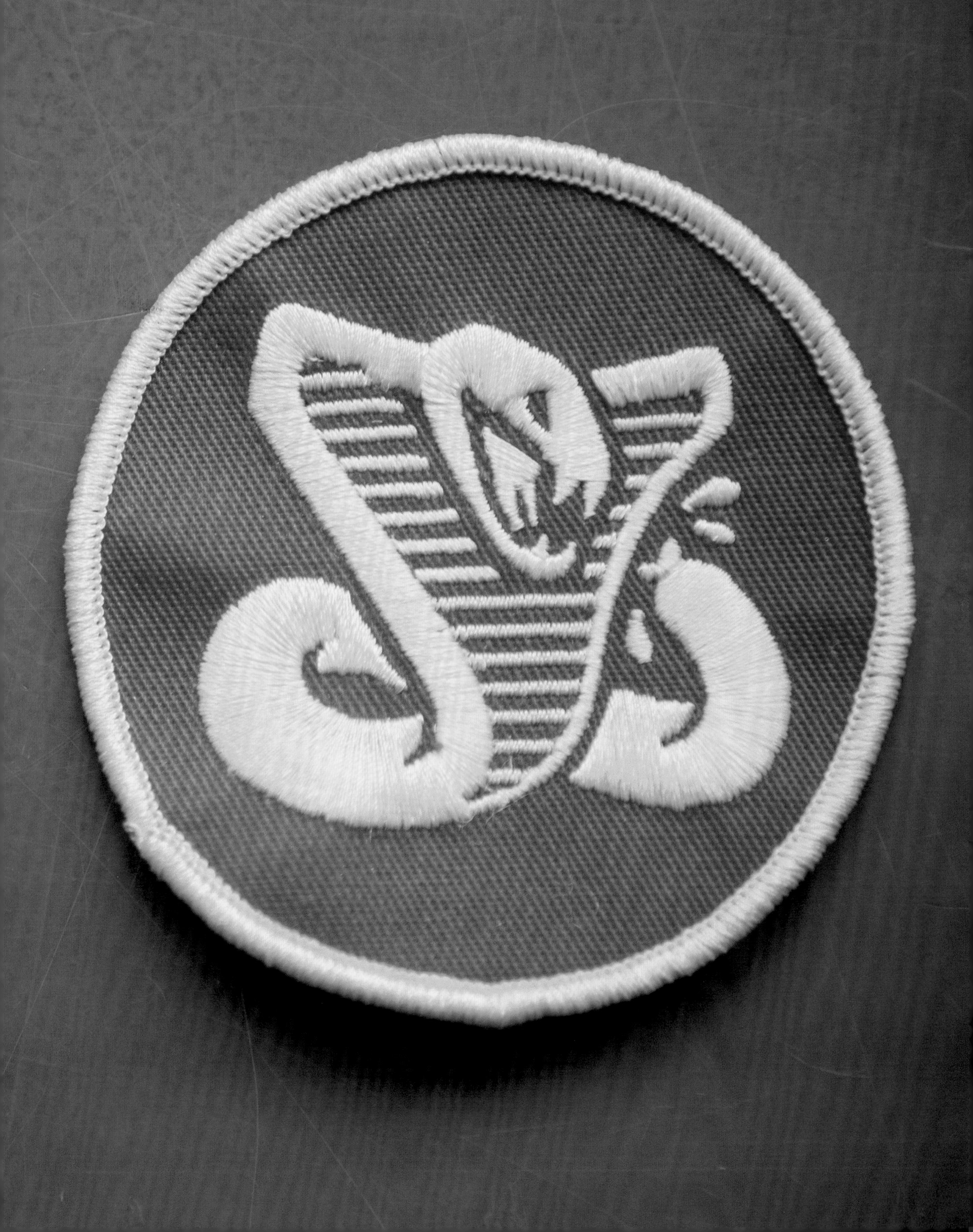

Cobra Dogs

This is one of my favorite stories I tell on the road. People are always smiling when I wrap it up. I hope you are too as you finish reading this magical tale. Let's go:

Back in the spring of 2008, my Portland buddy Cory Grove came to me in a bit of trouble. Turned out he was "using" the G.I. Joe Cobra Commander logo, with a little ketchup and mustard dripping off it, for a couple hats and T-shirts for his hot dog cart. Harmless stuff, really. He sold a sweatshirt to some punk kid whose power-attorney dad noticed the logo, alerted Hasbro, and the next thing you knew, Cory had a big-time cease and desist notice staring him down, threatening litigation and financial ruin. Freaked out, Cory set out to change the logo.

He hit up friends around town, and of course, with no budget to speak of, no one took on the job. The same people who told him, "Hey, if you ever need help, let us know." But when he called on them, they didn't have the time, were too busy, etc. Of course, though.

So he came to the DDC and hit me up. We had a quick chat, discussed where he'd like it to go and I took on the job and got to sketching. No big negotiations. No big plan. Just simple chit-chat.

Now remember, there was no money involved. I was just happy to be getting my buddy out of hot water. This wasn't about mortgage payments or a paycheck—this was a rescue mission.

And we made him a logo. Cory's loose brief detailed wanting a "cobra eating his own tail" or something. Pretty serious shit, right? I got going, sketched a bit, started refining and delivered Cory the logo. He freaked out, and we got cooking on the next couple deliverables.

And this is where shit got fun. With our "ketchup and mustard" color palette, rounded-edge typography and logo intact, the pieces started to design themselves. No fucking account managers breathing down our necks, complicating shit for the sake of complicating shit. No e-mails about e-mails. No meetings about meetings. This was just my buddy and me, building the pieces he'd need to get rolling for his summers up at Government Camp.

This is where you see the power of graphic design up close, free of the power struggles, arbitrary wavering and tricky compromises. It's not complicated. It's fun and fast and works.

And there's a powerful lesson here: Don't be afraid to work for your buddies. For a little bit of loot, or even no loot.

Because what matters the most in the end, you know? When I look back at my little career so far, I'm so proud I made room for the Cobra Dogs sort of clients. This is the stuff I remember and love the most. The big stuff? I can't remember the details, because, quite frankly, the moment that shit is off the plate you move on to the next thing. Those things pay the bills but aren't memorable.

I know you can't pay your mortgage with this stuff, but don't go through life missing design's golden opportunities.

It's a lesson of how powerful our mouse fingers are. My work on Cory's logo not only kept his ass out of court, but it gave him all the tools he needed to build his business. That's some powerful stuff. Imagine applying that to your church or to a local women's shelter or what have you. Donating time to actually help people with our design skills.

Think about how much time is wasted over the course of a week in the normal client back-n-forth. It's embarrassing, and I think we should all constantly check ourselves. For every five days on the job, I'm betting I throw away a solid day of it, due to having to save files down to antiquated software versions, hemming and hawing, missed e-mails, soothing people in regard to whether or not "I got their e-mail," and whatever other bullshit. A whole day, gone. And sure, I get a paycheck at the end of it, but it's a weird thing. How much time are we just throwing away?

I've always been open to doing stuff just because it felt right. Hell, before I ever made a buck, that's all I knew. Don't become the kind of designer who scoffs at this stuff. We are so lucky to do what we do. Be open to helping someone along using our skill set.

Just be open to the weird stuff. It's super rewarding to help people with our talents. Small contributions from us can really transform someone's project or business. That's a beautiful thing. There's gold to be mined from this kind of risky business.

Process sketches, trying to get Cory out of hot water.

Final mark for Cobra Dogs. 2008.

DDC

Draplin
Design Co.

Pretty Much
Everything

Aaron James
Draplin

File Under:
Extra Cobra Sauce

072
073

Park City, Utah. 2011.

Park City, Utah. 2011.

Sharing our Cobra Dogs story with the Spark Conference, San Diego. 2011.

WICKED HOT COBRA SAUCE

COBRA SAUCE

COBRA STYLE

COBRA DOGS FOODS, LLC
89018 Little Trail East, Government Camp, Ore. 97028
(888) HOT-STUF (www.cobradogs.com)

NET WT. 17 OZ. (1lb. 1oz.)(482g)

Cobra Dogs collab with Union Binding Co.

Cory with his mom, Doreen. 2009.

Gocco Print Black Belt

Back in 1997, I was lucky enough to head out to the Tamástslikt Cultural Institute in Pendleton, Oregon. I went there to help Native Americans set up computers and teach them how to use drawing programs to make packaging designs and materials for their crafts businesses.

Robbie and James Lavadour had built a beautiful studio at the institute, outfitted with so much cool equipment. One of the things that Robbie showed me was this odd little machine called a Gocco printer. "You have to see this!" she exclaimed, and had me sketch out a quick design in pencil. We trimmed it to the pad size, inserted the screen and bulbs and pressed down to shoot the screen. She pulled out the screen and had me spread a little metallic ink over it. And then we started printing little cards with the image. My mind was blown a million ways. Beautiful, oddly precise little prints! And with just enough inconsistency to give them this fresh feel.

Print Gocco machines were popular Japanese children's toys. Good for tricking out napkins and party favors for birthday parties. These were home-based

screenprinting machines, and it's estimated that one-third of Japanese households owned one. Kind of like a Spirograph in the States, but so much cooler.

As soon as I got back to Bend, I put my order in. I think it was $100 for the kit. Which was a splurge for me in 1997. I ordered a bunch of extra inks and got going. I had the power of screenprinting in my little room! Mixing colors, happy accidents and this charming little randomness to the quality of the impression from print to print. Dust and shit would get in the screen, and that would make for cool little screwups. The more the better.

I've rolled the odometer on my Gocco machines. Cracked plastic, repaired plastic, superglue and duct tape. I've made my initial investment back a number of times, through elaborate monthly card sets, business cards, concert tickets and all kinds of invitations for friends' events.

My favorite project was a four-color-process halftone print on French "Steel Blue" construction cardstock. But to get that halftone to pop off the gray paper, you

had to hit it with a flash of white ink. That allowed those CMYK plates to jump off the white! And, holy shit, considering all the factors combined, I pulled off some beautifully aligned dots! You'll see that rose on that old Portland card on the bottom of the facing page.

All these years later, I like to think I've got a black belt in Gocco printing. I still have a stash of the stuff, stocking up in 2007 when it was being discontinued. Sadly, the screens are slowly drying out and are pretty inconsistent when you burn the images in. Crusty, spotty, etc.

Almost twenty years later, I'm so thankful I was introduced to that amazing machine. I had fought so hard to get that computer and to free myself from analog restraints. And this little contraption taught me something so insanely important: Never underestimate the beauty, charm and power of ink on paper. Of losing control from print to print. Of surprises. This little contraption reminded me to stay dirty, just a little bit.

Thank you, Robbie Lavadour!

Assorted Gocco Christmas cards, birthday announcements, tickets and packaging. 2002-2013.

A poor man's split fountain print job.

Drying before that final silver hit.

And the back of the cards.

DDC

Draplin
Design Co.

Pretty Much
Everything

Aaron James
Draplin

File Under:
Gocco Black Belt

074
075

2001 Once-A-Month Card Series

2002 Once-A-Month Card Series

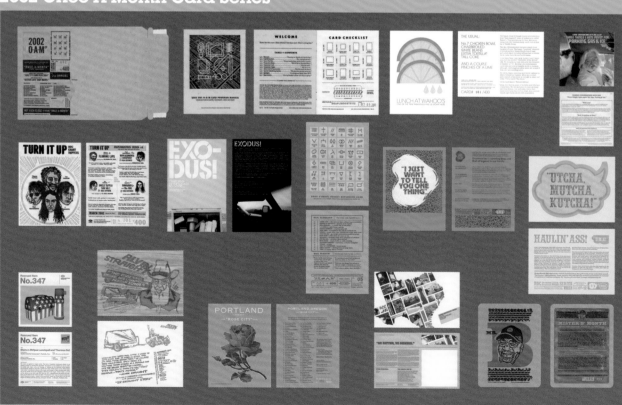

Gary Longfellow Draplin

Sure do miss little Gary. He was my first dog. I celebrated the little guy on my site, in my designs and with friends around the shop. Design-wise, dachshunds did it for me. The coat, the color and, man, that majestic length! I used to live over on Hawthorne Boulevard and this gal would walk by with her little wiener dog every now and again. I loved seeing that little guy pound down the sidewalk.

In May 2005, I decided I was ready for the purchase. I did some research, pored over thousands of web photos and started the hunt around town. Mom, being the savvy navigator, located a breeder in the far, outer reaches of Southeast Portland. We were greeted by a weary-lookin' mother, who invited us in, simultaneously corralling the herd of barking dachshunds. He shuffled up to us, so small, so skittish, and not quite able to climb the carpeted stairs just

yet. I practiced holding him and negotiated a price of $350. Money was no object at that point. I would've paid whatever they were asking. He was coming home with me at all costs. Spare no expense! And "Gary" was his name.

Gary was a barker. So shrill, those shrieks pierced the soul. But equally, he was loving and learned to ring a bell when he needed to go out back to pee. He loved tennis balls, chew toys and burrowing in blankets. When his little back went out—a spinal rupture of cartilage holding his vertebrae together—his little number had come up. I remember the vet—almost comically—explaining how Gary's back was like a hose with a kink in it, with no more signals going to his hind legs. (And how common this was, with little old ladies desperately trying surgery after surgery.) We were devastated.

We accepted Gary's new status and got on with life. Gary would drag himself along; a little front-wheel-drive ATV. He did pretty well on our hardwood floors and could "ghost walk" on grass. For a year and half, my girlfriend Leigh and I mobilized and kept little Gary as clean as we could, with nightly baths and "expressing" his little tootsie rolls off the front porch. But of course, only so much Simple Green could fight against the accidents. We drove him back home to Michigan that summer, feeding him cheeseburgers each night. He was given back to the universe on August 4, 2010. He was almost six. He's buried in Mom and Dad's animal graveyard. Dad and I made his casket.

It's hard not to be bitter. I'll find myself talking to random dogs in weird ways: "Hey you, dog, just be glad you can walk." I wish Gary was around, ringing that bell.

"DDC-Sanctioned"   **"All Things Gary"**

Official "Gary" Guide
WORLD CHAMPION MINIATURE DACHSHUND
Mean Streets, Portland, Ore.

April 2008   Portland, Ore.

"HOW IT ALL BEGAN"
I always wanted a dog. But of course, the transaction was an issue of timing. Apartment dwelling and college days just weren't gonna cut it. I vowed once I `started working out of my house, with enough time and resources to devote to a little guy, well, then I'd step up to the plate. This moment was realized in May, of 2005. Design-wise, the Dachshund did it for me. The coat, the color, and man, that length. Dachshunds are fiesty and have the guts to look at you and go, "No man, not today." Mean little bastards. My kind of dog. —A. Draplin

"WHY'D YOU CALL HIM GARY?"
I've got a theory about guys with the name of Gary, or Harry, Larry, and even Barry—just kinda, uh, "Gross." That and being completely disgusted with the narrow, predictable roster of cliche' dog names out there, well, I thought I'd err on the creepy side in my name quest. I mean, c'mon, if I meet one more "Marley" or "Sadie" I am going to puke. I thought I'd mix it up a little bit. Gary had an unsettling ring to it, and trampled all the "Dakotas" and "Maggies" and crap out there at the dog park. Gary's alright with it. —A. Draplin

Gary—Color Palette

Gary Fur 01	Gary Fur 02	Gary Collar	Gary Pee	Gary Poop	Gary Puke	Gary Blood	Gary Nose	Gary Fang
PANTONE 469 C	PANTONE 174 C	PANTONE 165 C	PANTONE 100 C	PANTONE 476 C	PANTONE 452 C	PANTONE 187 C	PANTONE Black 3 C	PANTONE 7499 C

Gary—Logo Corral

Gary Official	Gary Long Breed	Gary Modern	Gary Icon	Gary Profile

Gary—Specs

BREED	Dachshund.
SIZE	Miniature.
GARYDAY	December 28th, 2004.
BIRTHPLACE	Deep, Southeast Portland.
LENGTH	19".
HEAD HEIGHT	11".
BACK HEIGHT	7".
WEIGHT	7 lb, 8 oz.
COAT	Smooth, soft, clean.
HEART	Strong, pure, brave.
DEMEANOR	Protective, then friendly.
BREED COLOR	Smooth Red.
HANDLING	Loves to be held.
SNIPPAGE	Ball-less and proud.

Gary—Feisty Genetics

The Dachshund (pronounced "dak sund") originated in Germany many hundreds of years ago. "Dachs" is the word for badger. The Dachshund was bred to hunt and follow these animals to earth, gradually becoming highly-evolved, with shortened legs to dig the prey out and go down inside the burrows. Smaller Dachshunds were bred to hunt hare and weasel. Dachshunds have many feisty "terrier" characteristics. They are versatile and courageous dogs and have been known to take on foxes and otters, besides badgers.

Gary—Aliases

Gary goes by a lot of names. Due to his high level of intelligence, he completely understands each and everyone of these aliases with surgical precision.

01. "Gary Zissou." (For days on the coast.)
02. "Gary Ball."
03. "Little Buddy." (As in, "What's up, Little Buddy?")
04. "No Lick!"
05. "No man, not there!" (Aim and deposit.)
06. "Gary, get the hell out of there!"
07. "Little Gary."
08. "Gary America." (Our soil, our strength.)
09. "The Little Man."
10. "Gary Longfellow Draplin." (Official AKC name.)
11. "Goddammit, Gary!" (Common refrain.)
12. "Gary Goiter."
13. "Little Asshole."
14. "G-A-R-Y, he ain't got no alibi!"
15. "Little Wings."
16. "Gary, get over here…now!"
17. "G-Unit."
18. "Gizmo." (Accredited to Fran Badalamenti.)
19. "The Neverending Gary."
20. "Situation: Gary."
21. "Garold." (As in, "Harold.")
22. "Free Range Gary."
23. "Gary.com." (G-commerce site.)
24. "Director of Barketing."
25. "Sacco Di Pulce." ("Flea Bag" in Italian. Thanks Marty.)
26. "The One Who Can't Hold His Piss."
27. "Leaky Dick Gary." (Greeting issues…)
28. "G-Spot."
29. "GaryCare."
30. "Gare-Bear." (Like "Care Bear" but, with a "Gar"…)

Gary—How Gary Spends His Day

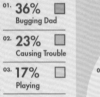

01. **36%** Bugging Dad
02. **23%** Causing Trouble
03. **17%** Playing
04. **12%** Fetching
05. **7%** Eating
06. **3%** Sleeping
07. **2%** Eliminating

Gary—Four Legged Affiliations

Gary's got a pretty colorful roster of pals all over the states. Sure, he prefers smaller breeds, and isn't afraid to take the time to win over bigger beasts too.

Dot   Toby   Zöe   Sofi   Donald   Otto

Enemy
Gary and Gus don't get along.

Gus

Gary—Destructive Tendencies

Gary loves tennis balls. It's love/hate thing cuz, in a moment's notice, he'll go from "fetch" to "destroy." So last summer I stocked up and bought 36 of the things. Cleared out the store. As this guide went to press, we were down to a mere seven balls still intact.

Lives to be fetched another day.

Destroyed and bound for the trash.

Gary—Official Portrait

File this look under: "Feed me, man." and, "Hey, I wanna go out!" and, "I just peed on Larry's laptop case." Hard to say "No" to that little face, eh?

David Nakamichi photo.

Gary—Loud As Hell

Gary's big little bark packs quite a punch. Don't let him fool you. That micro, compact torso has a set of lungs that can bring any human to their knees in excrutiating pain.

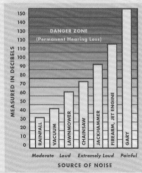

DANGER ZONE (Permanent Hearing Loss)

MEASURED IN DECIBELS: 150, 140, 130, 120, 110, 100, 90, 80, 70, 60, 50, 40, 30, 20, 10, 0

SOURCE OF NOISE: RAINFALL, VACUUM, LAWNMOWER, CHAINSAW, JACKHAMMER, FIREARM, JET ENGINE, GARY

Moderate   Loud   Extremely Loud   Painful

Heartfelt Testimony: "The G-Unit has been at my side for going on four years. Honestly, I don't know what I'd do without him. Part guard dog, part best friend, he's just part of the deal. There's been some rocky days, but, I'd never let the little man go, ever." —A. Draplin

Related Brands:

Owner: Aaron James Draplin
AARON JAMES DRAPLIN

DRAPLIN DESIGN CO., NORTH AMERICA
107 SE Washington Street, Unit No. 540, Portland, Ore. 97214

Contact Information: WWW.DRAPLIN.COM/GARY   GARY@DRAPLIN.COM

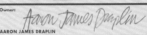
The Gary page from Ethan Bodnar's *Creative Grab Bag: Inspiring Challenges for Artists, Illustrators and Designers* book. 2009.

Draplin.com

I've had a website since 1997. And I owe that triumph to one guy: Cameron Barrett. I met Cameron at Northwestern Michigan College right out of high school. And we didn't hit it off. I was a punk from Traverse City and he was a nerd from Kalkaska. Due to my immaturity, I pounced on the guy a bit in class, unfairly. I still feel bad about that one. Little did I know what he was up against in the world outside of our goofy little community college program.

So I go out west, sow some oats, live like an animal, hit up Alaska, save for a computer and acquire one, and on my fall trips back to Michigan, I run into Cameron. He's got some horrific supermarket night-stocker job, but super fluent in all things Mac. The first night we hung out, Cameron and his twin brother, Damien, tuned up my Power Computing rig. They loaded new typefaces and enhanced its performance. And I was blown away.

Cameron had a bit of a name going for himself on the Web, and he showed me the power of The Internet, the personalities and the pitfalls. And how powerful one's personal expression could be online— how many people you could reach efficiently in one blast.

By 1997, I had a number of places I'd lived in under the belt. Traverse City, Bend, Government Camp and Anchorage. I was doing a crude newsletter called the Draplindustries Gazette and sending it out to all my friends via e-mail. Cameron helped me build my first site, and showed me how one post could reach so many people. And I started "blogging" right away with fun posts and updates.

I think I finally went daily sometime in 2007. I remember my buddy Bry Aleshire laying into me about it. I must've written "daily" somewhere, he saw it and reminded me of my claim. From that day on, I've tried to post something every day.

All too often, I'll let it slip. Be it being on the road doing gigs or being too busy when I'm in the shop, the site's the last thing on the radar. I always manage to get the thing back up to speed, though.

Thoughts on Technology

I've had a cast of characters slam my site over the years. First it was about using "Flash," then it was about "Web 2.0," and now folks are on my case to make my site "responsive." I get it, I get it, but c'mon, relax. Our code is our code. Might not be pretty, but it still works and I can control it. The code, the format and my ability to update the thing somewhat efficiently. Sure, it might not be the prettiest thing, but it still does the job.

Have you ever had your hands handcuffed by a shifty web developer? I have. The excuses. The coaxing. The bullshit terms. The bald-faced lies. I've been there and it was terrifying. I can handle vectors and will keep it that way. To web developers: You have great power and should use it respectfully. You'll inherit the earth! So be cool with that privilege.

And the little DDC merch section, and those embarrassing PayPal links? As this book went to print, I was averaging 100 to 120 orders a week. That's big for a one-man band. So something's working. Any more than that, and I'd be in trouble— I wouldn't be able to fill all the orders!

Daily Graphics

Plus, I liked the idea of always finding time to post some kind of daily graphic. Either something I whipped up on the spot, or some old nugget I found out there. I'm proud of being able to make that time. So many blogs started with big wind in their sails and then petered out a year later. The shit takes work, you know? By smart people, too… who would let me have it about my rudimentary site and topical posts. And where are they now?

I love lists. Grocery lists, checklists, things to do, things to see, things to not forget. My website got away from me years ago after I naively went after movies, records, bands and whatnot. It's a full-time job keeping that shit updated. Phew.

I have to give credit to Ryan "Ryno" Simonson for the "Things I Love"/"Things I Hate" lists. That curmudgeon did it first, and I hijacked it from him and got it on my site. And that reminds me to add him high on the "Things I Hate" list.

I had a guy come up to me at a show earlier this summer and say, "Thanks for doing your site, Draplin. I've always enjoyed how every time I came back, there is something new to see." And that was enough validation for me. I don't know who's coming to Draplin.com, but I sure do thank you guys for digging our bandwidth.

We've had a website since 1997. And you?

The DDC Merch section! Junk PayPal links, and working fine.

Archives, archives and archives. All the warts and moles.

OUR PLEDGE:
GETTING OUT MORE
DDC SUMMER

Duck

DDC GOOD H...OD

PNW USA:
YOU BET!

THE DRAPLIN DESIGN CO.
"ALMOST SUMMER"
GET-TOGETHER.
GOT-TOGETHER.

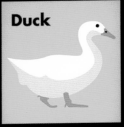

INSIST UPON
"DDC"
BRAND
GRAPHIC DESIGN
(TRADE MARK REGISTERED)
Draplin Design Co.
PORTLAND, OREGON, USA

ALL DAY TODAY:
JOHN MORELAND DAY
ON THE DDC FACTORY FLOOR

SUMMER FUN WITH THE
UNION BINDING COMPANY

THE DRAPLIN DESIGN CO. PROUDLY PRESENTS
AVIATION MUSEUM
McMINNVILLE, OREGON
14 VIEWS IN FULL COLOR

Today, the DDC offers an obligatory, "Out The Window of an Airplane" image to give thanks for getting home safe.

Those are some French Alps below, man!

"FRIDAY, YOU DO US RIGHT."

"FRIDAY, YOU GIVE US HOPE."

"FRIDAY, THE INSPECTION."

"FRIDAY, THE SPIRITS LIFT."

"FRIDAY, ALL DAY LONG."

"FRIDAY, CA$H THO$E CHECKS!"

"FRIDAY, WE GO 'COASTAL.'"

"FRIDAY IS ON YER SIDE."

"FRIDAY IS REAL GOOD."

"FRIDAY, OH SWEET FRIDAY."

"FRIDAY, TAKE ME HOME."

"FRIDAY, WE NEEDED YOU."

"TURN IT UP" SOLID STATE
GARY
10 11
9
8
7 6 5 4
1
2
3
VOLUME
DRAPLIN DESIGN CO., NORTHEAST PORTLAND

Officially Official.

BAD SANTA

FLAT FILES

DDC in 2004!

Oh YEAH

GARY
Natural Barking
INSTANT WEINER DOG
LONG, LEAN, -&- MEAN.
NET WT. 128 OZ. (8 LB.)

VIN vs. DDC

Wet Dreamers

BIONIC DOLPHIN

Key Command:
Apple-G

DDC VERSUS FLAMING LIPS

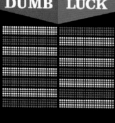

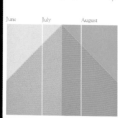

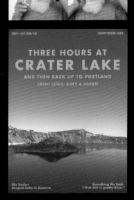

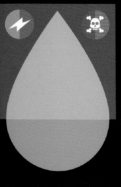

ANOTHER BANG-UP JOB
by our buddies at the
U.S. POSTAL SERVICE

DDC SHIPPING DEPT. DDC DDC MERCH ARCHIVES

SINUHE
XAVIER
Grand Canyon

DDC2013
DDC2013
DDC2013
DDC2013
DDC2013
DDC2013
DDC2013
DDC2013
DDC2013
DDC2013

"UNDERSTANDING"
IN ARABIC
AS INTERPRETED BY THE
DRAPLIN DESIGN CO.

LEAH30

OLIVER
SUMMER

MOM & DAD
VISIT

SHIPPING
SHIPPING
SHIPPING
SHIPPING
SHIPPING
SHIPPING
SHIPPING
SHIPPING
SHIPPING
SHIPPING
SHIPPING

MERCH TABLE
MADNESS!

THANK YOU, R+I+TI DDC ROCHESTER, N.Y.

WAY RARE.
FIELD
KNOTS

BUNNY
BOOTS

SUCK IT
NAKAMOTO

ACL vs DDC

San Diego
"The Flight Path City"

FUCK
YEAH
OHIO
KNIFE

"WWW.DRAPLIN.COM"
DDC800

DRAPLIN DESIGN CO. NORTH AMERICA
NORTHEAST PORTLAND, ORE.

CONGRATULATIONS, LEIGH!

12-24
MONTHERS
HARD
TO PART WITH
EERO
BRITCHES

Just Confirmed:
Final-Leigh!
Moving Leigh Out West
January 23–26, 2008
Wild, Young and Free.

DRAPLIN
DESIGN CO.
PORTLAND, ORE., USA

GRAPHIC DESIGN
SERVICES

WWW.DRAPLIN.COM

40

2002
O·A·M
DRAPLININDUSTRIES DESIGN CO.
ONCE-A-MONTH CARD SERIES
NOW SHIPPING.
12 MORE REASONS TO KEEP LIVING.
"WE'LL SHIP ONE ANYWHERE." ONLY $5

Fourth Annual
Draplin Design Co.
North American Fall Tour
Day 02
Long Haul
Dates to Salt Lake

TOBY
2001–2013

SUMMER HUMP DAY

CHICAGO
A PLACE WITH
DANGEROUS-LOOKING
BACK PORCHES.

CONFLICT
FREE
SINCE
SEVENTY
THREE

Rappin'
with
Draplin
Saturday, October 4
11:00am–12:30pm
$30 / 30 spots available
21-and-up only
Brunch Provided
(Eggs, bacon, hash browns &
pancakes! Breakfast stuff!)

MIDWESTERN UNITED STATES
"EIGHT
CITIES
EIGHT
WEEKS"
DDC FALL TOUR

CHRIS COYLE BARBARIAN

DDC – 09/16/14   PORTLAND, ORE.

ALL PURPOSE
DDC BRAND
"SHOP RAG"
CLEAN-UP ON AISLE 73!
LET'S SOP
SOME SHIT
UP WITH
THESE
FUCKERS

FILE UNDER: FEBRUARY:
Way Absorbent.   Always spilling shit.

GREETINGS FROM
ROAD RASH, ORE.
INTERSTATE 84

DOING BUSINESS AS:
"DDC"
in
'08*

YOU KNOW, MORE OF THE SAME:
Simple living, working hard,
saving loot, spending loot,
fighting the good fight,
making stuff, trying new shit,
staying honest, staying true,
hoping for change, wondering,
and crossing our fingers.

[*]
OUR PLEDGE:
To keep this deal going
STRONG and PROUD
for another long year.

THE DRAPLIN DESIGN CO.
"ALMOST SUMMER"
GET-TOGETHER
Saturday, May 26th, Pretty Much All Day

DDC BACKYARD
WRESTLING

GREETINGS FROM
BLACK ICE, WYOM.
INTERSTATE 80

CLIMBING
PALM TREES
IN
THE KEYS

"GARY ACROSS
AMERICA"
NORTH AMERICAN FALL TOUR
"GO DAYS ON THE ROAD
WITH THE DDC"

GREETINGS FROM
FROSTBITE, IOWA
INTERSTATE 80

10

DDCBRAND

Ninety **Fuckin'** Inches

FOUR-LEGGED
FRIENDS
draplin.com/gary

SHHH!

DDC Merch

"Things you need."

DDC
Action Cap

$29.99

[DDC]

Draplin
Design Co.

Pretty Much
Everything

Aaron James
Draplin

File Under:
A Proud Offering

084
085

DDC Merch

I'm always kind of taken aback when people ask me, "Why do you make all this stuff?" They'll be digging through the merch section in the shop, utterly confused by the array and volume of our spirited assortment. And it all makes perfect sense to me. First off, I use this stuff. Ferociously. That's the main thing. Does it help me along in my day? That's why I made the stuff in the first place, to serve a need I had.

Second, I like the idea of sourcing the classic items from the tricky American promotional landscape. It's sad to me how the simpler the item is, the harder it is to make. Things like socks. Turns out America sold the looms to places far away, and now it's harder and harder to make a simple pair of socks. I find that incredibly disheartening. If we can't make the simplest of stuff, what's that say about the state of American manufacturing? So many times, I've been forced to ship a catalog file far, far away. Out of my hands. We couldn't beat Asia's prices, and that's just business, I'm told. But with little promo items, there's something gratifying about knowing your carpenter pencil is still made in Texas.

Third, it's just fun to make stuff. And to put your name on it, or trick out the copy to make it fun, or what have you. There's an absurdity to making a thousand combs, knowing that combs just aren't a thing people use anymore, you know? But then they pick it up, and they smile, and it evokes an old fond memory from growing up. I've sold over three thousand of my DDC-035 "Hair Organizer" comb! Take that, eye rollers!

Growing Up with the Stuff
A big part of my love for this stuff comes from where I grew up. My childhood buddy Ronnie Mortensen had an uncle who worked for a grain elevator in southwestern Michigan. He'd load us up with the coolest hats and jackets and stuff. Kent was the brand. The products were starchy and rigid, and then you'd see some old-timer who took the time to break the stuff in, riding his combine through his fields. That's still the best. An authentic product in an authentic moment.

That stuff was the currency of the American farmer. Go back and dig up the old Farm Aid footage. Like, 1983 or something. And just check out the hats all the people in the crowd were wearing. Or, even scarier, as the family farms started to decline, I remember the footage of farmers standing around, huddled, discussing things. And the hats they wore? Your classic American seed cap. Sad, but beautiful

in its simple functionality. That's the stuff I love the most. Still works today.

I remember my dad being wooed by the power of simple merch. He'd be on the fence with some proprietor over some price, and the guy would throw in a couple hats and tchotchkes, and that would be enough to seal the deal. That's an old way of doing business. And I'm betting Dad enjoyed snowblowing the driveway that much more in his John Deere beanie.

Bottomlineism
I think I might've made that word up? Out of disgust, of course. Disgusted with the climate I'll find myself in. Bar codes on everything. Or that time I'm visiting a guy's design shop, load him up with Field Notes, and in return he's handing me shit here and there, and then I get a PayPal invoice from their bullshit assistant later on? So yeah, "bottomlineism." Everyone's worried about their bottom line, all the time, and damned if the stuff they make doesn't always have some electronic tendril attached to it.

I don't mean you should just give out your stuff for free. No, but c'mon, every now and again, just let some little bullshit trinket go, you know. Because here's the deal: Every little piece of DDC merch, once it leaves the shop, it's got a pretty distinct job to do. Each are little reminders of what we're all about. About how we work and the work we do and how we pull it all off.

And that's no different than the feed and seed down the street, or that tire shop on the corner. They'd give you a little calendar or coin purse or whatever, with their number on it. Simple, simple stuff. And you'd use that little thingamabob in the coolest of ways—when you weren't thinking about it—and the little thing made your life a little easier. Be it an ice scraper, a reversible screwdriver or a bullet pencil. The stuff worked, and that pure functional integrity, that's something that I love about American business and promotion.

When I was getting into design, there were just a couple guys who knew how to take the edge off of stuff. Charles Spencer Anderson and House Industries come to mind when I think back. What I loved the most about their work was that it had a certain charm to it. Not only was it functional, but it was fun. Fun to read, look at, emulate and show my dad. Even Dad could enjoy their work. So much of design can be this odd, elite thing, almost purposely angled to go above people's heads. That shit freaks me out. Chuck and

the House guys made design fun.

A Lesson
This stuff can get tricky, too. There've been many instances when the merch game bit me back: the first time a link featuring DDC merch went up on Uncrate and exploded into a thousand orders, or the time Brad gave our USA hats to the United States soccer team and we sold four hundred of the things in an afternoon, or when a big order came in with a typo or another mistake. There's nothing worse than riding high on anticipation, and you finally get the stuff in and there's something wrong with it. Such a bummer.

One thing I've learned about merch deals is with quantities. Always buy extra. There's so many factors working against you, even when making the smallest of items. The lead time, the elusive and devastating "art department" who tweaks the art and always fucks it up, and shipping times can all add up to heartbreak. Be clear with the middleman, show good comps showing the imprint on the item, and, here's the most important part: Always buy more than you need. The stuff will move. You get a volume discount, and when you sell out of the stuff, it takes forever to replenish the supply. Always buy more.

And Back to Dad
My dad understood the power of this stuff. He had little items he'd use for his Draplin Tool Supply business, and would "take care" of the guys in the shops by giving them little extras and goodies. That was a good lesson for me. It made them love and trust Dad, and, hell, every guy needs a little precision ruler in his tool kit.

Or with my dad's treasures. He had this really generous side to him. Be it lending out tools to neighbors or noticing when someone liked something in his garage. He'd just say, "You like it? Take it." And they'd freak out. I apply that same quality to the moment I notice someone marveling at a Field Notes three-pack or playing with whatever of my latest trinkets that's come into the shop. Just take it, use it, enjoy it and remember that there can be room to breathe in this stuff.

I'm so lucky to make good loot. More than I ever thought I'd make. And the idea of bean-counting every little purchase, piece of merch or transaction is just kind of sad and deflating. I don't want to live like that. Leave a little room for that moment when you just like someone and want to flip them a couple freebies. People remember that stuff.

DDC

Draplin
Design Co.

Pretty Much
Everything

Aaron James
Draplin

File Under:
Promotional Goods

086
087

Complete DDC Merch Roster

Draplin Design Co. | Pretty Much Everything | Aaron James Draplin | File Under: Holy Fucking Shit | 088 089

DDC-073 2012 — Heavy Duty Torso Cover
DDC-074 2012 — DDC 2012 Fall Tour Torso Cover
DDC-075 2012 — Iowa All The Way Poster
DDC-076 2012 — Badass Buffalo Poster
DDC-077 2012 — Your Utah Poster
DDC-078 2012 — Super Chicago Poster
DDC-079 2012 — Solidly South Dakota Poster
DDC-080 2012 — Oregon, Oh Yeah Poster

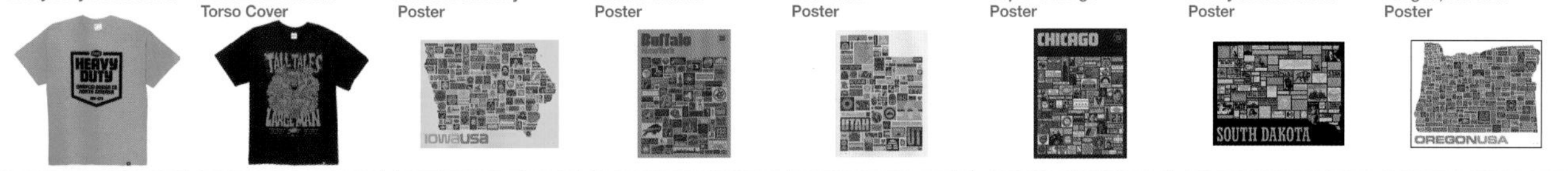

DDC-081 2012 — Oregon Torso Cover
DDC-082 2012 — Oregon Decal
DDC-083 2013 — Idaho, All The Way Poster
DDC-084 2013 — Florida, Full-On Poster
DDC-085 2013 — Maximum Montana Poster
DDC-086 2013 — DDC Jean Jacket Pin
DDC-087 2013 — Nuthin' But North Dakota Poster
DDC-088 2013 — Nevada Neverending Poster

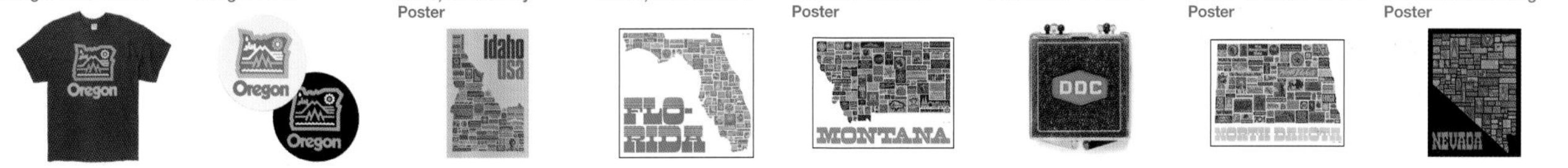

DDC-089 2013 — California Compiled Poster
DDC-090 2013 — Space Shuttle Tribute Poster Kit
DDC-091 2013 — Space Shuttle Tribute Torso Cover
DDC-092 2013 — Space Shuttle Tribute Patch
DDC-093 2013 — Space Shuttle Tribute Action Cap
DDC-094 2013 — Notable North Carolina Poster
DDC-095 2013 — Nebraska Nonstop Poster
DDC-096 2013 — Kansas Kollected Poster

DDC-097 2013 — Wonderful Wisconsin Poster
DDC-098 2013 — Summer Sun Torso Cover
DDC-099 2013 — Necessarily New York Poster
DDC-100 2015 — Pretty Much Everything Up To January 9, 2015 Poster
DDC-101 2013 — DDC Stuff Sheath
DDC-102 2003 — Draplindustries Pong Div. Ping Pong Ball
DDC-103 2013 — Incredible Indiana Poster
DDC-104 2013 — Oklahoma Overload Poster

DDC-105 2013 — COAL x DDC x USA Action Cap
DDC-106 2013 — USA Patch
DDC-107 2013 — Shop Rag (3-Pack)
DDC-108 2014 — Sweatshirt
DDC-109 2014 — Sweatpants
DDC-110 2014 — Fluids Unit
DDC-111 2013 — Meandering Mississippi Poster
DDC-112 2013 — Mostly Maine Poster

DDC-113 2013 — Thick Lines Edition Playing Card Set
DDC-114 2014 — Thick Lines Poster Series
DDC-115 2014 — Volcano Choir 2014 West Coast Tour Poster
DDC-116 2014 — Markedly Missouri Poster
DDC-117 2012 — Iowa Landscape Poster
DDC-118 2014 — Plentiful Pennsylvania Poster
DDC-119 2014 — Michigan Magnificent Poster
DDC-120 2014 — All-Out Alabama Poster

DDC-121 2014 — Thick Lines Magnet Set
DDC-122 2014 — Pacific Northwest Torso Cover
DDC-123 2014 — Mt. Hood Thick Lines Torso Cover
DDC-124 2014 — Get Cosmic Torso Cover
DDC-125 2014 — Get Cosmic Patch
DDC-126 2014 — Get Cosmic Decals
DDC-127 2014 — Get Cosmic Action Cap
DDC-128 2014 — Portland Sunny Day/ Rainy Day Torso Cover

DDC-129 2014 — Oregon Kids Torso Cover
DDC-130 2014 — Oregon Stack Torso Cover
DDC-131 2014 — Oregon Stack Embroidered Patch
DDC-132 2014 — Oregon Stack Action Cap
DDC-133 2015 — Snack Clamp
DDC-134 2015 — Jim Draplin Torso Cover
DDC-135 2015 — Vive La Louisiane Poster
DDC-136 2015 — Mighty Maryland Poster

DDC-137 2015 — Marc Maron Aladdin Theater/Revolution Hall Poster
DDC-138 2015 — D Thick Line Souvenir Patch
DDC-139 2000 — DDC Thick Line Souvenir Patch
DDC-140 2015 — DDC Freight Div. Souvenir Patch
DDC-141 2015 — DDC Freight Div. Action Cap
DDC-142 2014 — Way Washington Torso Cover
DDC-143 2015 — Box of Matches
DDC-144 2013 — DDC Pinback

It's One Thing to Make and Sell the Stuff, and Another Thing to Get It Out the Door

I'll tell you this right now: Until you've stood in a holiday shipping line at the post office with fifty pissed-off people behind you, rolling their eyes, emitting audible groans, while the checked-out clerk robotically drones through the one hundred poster tubes you lugged in that night, well, you haven't lived.

Tough stuff. And we endured that shit for years. But it wasn't always like that. When it first started out, I'd just wrap each order up and mess with the customers with fun nicknames. Each week, it'd be ten to twelve pieces and Eric Lovejoy would take it down to the post office on Fiftieth Avenue.

Every order got extra shit thrown in. I learned this from the mail-order experiences I had growing up.

Record, skateboard and BMX companies always surprised you. Sub Pop record packages came with extra stuff. Stickers and catalogs and stray promo 7-inches. That stuff meant the world to a scrub in Michigan. Stuff you didn't expect. I always try to throw in extra stickers and shit. But of course, as this thing has exploded, that has got away from me. When I can, I'll sprinkle stickers into tubes while Leigh isn't looking.

That's what it's like shipping merch. Well, at least until we got our shit together and got an Endicia shipping station, which allowed us to automate the labeling, blast out consistent shipping notifications and have USPS come pick the mess up the next morning. Hours and hours gained. And I owe that leap up the food chain

to Leigh McKolay. She took matters into her own hands, if anything, just so she wouldn't have to endure those brutal trips out to the airport post office. Things get heated in those lines! Brutal, brutal stuff.

Fulfillment is a weird thing. It sneaks up on you and bites you in the ass. Each year, the DDC merch onslaught grows. I have great respect for outfits who have their shipping practices dialed in. Things are a little rusty at the DDC, but we're always trying to do better. Special thanks to Eric Lovejoy, Andy Forgash, Dale Allen Dixon and the "merch mistress" herself, Leigh McKolay, for helping me get all the stuff out the door all these years. And to those waiting for a package to show up, the shit's on its way! Stay tuned!

Cargo van filled to the brim with posters to be shipped. Fuckin' beautiful. May 2009.

DDC

Draplin
Design Co.

Pretty Much
Everything

Aaron James
Draplin

File Under:
Now Shipping

090
091

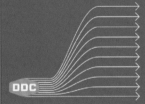

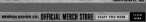

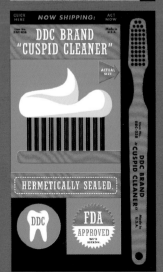

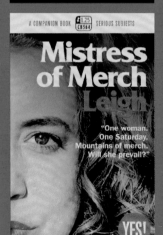

Little web blasts to help push merch items along. 2002–2015.

DDC Action Cap and Torso Cover Archive

DDC Carhartt/Khaki Mesh. 2003.

DDC Orange 6-Panel Foam. 2003.

DDC Black 6-Panel Foam. 2007.

DDC Brown/Khaki Mesh. 2007.

DDC Black 6-Panel Foam. 2012.

DDC Gonna Rain Gray 6-Panel Foam. 2012.

DDC Storm Cloud 6-Panel Foam. 2012.

DDC Orange/Orange Mesh. 2006.

DDC Carhartt 6-Panel Foam. 2013.

DDC All-Black 6-Panel Foam. 2013.

DDC Green Mind Green 6-Panel Foam. 2015.

Open Road Div. Denim/White Mesh. 2008.

Open Road Div. 6-Panel Denim. 2008.

Open Road Div. Blue/White Mesh. 2013.

Open Road Div. Red 6-Panel Foam. 2013.

Pacific Northwest Green/White Mesh. 2013.

Pacific Northwest 6-Panel Foam. 2013.

Space Shuttle Gray/Gray Mesh. 2014.

Space Shuttle 6-Panel Foam. 2014.

Space Shuttle Yellow 6-Panel Foam. 2014.

COAL x DDC x USA Navy/Navy Mesh. 2013.

COAL x DDC x USA Blue/White Mesh. 2013.

Oregon Stack Brown/Goldenrod Mesh. 2014.

Oregon Stack 6-Panel. 2014.

Get Cosmic Black/Silver Mesh. 2014.

Get Cosmic 6-Panel Foam. 2014.

DDC Thick Lines Orange/Yellow Mesh. 2016.

DDC Freight Div. 6-Panel Foam. 2016.

Pretty Much
Everything

Aaron James
Draplin

File Under:
Durable Fibers

092
093

DDC Pop-Up Shop

Portland is an amazing town; with its DIY sensibility and acceptance of quirky ideas, it always surprises me. When I first started coming here in 1993, I quickly noticed all the cool indie businesses. Restaurants, record stores and weird boutiques. People doing things on their own terms, and this was twenty years ago! The town was way ahead of its time.

In the summer of 2014, we met with Lisa Frisch and Cori Jacobs from the Portland Business Alliance about their yearly pop-up shops program. The city would find retail spaces that were in between leases, cover the rent and we'd load in and build out a pop-up shop. We submitted our ideas and we made the cut! We'd be doing a pop-up along with North St. Bags (Portland-made bicycle panniers) and Omiyage (Asian-inspired gifts and crafts). We'd be sharing the space. The pop-up went from November 13 to December 22, 2014, covering the Thanksgiving and raging holiday-shopping seasons.

We had a small budget to paint and outfit the joint. In a couple heated days, we scrubbed the floors, loaded in the merch, painted and organized the store into a proud offering. Posters, hats, torso covers, trinkets and the world's biggest wall of Field Notes! And we pulled it off. So much orange paint went up.

This was a new one for us and we learned many lessons about retail. Be careful what you ask for! Or, be careful what shop hours everyone agrees on. It's one thing to trick out the place, it's another to man it when things are slow. And when things are nuts, it's an uphill battle to take care of everyone. But we pulled it off, proudly.

Special thanks to Leigh for initiating the idea to reach out to the PBA, developing the shop, painting, cleaning, restocking, organizing help and running the joint. Buchino, Jenna and Jesse, too! A Grand Canyon of appreciation is felt to all the family, friends and customers who came in to the DDC Pop-Up Shop to hang out.

Initial walk-through.

Confident mock-up.

The real thing!

Customers, holding me to it.

With J Mascis and Otis "O" Bartholomew! Feel the pain.

I hand-painted all the A-boards. That shit took forever.

With Josh Higgins and Milo Ventimiglia!

A proud offering.

Draplin
Design Co.

Pretty Much
Everything

Aaron James
Draplin

File Under: 094
Closed Mondays   095

Leigh holding it down, just minutes after opening. 11:02 A.M., November 13, 2014.

Hear that?
That orange sound?
That's the sound
of the Draplin Design
Company Pop-Up
Shop coming to life.
Get used to it.

DDC Pop-Up Shop
Nov. 13 to Dec. 24   DDC   11 NW 5th Avenue

We're just a block away
from Ground Control.
Go play some Galaga,
then come over and
check out our spirited
offering of rad shit.

DDC Pop-Up Shop
Nov. 13 to Dec. 24   DDC   11 NW 5th Avenue

Be it hell, high water
or fuckin' ice storm,
nothing is getting
in the way of us
"opening at 11am"
today. Nothing.

DDC Pop-Up Shop
Nov. 13 to Dec. 24   DDC   11 NW 5th Avenue

We were just in
Toronto. Now we're
in Jacksonville.
And wait, Nashville
on Tuesday? Yep.
Portland on Thursday?
You bet. Mandatory.

DDC Pop-Up Shop
Nov. 13 to Dec. 24   DDC   11 NW 5th Avenue

No mixologists.
No brunch lines.
No goats.
No artisanal ice cubes.
No birds on stuff.
No infusing of anything.

DDC Pop-Up Shop
Nov. 13 to Dec. 24   DDC   11 NW 5th Avenue

Just nine days until the
grand opening
of the Draplin Design
Company Pop-Up
Shop, Portland.
That's a Thursday night.
See you there.

DDC Pop-Up Shop
Nov. 13 to Dec. 24   DDC   11 NW 5th Avenue

Thick Lines Thursday!
Thick Lines posters are $25
in the DDC Pop-Up Shop today!

DDC Pop-Up Shop
Nov. 13 to Dec. 24   DDC   11 NW 5th Avenue

BLACK FRIDAY!
BLACK FRIDAY!
BLACK FRIDAY!
BLACK FRIDAY!
BLACK FRIDAY!
(Tomorrow, 11am-7pm!)

DDC Pop-Up Shop
Nov. 13 to Dec. 24   DDC   11 NW 5th Avenue

What happens
in the DDC Pop-Up
Shop, stays in the
DDC Pop-Up Shop.
Until it spills out
on to 5th Avenue.

DDC Pop-Up Shop
Nov. 13 to Dec. 24   DDC   11 NW 5th Avenue

And yes, we're making
our little zone
"as orange as possible."
If yer wondering,
"Orange 021" from the
Pantone color cartel.

DDC Pop-Up Shop
Nov. 13 to Dec. 24   DDC   11 NW 5th Avenue

Things you need:
Pens, pencils, magnets,
way limited edition
Field Notes, mugs,
weird plastic things and
Northwest-specific items
at Portland-only prices.

DDC Pop-Up Shop
Nov. 13 to Dec. 24   DDC   11 NW 5th Avenue

We'll talk to you.
Offering up general
conversation, loose
chatter, uncomfortable
pauses, bullshitting,
risky speculation and
free advice. Try us.

DDC Pop-Up Shop
Nov. 13 to Dec. 24   DDC   11 NW 5th Avenue

Decimal points in our
pricing? You bet.
And, this thing called
"Customer Service."
Yeah, even that.
What you gonna do
about it, Portland?

DDC Pop-Up Shop
Nov. 13 to Dec. 24   DDC   11 NW 5th Avenue

And that's a wrap!
The DDC Pop-Up Shop
is officially closed.
Thank you to everyone
who came in, hung out
& grabbed some stuff.
Very appreciated!

DDC Pop-Up Shop
Nov. 13 to Dec. 24   DDC   11 NW 5th Avenue

Now we'll return to our
normal DDC broadcast
of painful coffee photos,
reality-bending selfies,
crooked horizon vacation
pics and "this happened"
sorts of stuff. Phew.

DDC Pop-Up Shop
Nov. 13 to Dec. 24   DDC   11 NW 5th Avenue

A selection of our daily DDC Pop-Up Shop Instagram blasts.

Setting Up Shop

A hard rain fell. A dry Leigh is a happy Leigh. Portland Renegade Craft Fair. July 2015.

Leigh stays on top of her Facewhizzery. Portland Bazaar. December 2014.

Field Notes's Matt Jorgensen mans the booth. American Field. Boston, MA. September 2014.

Portland Bazaar brown paper bag special. December 2012.

Field Notes

"I'm not writing it down to remember it later, I'm writing it down to remember it now."

Draplin
Design Co.

Pretty Much
Everything

Aaron James
Draplin

File Under:
Durable Materials

098
099

Field Notes, the Complete Story

First off, if you are recognizing the memo books in this section, that isn't because of me making the first couple hundred in my basement. It's because of that fateful moment when I handed them to my buddy Jim Coudal, and he saw something in them that I couldn't quite see just yet. That's why you know about Field Notes. And I want to start out this little section by saying precisely that, thankful as hell.

History of Jotting Things Down

I've always had some kind of sketchbook, memo pad or journal going. That goes all the way back to high school. My first journals were started in ninth grade, detailing skateboard tricks, gym class jitters and bands I was discovering. I'll go back and re-read passages from those old days and cringe. So painful and embarrassing, but equally, I'm so thankful I wrote it all down. I always had a sketchbook going for drawing, too. Every school notebook cover was an opportunity to customize it. I'm a big list-maker. That's how I kept all my shit together back then, and all the way to the present day.

Over the years I used off-the-shelf stuff like Muji and Moleskine and old memo books found in estate sale junk drawers, and eventually started building my own books to use. I learned how to build and bind books at MCAD and would make my own journals. You can see those on the facing pages. I always had one close by, pocket-size, for keeping track of everything in my little world.

I went to Italy in November 2004 for the first time to work on Union Binding Company stuff. On a day off, while in Milan with Martino and George, I saw Moleskine books for the first time and popped for a couple hundred bucks' worth to drag back to the States. They had this big story about Van Gogh using them! Cool, right? When I found out that was bullshit, that broke my heart. Plus, they were made so far away. Such a simple item? We used to make this stuff in the States. Frustrated by the feeling that I was being taken by some schlocky marketing plan, I started drawing up plans for my own books.

I made the first run of two hundred in January 2005 using my Gocco printer. Each panel was a separate print. Once the cover was printed, I would score it, then staple in a stack of innards. That first run, I used basic architectural-grade graph paper, and for the cover, French Paper samples scraps, chipboard scraps or whatever I had around the house. Once I had everything collated and stapled,

I scored the spine, folded it and trimmed it down to the final size. Then I'd hit the upper right and lower right corners with a corner rounder and I was done. Next book! I did these to populate my little annual trade show DDC Appreciation Kit I'd give my clients and pals. Pens, pencils, stickers and a little memo book as a way to acknowledge my appreciation for the work they were sending my way.

That first two hundred went quick. I gave them to friends and colleagues, burning through the stack in a month or so. And everyone started asking for more. My next step was to get a run professionally printed. I got an order going with friends at the local Portland printshop Pinball Publishing. Two thousand books for $2,000! That first run sounded pretty big. I remember thinking that would last me a lifetime. Little did I know how quick that first official batch would go.

I went with home-state heroes French Paper with a one-color Dur-O-Tone Packing Brown Wrap cover and one-color graph paper print on Boise Offset Smooth 50#T for the innards. Like the covers say, "Durable Material/Made in the U.S.A." I was so proud to support domestic companies for the materials, printing and binding. That meant a lot to me. I watched my dad's business decline in the '90s, due to manufacturing being shipped overseas. I still remember that first call I got from a printer in Taiwan. They offered me a slick deal for pennies on the dollar. But I stuck to my guns. "Thank you for reaching out, fellas, but I'll be making my books in the States. Forever."

The Thinking Behind Them

The idea behind the design of Field Notes was to not make something complicated, but to make them feel "undesigned." The decision to use Futura Bold and Futura Bold only was really out of respect for the old memo books that I would see in the Midwest, on my way from Portland to Michigan and back. I'd see these wonderful examples of dead, agrarian communication devices. They'd use one typeface, because that's all they needed.

So, when designing those initial versions of Field Notes, it just came down to "How functional could these be?" When stripped down (and, yet, I know, they still feel pretty "designed"), they didn't need anything else. That kind of confident restraint was something I couldn't find out there on the shelves. To strip it all the way down freed the books up. The voice wasn't competing with how the things

looked. If something is witty, in kind of an understated way, that can almost be more fun than when it's forced, or punching you in the face. Sorta like life?

Becoming a Real Company

I'd been a fan of Coudal Partners for some time and reached out to see if I could meet them the next time I rolled through Chicagoland. Jim wrote me back and said I was on his radar, too! We became buddies, and before I knew it, I was a guest contributor for their Fresh Signals link feed, a co-conspirator on the SHHH cards and even wrote an essay for their *Field-Tested Books* book.

In late January 2005, I sent a stack of the first official two thousand print run to Jim. Here's the reply from him that planted the seed for Field Notes becoming a real thing: *FIELD NOTES is brilliant. Thought you'd want to know that. Later. —Jim.* The thing is, I didn't know that. I was using them and was just having a good time seeing them take off with friends and colleagues.

As the first two thousand dwindled away that summer, I printed the next couple runs with Pinball and Ann Frank from Think*Plan*Deliver. And then I would ship chunks to Jim. Shipping reams of paper back and forth can get pretty spendy. As the thing took off, it made better sense to do all the printing in and around Chicagoland, near the source.

How We Make Them

I'm in Portland, and Jim and the Field Notes crew are in Chicago. We call the two camps Field Notes Northwest and Field Notes Midwest, respectively. My camp is considerably smaller. We collaborate on new stuff over e-mail and quick phone calls. Ideas come in from all angles, and we settle on our newest sets based on the things that feel unique, exciting and most fun to make.

Sometimes I'm on the road going apeshit and will be out of the loop. There's been a couple sets that I didn't have any input on. And that's fine! I trust Jim and the gang with my whole heart. They always blow me away. Our secret weapon is Bryan Bedell. That guy is always coming up with cool surprises for the books.

Special Editions

We release a new limited-edition set every quarter. Every three months, there's a chance to go after weird themes, try new papers, or just see if we can surprise our subscription customers. As this book

Gocco printing on to existing books. 2003.

With Field Notes co-founder Jim Coudal. So much grip on his shoulder. Summer 2015.

Where it started! Gocco printing on shop scraps. 2005.

Field Note No. 001. 2005.

No. 001/200.

Back cover.

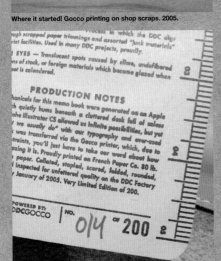

A decade later, Evan Rose is still using the first one I gave him. Weird.

Real "misty".

Assorted journals, books and sketchbooks from growing up.

Field Notes

went to print, our twenty-eighth seasonal offering hit the shelves. In the spirit of autumn, the "Shenandoah Edition" featured three versions of our very own duplex paper made by the French Paper Co. in Niles, all of which were inspired by the most common trees that change color in the Shenandoah Valley. One side of the paper represents the summer leaf color and the other the fall's. Another beautiful ode to the best season of all—fall!

My favorite set is still the "Expedition" with its indestructible paper and bright orange covers. Or maybe it's "American Tradesman" with the great, textured cover. Wait, "National Crop" is high on the list, too! And the "Shelterwood" cherry wood covers? I'm proud of all of them. There's not enough time in the day to enjoy them all!

The set I'm still most proud of is the "Two Rivers" edition made in partnership with our buddies at the Hamilton Wood Type & Printing Museum in Two Rivers, Wisconsin. The three-pack featured a variety of covers printed with hand-set wood-type designs, where no two covers was the same. Our first benefit set, we raised a pretty sizable chunk of loot for the museum. Readers of this book: Get your asses over to Two Rivers and hang out at the Hamilton Wood Type museum. Mandatory stuff, people!

All Those Movies
One of my favorite parts of our seasonal updates are the movies that go with each release. That credit lands squarely in the laps of Steve Delahoyde and Bryan Bedell. Those guys have made some beautiful pieces over the years. There's such a power to the films they've made. I sorta forget they have anything to do with Field Notes! Notables have been the "Night Sky" with its dramatic cosmic shots. And the panning shot in the "Drink Local" piece? I still don't know how they changed the colors in that one. Some kind of video effects or something? Let it remain a mystery. Hands down, my very favorites have been the "Expedition Experiments." Twelve tests! The type, the sets and the peculiar results! And the weird, ambient "lab setting" noise, too. Incredible stuff. This is the part of Field Notes that always surprises me, and I look forward to each release day to get that buzz.

The "F" Word
Don't mess with the "F" word. And folks, I'm talking about "fulfillment" here. Each year, Field Notes grows and grows.

Both in demand and staff. The last time I was in Chicago at Field Notes Midwest, I spent the most time just hanging out in the shipping room, marveling at how the fulfillment outfit has taken shape over the years. At the height of our Christmas season there's a full team in there getting the orders out the door. When the new seasonal releases come out, the place is bonkers for a month. It's a dance, choreographed, with extras thrown into each order. Even as official as Field Notes is becoming, we still find time to throw a little surprise in. That's what I've tried to do with the DDC since day one.

DDC Curveballs
Sure, Jim and the gang have the year's onslaught beautifully mapped out, but I'm always scheming up weirdo DDC editions from my end. Little monkey wrenches to throw into the gears. In November 2014, 1,750 DDC sets went up on my site, and I sold 1,400 sets in four hours. So, so cool. And, uh, completely terrifying! That afternoon blew my mind.

Ferocious Field Nuts!
A couple years back, a group of Field Notes fans started a little Facebook club called "Field Nuts." There were a couple hundred folks on board pretty fast. And the next time I checked, it was a couple thousand. And they are ferocious. In a fun way. Paper, design and theme speculation. Tips and tricks. Usage stories. Unboxing videos. Laments. The whole gamut of Field Notes enjoyment, excitement and usage. I just love seeing people dig the books. I'll lurk on there every now and again to pick up the pulse. Thanks for diggin' us, you Field Nuts!

Shady Economics
It's been surreal to see our little books show up on eBay. Especially when I get sob-story e-mails about a set someone missed out on—one of my rogue DDC editions or whatever. And I'll gladly send them a set from my stash. But this one time, something felt a little fishy. The story was a little too tear-jerking, and felt oddly desperate and a bit choreographed. I wrote the belly-band number down when I sent it, curious. And wouldn't you know, I see the same set show up at some big price on eBay a week later. That's the last shipment to that turd. I go out of my way all the time to make people happy with these things. I guess you are going to get burned every now and again.

My Favorite Part
I get great satisfaction from making a big list and chipping everything off it over the course of a day. I have my latest book at arm's length at all times. I've got a decade's worth archived in my shop, and on some level that's the record of my life. Those little pages mean so much to me. I made the books for simple reasons. Seeing people enjoy them in new ways always blows me away. I'm really proud to see our little books out in the world, doing the job.

Thanking the Field Notes Gang
Thank you to Jim Coudal for rolling the dice on me. To Michele Seiler for infiltrating Field Notes into the retail landscape and fighting for our nerdy design requests. To Bryan Bedell for his design chops, wit and press check wizardry. To Steve Delahoyde for making the brand come alive with amazing films. To Joe Dawson for outfitting us with a beautiful website. To Trina Foresman for her customizing prowess. To Matt Jorgensen for saving my ass so many times with potent drop shipments to me out on the road. To Jerry and Brian French of the French Paper Co. in Niles, Michigan, for providing the greatest paper in the world. To the good printers of eDOC Communications in Mount Prospect, Illinois, for doing such an incredible job printing our books. And finally, our growing Memo Book Archive owes a debt of gratitude to Eric Lovejoy for scanning in a thousand books, to Leigh McKolay for painstakingly clipping them all out and of course Joe Dawson for getting them up on the site.

These people have built a wonderful brand. I'm forever indebted to their efforts, bringing Field Notes to life like they have. Thank you, Chicago.

Some Rules for Field Notes Usage

01 Peel off all the stickers on stuff. And then stick them in your Field Notes. If they stick, stick 'em. There's a scrapbook quality to the way I fill the books up. If I had a nickel for each banana or apple sticker, I'd have roughly $635.85.

02 My policy for "When to start a new Field Notes memo book" is pretty simple: When I complete a book, it's time for a new one. I use the books all the way to the last page. A couple days before all that, I'll pick out the new one and carry it with me to break it in a bit.

03 Fill out the "Pertinent Coordinates" section at the start. We've heard many stories about the books being returned to people who lost them out in the world.

04 If the spine starts to tear or fall apart, hit it with some shipping tape. The light stuff will be enough. These are paper, and paper wears out.

05 Use them ferociously.

06 Tell one thousand of your closest friends about Field Notes.

| Draplin | Pretty Much | Aaron James | File Under: | 102 |
| Design Co. | Everything | Draplin | Durable Materials | 103 |

Scenes from our first print run! 2005.

Making buddies with the guy who dropped off the first run. 2005.

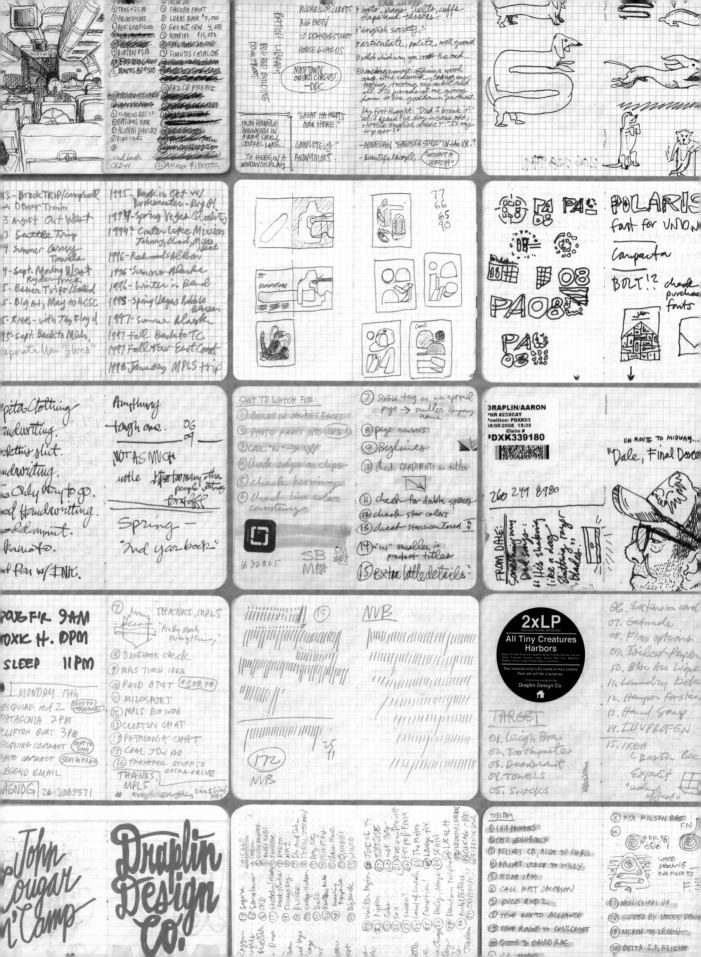

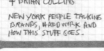

Field Notes Color Editions

Field Notes spine spectrum!

Field Notes "Neon Ice Pop Pack." 2010.

Field Notes COLORS "American Tradesman." Summer 2011.

Field Notes COLORS "County Fair." Summer 2010.

Field Notes COLORS "Grass Stain Green." Summer 2009.

Field Notes "Steno Book." 2010.

USEFUL INFO

LENGTHS:

....	5,280 feet
....	660 feet
....	16-1/2 feet
....	6 feet
....	4 inches
....	39.37 inches
....	.305 meter

STANCES FROM SUN:

....	35,980,000 miles
....	67,200,000 miles
....	93,000,000 miles
....	141,620,000 miles
....	483,780,000 miles
....	890,755,000 miles
....	1,784,860,000 miles
....	2,793,100,000 miles

PACIFIC 3 PM

"Steno Book" inside cover detail.

ⅅⅅℂ

Draplin
Design Co.

Pretty Much
Everything

Aaron James
Draplin

File Under:
Limited Editions

108
109

Assorted launch advertisements. 2008–2009.

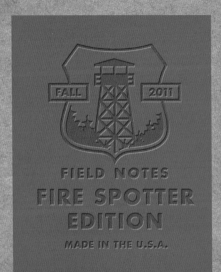

Field Notes COLORS "Fire Spotter." Fall 2011.

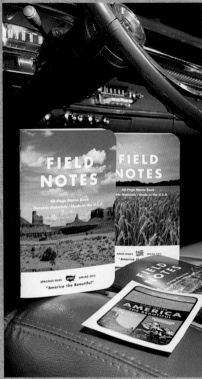

Field Notes COLORS "America the Beautiful." Spring 2013.

Field Notes COLORS "Packet of Sunshine." Spring 2010.

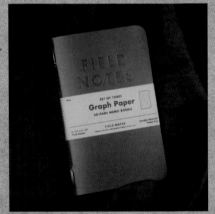

Field Notes COLORS "Ravens Wing." Fall 2010.

Field Notes COLORS "National Crop." Spring 2012.

Field Notes COLORS "Balsam Fir." Winter 2010.

Field Notes Color Editions

Field Notes COLORS "Traveling Salesman." Fall 2012.

Field Notes COLORS "Cold Horizon." Winter 2013.

Field Notes COLORS "Night Sky." Summer 2013.

"Night Sky" staple detail.

Field Notes COLORS "Shelterwood." Spring 2014.

"Drink Local" staple detail.

"Drink Local" letterpress coasters.

Field Notes COLORS "Drink Local." Fall 2013.

| Draplin | Pretty Much | Aaron James | File Under: | 110 |
| Design Co. | Everything | Draplin | Fringe Benefits | 111 |

Field Notes COLORS "Two Rivers." Spring 2015.

Field Notes COLORS "Arts and Sciences." Summer 2014.

"Arts and Sciences" buttons.

Field Notes COLORS "Ambition." Winter 2014.

Field Notes COLORS "Unexposed." Fall 2014.

"Ambition" gilded edges detail.

"Workshop Companion" staple detail.

Field Notes COLORS "Workshop Companion." Summer 2015.

My Complete Field Notes Cover Stash

FIELD NOTES
DDC OPEN ROAD
DOGS
OREGON
AARON JAMES DRAPLIN
DRAPLIN DESIGN CO.
DDC USA
"SHITCHYAH!"
Philadelphia
DRAPLIN DESIGN COMPANY, NORTH AMERICA
GRAPHIC DESIGN!
STANDARD ISSUE DDC FACTORY FLOOR MEMO BOOK
"NATIONAL CROP" EDITION
SOYBEANS
KENNEDY
MYSTERY PACKET
PAHASKA TEPEE
WYOMING
Freedom is something you take.
with love, Victore
DECORCAL INC.
Sasquatch!
"America the Beautiful"
VANS "OFF THE WALL"
Space Shuttle
DRAPLIN DESIGN COMPANY NORTH AMERICA
MICHIGAN
CREATIVE WORKS
COMMIT TO CRAFT
Oregon
DDC

Rock-n-Roll Efforts
"Always have a record playing in the shop.

megafaun HT047

ELC901 THE DELINES COLFAX EL CORTEZ RECORDS

RICHMOND FONTAINE THE HIGH COUNTRY ECR14T

ARRCO RICHMOND FONTAINE "WE USED TO THINK THE FREEWAY SOUNDED LIKE A RIVER" No. ARE-071

Rhett Miller The Traveler ATO0275

ATO0232 OLD 97'S – MOST MESSED UP ATO RECORDS

Scott Sullivan The Crushwater Symphony

No. 78176-1 VIVA VOCE / THE FUTURE WILL DESTROY YOU VANGUARD

DIVIDED & UNITED THE SONGS OF THE CIVIL WAR

All Tiny Creatures Harbors

CASEY NEILL & THE NORWAY RATS – GoodBye to the Rank and File

CASEY NEILL AND THE NORWAY RATS ALL YOU PRETTY VANDALS JR101

Kevin Lee Florence GIVEN Fluff & Gravy Catalog No. EnG002E

A JOCKEY'S CHRISTMAS WILLY VLAUTIN

HUB002-2 Dawes STRIPPED DOWN AT GRIMEY'S HUB RECORDS

CHUCK PROPHET dreaming waylon's dreams decor

JIMIJAZZMUSIC THE JIM PRESCOTT TRIO DOGS & ROSES JJM-001

MISSION SPOTLIGHT KEEP THE GOOD ONES CLOSE

RECALLSEVEN RS002

DDC

Draplin
Design Co.

Pretty Much
Everything

Aaron James
Draplin

File Under:
Audiophile Itch

114
115

Our record collection back at the ranch.

Turn it Up

I've got a monster tape, record and CD collection. Been at it since the late '80s. Quiet Riot's *Metal Health* was the first tape I bought. Men at Work's *Business as Usual* was the first record. Minor Threat's *Complete Discography* the first CD.

Mom raised us with music. Tunes were always playing in the car, and around the house while we playing. Most important, it was my mom's musical bravery that allowed for weird stuff and punk rock to enter the household. Remember parents barring it from homes? Satanic heavy metal and all that? Warning stickers? Tipper? My mom wasn't caught up in all that shit. I remember her being concerned about the Cult. And a little about Metallica's darker lyrics. But I explained it all to her and we were all right. I owe so much to my mom for being a cool mom. So many kids have it the other way around.

Crucial Rock Influences

I remember peering into my Uncle Kevin's bedroom to see scary posters, records and guitars. All off-limits to a six-year-old, of course. But what I'm thankful for, my Uncle Kevin was my introduction to the mighty Led Zeppelin. Zoso!

My cousin Patrick Draplin has maybe seven years on me, so when the '80s hit, he introduced me to U2, the Police, Sting, Duran Duran and Men at Work. I was ten to eleven years old and listening to U2's *Under a Blood Red Sky*. That record is still one of my favorites off all time.

As high school started, I owe a nod to Edgar Barlan. He taped me R.E.M.'s *Document*. That'll be one of my favorite records forever. It opened me up to the world of "college rock." That one little tape. Thanks, man.

I worked with a couple heshers at my high school pizza job. Hair, leather jackets and shitty tattoos . . . and those guys led me to Metallica, Anthrax, Suicidal Tendencies and the mighty Black Sabbath.

Skateboarding introduced me to punk rock. Minor Threat, Black Flag, the Misfits, 7 Seconds and my very favorite band from high school, the Dead Kennedys. Jello Biafra changed me. I'll never look at the American government the same.

I graduated high school with Phil Lieffers and he worked at Traverse City's only record store, New Moon Records. He turned me on to Uncle Tupelo in 1992. Record store guys could be such dicks. I was lucky to have Dave VanOcker and

Phil feeding me new stuff each week. That primed me for Son Volt, Wilco, the Bottle Rockets and the Jayhawks. Which led me to the Replacements, Hüsker Dü and all the Midwestern stuff I missed growing up. I was just too young. The greatest stuff wasn't from Los Angeles or New York! It was Minneapolis? Yes.

College was where I smashed my head on the indie rock. My high school buddy Steve Brydges always knew the cool bands to go after. He introduced me to the Red House Painters, Sebadoh and the goddamn Jesus Lizard. Those bands changed me.

Those introductions led me to the loud, fuzzy, atmospheric stuff. Mercury Rev, Spacemen 3, Swervedriver and our very favorite band of all time—Oklahoma City's very own—the goddamn Flaming Lips. They grabbed hold of me in 1992 when I saw them at Val Du Lakes opening for the Butthole Surfers. So loud, freaky looking and fucking great. To this day, the records from the early to mid-'90s are my favorites. I was twenty-two when I first heard *Transmissions from the Satellite Heart*. The kind of record that makes you thankful to be young. And aware. And alive. You could tell they had complete creative control over the music, the album art and the hand-screenprinted posters that Wayne Coyne would pull in his garage. Beautiful, folky, wobbly and perfect. Thank you Wayne for inspiring me to make my world what I wanted it to be. And thank you to Steven Drozd's drumming on those records. Those are my favorite drums on any records, ever. The best. Turn it on!

When we got out west, grunge was exploding in Seattle. By the time we got up there, you knew better than to divulge your love for Pearl Jam or Soundgarden. Of course we loved that shit! We were from Michigan. I remember seeing the politics from that era up close and being freaked out by how cynical it all was. Like, the town was embarrassed by it? So poisonous. Mudhoney, the Screaming Trees and TAD were my favorites from the grunge explosion. Those records still hold up. *8-Way Santa* still rules.

Rock Rags

I grew up reading *Rolling Stone*. As far back as I can remember, that mag showed up at the house. When I go home these days, I'll lay on the couch and go through the last couple months' worth. *Maximum Rocknroll*, *Spin*, *Ray Gun*, *Motorbooty*, *Punk Planet* and *Copper Press* were the music rags I sought out. *Chunklet* was

my favorite rock rag. That mag's snarky, creative perspective turned me on to so many bands. Thank you, Henry Owings.

Our Own Vinyl Reintroduction

I got back into vinyl in 2006. Due in part to one Mark Phillips lighting the fire under my ass. He sized up my CD collection, and then we flipped through the lone stack of records I had from growing up.

All those years since leaving Michigan, I amassed a couple thousand CDs. I'd buy a few each week. A coping mechanism, on some level. Even in the toughest of times, I could find thirty bucks to get a couple new albums. I remember buddies complaining about spending all their cash at the bar. I've never been much of a drinker, and I was proud to make as little money as I did and still have some cash for music.

And remember how records used to be cheaper than CDs? I remember picking up a record, checking out the artwork and track listing and then going to find the CD to purchase. Vinyl weighed too much for my missions back and forth across the nation. Of course, when that iPod came out, my wall of CDs went quiet. I burned 99 percent of them into my machine and they've just sort of sat there ever since. That's sad to me. I miss those discs. The art, the feel, the intricate packaging.

Making the Sausage

Being able to design a CD or record for a band or buddy? Before I ever got to make a record, I had heard enough from other designers about how little money they could make designing them. That didn't matter to me. I was just jealous they even got to do it!

Records are my favorite projects to work on. They are real. Tactile. Little blasts of creativity, timing, hard work and showmanship. It's almost too much to handle in that little kit. The art is big and you enjoy it so much differently than another click in your iTunes.

I've been lucky to do a couple a year the last seven to eight years, and each one is a shining jewel in my workload. Still my favorite thing to do. I'm working on records for Richmond Fontaine, The Delines and Belle Adair as these words go to print.

A word to the designers out there making the records I buy: I'm watching you with an eagle eye. You are of the LUCKY FEW. Don't let the band, rock and roll at large, yourself or, hell, little ol' me down.

Danava / Earthless / Lecherous Gaze split 12-inch. 2010.

Danava / Uncle Acid & The Deadbeats split 7-inch. 2011.

Danava - *Hemisphere of Shadows*. 2011.

Casey Neill and the Norway Rats - *All You Pretty Vandals*. 2013.

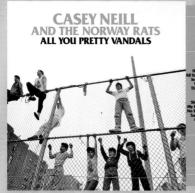

Viva Voce - *The Future Will Destroy You*. 2011.

Richmond Fontaine

Hands down, this spread just might be very favorite of the book. I've been a Richmond Fontaine fan since 1995. Saw them open for Mike Watt and was blown away. I bought their little six-song demo cassette from Watt's merch table that night. I wore that tape out, it met its untimely death at the hands of a roasting backseat window and the relentless Las Vegas heat. Sure, I was raised on punk rock, but somewhere in that mess I found Uncle Tupelo. And before I knew it, they were broken up and starting their own bands. When I got out to Portland, these guys became my Uncle Tupelo.

I'd see them in Portland, and even one time in Minneapolis. Ryno and I were in the "crowd" for their 7th Street Entry show. Pretty sure it was Ryno, myself, a couple stragglers, the sound guy and the band. I don't think there was even a bartender at the bar. They played some songs, and finally Willy Vlautin, the lead

singer, leveled with us: "Aw, hell, let's go see Blue Mountain in the big room!" And we all headed over to catch the rest of their set.

So you have to understand, when you go from being one of the four people in the crowd, to someone having the privilege of working on their design? It's kind of a big thing for a fan like myself. I just never thought that would be the case.

Willy Vlautin is prolific. Writing and playing on all the Richmond Fontaine records over the years, and now with The Delines. He's currently working on his fifth novel! It's just a special thing to be connected to someone who makes the art, records and stories you love. Willy's one of those guys in my little life. One of our greatest treasures in the Pacific Northwest.

I got to work for my favorite band from Portland. And became buddies with Willy

and the boys. Hell, Fred Green and I were even in a video! One time, with Ryno Simonson, CEO of the Greater Minneapolis Richmond Fontaine appreciation club, we went and joined Willy for tacos up in Portland's St. Johns. One cool lunch.

With each new record I get to work on, the very coolest part of the project is that I get to listen to it months before it comes out. I'll never get over how cool that is. Willy will warn me, "Hey, man, be careful listening to those new songs. They get a little dark, so don't get depressed." So far, so good. Thank you for the privilege to roll my sleeves up for Richmond Fontaine! I need to thank my old Cinco buddy Sunny Burch for connecting Willy and me. She's the one who tipped them off to my mess.

I've been lurking in the Northwest since 1993. And hands down, Richmond Fontaine is still my favorite Portland band.

Richmond Fontaine - *We Used To Think The Freeway Sounded Like A River*. 2009.

Big time client meeting with Willy.

DDC

Draplin
Design Co.

Pretty Much
Everything

Aaron James
Draplin

File Under:
White Line Fever

118
119

Richmond Fontaine - *The High Country*. 2011.

Willy Vlautin - *A Motorcycle For A Horse*. 2011.

Richmond Fontaine - *Live At Dante's*. 2010.

The Delines - *Colfax*. 2014.

The Delines - *The Oil Rigs At Night 7-Inch*. 2014.

The Delines - *Scenic Sessions*. 2015.

Assorted T-shirt designs. 2007-2014.

ATO Records

OLD 97s - *Most Messed Up*. 2014.

ATO0232

OLD 97'S
MOST MESSED UP

OLD 97'S – MOST MESSED UP Twelve songs in total: 1. Longer Than You've Been Alive 2. Give It Time 3. Let's Get Drunk & Get It On 4. This is the Ballad 5. Wheels Off 6. Nashville. 7. Wasted 8. Guadalajara 9. The Disconnect 10. Ex of All You See 11. Intervention 12. Most Messed Up. Produced by Salim Nourallah. Album length: Thirty-nine minutes, fifty-seven seconds. Play this album real loud. We're found online at "www.old97s.com" and "www.atorecords.com". ℗&© 2014 Old 97's under exclusive license to ATO Records, LLC. All Rights Reserved. 0882198718

Rhett Miller - *The Traveler*. 2015.

Rhett Miller   The Traveler
with Black Prairie

01. Wanderlust 02. Jules 03. Most In The Summertime
04. My Little Disaster 05. Fair Enough
06. Kiss Me On The Fire Escape 07. Lucky Star
08. Escape Velocity 09. Dreams Vs. Waking Life
10. Wicked Things 11. Good Night 12. Reasons To Live

Divided & United - *Songs of the Civil War*. 2013.

Rayland Baxter - *Imaginary Man*. 2015.

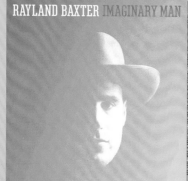

DDC

Draplin
Design Co.

Pretty Much
Everything

Aaron James
Draplin

File Under:
Adam Loves Sara

120
121

All Tiny Creatures - *Harbors*. 2011.

All Tiny Creatures

Harbors

Holography
An Iris
Cargo Maps

Valves or Hatches
Glass Bubbles
Breathing Set

Aviation Class
Triangle Frog

Reservoirs
Tine Feature
Plankton March

Megafaun - *Megafaun*. 2011.

real slow
these words
get right
hope you know
isadora
second friend
resurrection

kill the horns
scorned
serene return
you are the light
state/meant
postscript
everything

Hometapes

Adam Heathcott from Hometapes met me at my art show at Office in 2009. He gave me this incredible mix CD, both for the tunes and the design. Wore that thing out.

A year later, Adam and his wife, Sara, approached me about doing a record for a band from Milwaukee called All Tiny Creatures. Turns out I went to college with Thomas Wincek, their keyboardist. I can remember him hanging out in the computer labs, but we never really hung out.

So I dug in, started listening to the record and got the first couple waves of comps to present to the band. The Sea and Cake and Stereolab came to mind, so it was hard not to go down those respective graphic wormholes. We went back and forth with a couple rounds, to no avail.

A little flustered, I whipped up a colorful comp with simple, colorful shapes in a complex cluster. That's what you are seeing above. A quick comp, just to show

color on white space. A gesture, really.

And they went with it! I was blown away. One part *Spinal Tap* Stonehenge set, one part completely awesome. And with that comp, I invented a new style for myself to start playing with: Thick Lines stuff. But you know what I remember most about this project? Adam and Sara went with Stoughton packaging. I'm still impressed by that decision. Perfect. And, man, I love that record! Thanks, All Tiny Creatures.

Draplin
Design Co.

Pretty Much
Everything

Aaron James
Draplin

File Under:
Valves or Hatches

122
123

Chunklet, Rock-n-Roll Stuff and Festivals

We've got a soft spot for projects that fall into the "Rock-n-Roll" category. No matter the timelines, budget or rockers behind the project, I'll take it on.

I've been reading *Chunklet* since I was a wee lad, and when I met Henry Owings at Bonnaroo 2006, I thought he'd be nasty, cynical, and rip me apart. Quite the opposite. The man's a big Georgia peach, and we hit it off right away. He's called on me over the years and I've been lucky to do a 7-inch for Man or Astro-Man?, the cover and a good chunk of pages for *The Indie Cred Test* book, and consulting on various projects Henry is working on.

I went to the Sasquatch! Music Festival in 2002 to see the Flaming Lips, Calexico, Kathleen Edwards, and Death Cab for Cutie. When I got the call from Adam Zacks to work on the 2013 festival, I freaked out, on the side of the road in backcountry Iowa. A Northwest classic! I instantly said, "Yes!" To see those graphics up close the day of the big event was mind-blowing. I floated through the place and hell, even got to meet Tame Impala backstage! Nice guys.

A couple years back, I did a tour poster for Volcano Choir band member and old MCAD buddy Thomas Wincek. That rubbed off, and the summer we built this book,

I got to work for Justin Vernon, Michael Brown, Brian Appel and their Eaux Claires music festival. What started with a logo turned into posters, banner ads, signage, and backstage passes. Sadly, I missed the festival due to building pages in this here book. It doesn't take much to get me to go to Wisconsin, but duty was calling.

I've been lucky to do some really cool rock-n-roll work. I'm just waiting for my buddy George Salisbury (the designer for the fuckin' Flaming Lips!) to call upon my services to help out Wayne and the boys! Then our contribution to the Indie Rock will be complete!

Man or Astro-Man, *Analog Series* **for Henry Owings of Chunklet Industries. 2012.**

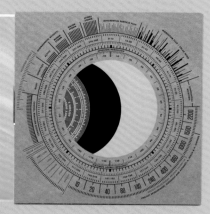

The Indie Cred Test, designing for Henry Owings of Chunklet Industries. 2011.

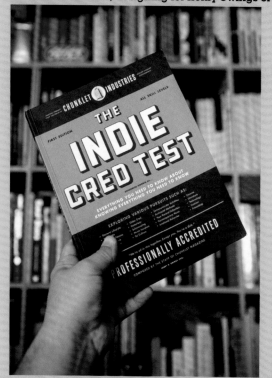

DDC

Draplin
Design Co.

Pretty Much
Everything

Aaron James
Draplin

File Under:
Backstage Lurkers

124
125

Sasquatch Festival event graphics for Adam Zacks. 2013.

Volcano Choir poster. 2014.

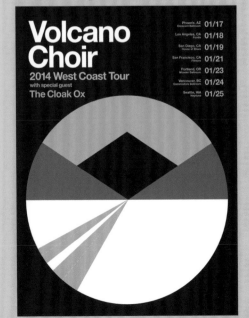

Eaux Claires Music Festival logo and event materials. 2015.

EAUX CLAIRES

EAUX CLAIRES

JULY 17 & 18, 2015

EAU CLAIRE, WISCONSIN

AERO FLYNN	ALLAN KINGDOM	BLIND BOYS OF ALABAMA	BON IVER	BOYS NOIZE
CHARLES BRADLEY & HIS EXTRAORDINAIRES	COLIN STETSON	CORBIN	DOOMTREE	ELLIOT MOSS
FIELD REPORT	FOUND FOOTAGE FESTIVAL	FRANCIS AND THE LIGHTS	GIVERS	GRANDMA SPARROW
HALEY BONAR	HISS GOLDEN MESSENGER	INDIGO GIRLS PERFORMING SWAMP OPHELIA	LITURGY	LIZZO
LOW	MARIJUANA DEATHSQUADS	MELT-BANANA	MINA TINDLE	MUELLER
NO BS! BRASS BAND	PHIL COOK	PHOX	POLIÇA	RAGNAR KJARTANSSON
RETRIBUTION GOSPEL CHOIR	ROSENAU	S. CAREY	SAM AMIDON	SPOON
STURGILL SIMPSON	SUFJAN STEVENS	SYLVAN ESSO	THE LONE BELLOW	THE NATIONAL
THE STAVES	THE TALLEST MAN ON EARTH	YMUSIC		

WE'LL JOIN YOU THERE...
EAUXCLAIRES.COM/TICKETS
@EAUXCLAIRESWI

Vectorized Living

"Logos, logos, logos, logos."

Making Logos

I'm amazed when I get that e-mail explaining how frustrated people are with their uptight designer and the making of their logo. All the wasted time and resources resulting in broken hearts. Of all things, coming up with a logo should be one of the funnest parts of starting a business. And I lay blame on knucklehead logo designers who don't put the time in. It's our job to give good options for the client to pick from. I can't tell you how many times I've heard that classic designer's lament: "We showed the client the stuff, and of course, they picked the shitty one." And I'm bristling, thinking, *Why'd you show them shit?* That's shameful. When I show logos, I don't show a thing that doesn't have my full blessing behind it. The client could pick any of them and make it work, or keep pushing on the iteration until we hit gold. It's my job to make them something they can use confidently and fall in love with. Right? Right. People always ask me about how I work, so I'm gonna try to boil down my process.

Initiation
It all starts with an e-mail, or a friend of a friend calling me. I'll hear them out, asking them as much as I can about what they are hoping to do with their project. It's important to get to know the people behind the project—the logo will be representing them. While we are bullshitting, I'll be taking notes. These initial pointers are the things I that guide me when getting the project going.

Get an Estimate Going
Let the client know what you are thinking for the fee. And no, there's no science to it. At forty-two years old, with twenty years of this stuff under my belt, I'm still freaked out by this part. There's so many factors to consider. So what if they don't have a big budget? I mean, who does? The bigger the client, the bigger the problems. Funny how that goes. Here's how it usually works: They'll throw out a number and I'll react. If it's too low, you push back, as articulately and professionally as possible. If people continue to lowball you, then that says a lot about who you will be working with.

Here's where things get weird: Be open to just sort of "going for it." Say the money is a little off, or the timing is tight. Part of the battle is knowing that there's always gonna be something compromised. Be it timing, loot or subject matter, rarely do all things line up. Just be open to things being a little weird. Don't be afraid to hammer on something all weekend long. Or to deliver something by the next day. I've been told that cheapens the game for everyone else. I disagree. My clients, for the most part, are friends and acquaintances and they don't fall into the same category. Most of the time, they are as big of an animal as I am, so we can work quick or pull an all-nighter. The fact of the matter is: This shit is a hustle. And the more jobs I've been able to pack in, the quicker I've gotten ahead. Sometimes for tons of loot, and sometimes, not one red cent. I'm open to both.

Determining a Schedule
Once we agree on a price, I'll work out a schedule. Depending on the level of the client, I'll stick to it to the minute. See, if it's your buddy, or it's for free, then they go to the bottom of the list. That's only fair, and I explain that to them. The paying clients go to the top. They are expecting the e-mails, check-ins and all that, and that's a service I work hard to provide. But if it's your buddy? They can chill the hell out.

Open Lines of Communication
From the initial call, I try to keep things as relaxed and fun as possible. I want people to be comfortable, because this is crucial for when things heat up and they need to assert their likes and dislikes. Tell me what you like and don't like. Tell me where you want to see it go. But there's a limit to this stuff. If you are hearing too much wavering, chances are you aren't showing the client the right stuff. You'll know pretty quick.

That First Presentation
I start by sketching in my Field Notes. Be open to the first idea that comes into your head. Over the years, a couple of those won out for me in the end! Document that magic. The whole time, I'm going back and forth, researching the client's history, their competition and the market they'll be operating in. If the competition has a specific color to their logo, you'll want to show things that react against it. Once I've got some pages of sketches refined, I'll jump into Adobe Illustrator to start building the logos, pairing up typefaces and picking initial colors, racing toward sending that first presentation.

As much as I'd love to make things I'm most comfortable with, first and foremost, when I am on the clock for a client, I make them what is appropriate for their needs. Of course, if they ask for things that are "in my wheelhouse," then that makes it a bit easier. But sometimes, it calls for inventing something you didn't see coming. And I love this. It takes work, sketching, research, thinking, flipping, flopping and tons of refinement. Some of my favorite logos surprised not only the client but me too! But know this: You have to put the work in. And then take the time to build it into a beautiful, logical presentation.

Don't start off a project sending the client some lumbering 147 MB Photoshop file! A simple PDF does the trick.

The first round is always the hardest one. It's where the client gets to see that first glimpse of the brand coming to life. So you better be on your "A" game. For that first offering, I try to show a range of options. I call it a "volume knob" approach. Say that volume one is something conservative, and as stuff gets louder, the logos get a little more complex. Then the client has a range to pick from. Right out of the gate, that gets me close to the target. I'm just trying to gauge their comfort level.

Harnessing the Feedback
Whatever the feedback is, before I indulge in the ol' "the client doesn't know what they are doing" riffraff, I try to look at the project through their eyes. Let them react. And document that exchange. Every bit of input is gold. I take their suggestions and concerns and dig into the next round. Now you can start refining things. Or adding something to the mix that is like-minded to the things the client picked out of the gate. Every now and again I'll throw out a curveball at the end of the presentation, and am always careful to explain the thinking behind it. I can usually nail something in three to four rounds of presentations. Occasionally, it takes longer. It's our job to ride it out. And, hey, if they hem and haw, then you have to size that up and react accordingly. But here's the deal: As long as you show smart, versatile solutions, all will be well.

And Finally, Completion
When you land on the final mark, then it's time to build out the kit. I rebuild the logo with the cleanest architecture possible, and supply simple, clean files, backing their work up for life on external drives.

Sometimes You Nail It
Every now and again, the client will dig something from the very first round and pick it. Which is so fun. Usually, this stuff takes a lot of work. Plain and simple. I'm always thinking about my open jobs. Sometimes an idea or refinement will come to me off the clock. I've trained myself to document those instances, and then reflect them in the work the next morning. When I'm on the clock, the stuff haunts me until I feel good about showing it to the client.

I've been able to make many logos over the years. For big companies and for tons of friends. For every big gig I did, I was able to make ten for the little guys. I'm proud to have been able to make time for both!

DDC

Draplin
Design Co.

Pretty Much
Everything

Aaron James
Draplin

File Under:
Jamestown, NY

128
129

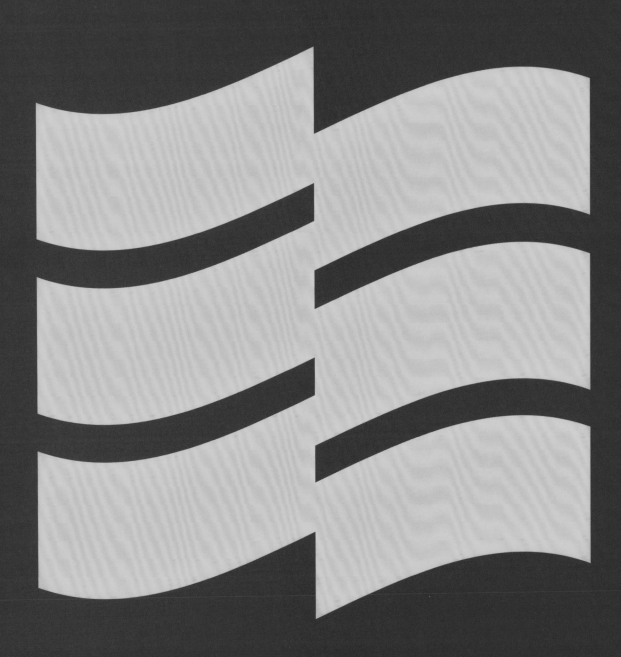

Suburban Blend. 2007.

Logos

Argonaut Cycles. 2012.

Timberline 75th Anniversary. 2011.

Coal Headwear. 2002.

Consolidated Fiction. 2008.

Wired Tasted & Rated. 2010.

Union Binding Company. 2004.

Insieme. 2014.

Field Notes Colors. 2009.

Westwood One. 2013.

Exit Real World. 2007.

AOL Autos: Lee Iacocca. 2010.

Giro One Step. 2011.

State of the Riesling. 2009.

Redwing Farms. 2008.

Patagonia. 2010.

Bold Development. 2010.

Fiender. 2012.

Koll Guitar Co. 2015.

New York Times Super Bowl XLIII. 2009.

Nike Air Max 360. 2005.

DDC

Draplin
Design Co.

Pretty Much
Everything

Aaron James
Draplin

File Under:
Proud Little Bursts

130
131

Carmagnum. 2011.

License Lab. 2011.

Megafaun. 2011.

Sasquatch Festival. 2013.

Beep Industries. 2011.

Matt & Leigh. 2014.

Resolved. 2014.

Forum Snowboards. 2006.

Drink Water. 2011.

Re:volve Project. 2006.

Red Pop. 2011.

Serious Electronics. 2010.

Skookum Digital Works. 2011.

Ride Decade. 2004.

Union Custom House. 2007.

Finex Cast Iron Cookware Co. 2013.

Crowd Compass. 2011.

MiniMini. 2015.

Ambission. 2006.

The Peoples Sandwich Republic. 2009.

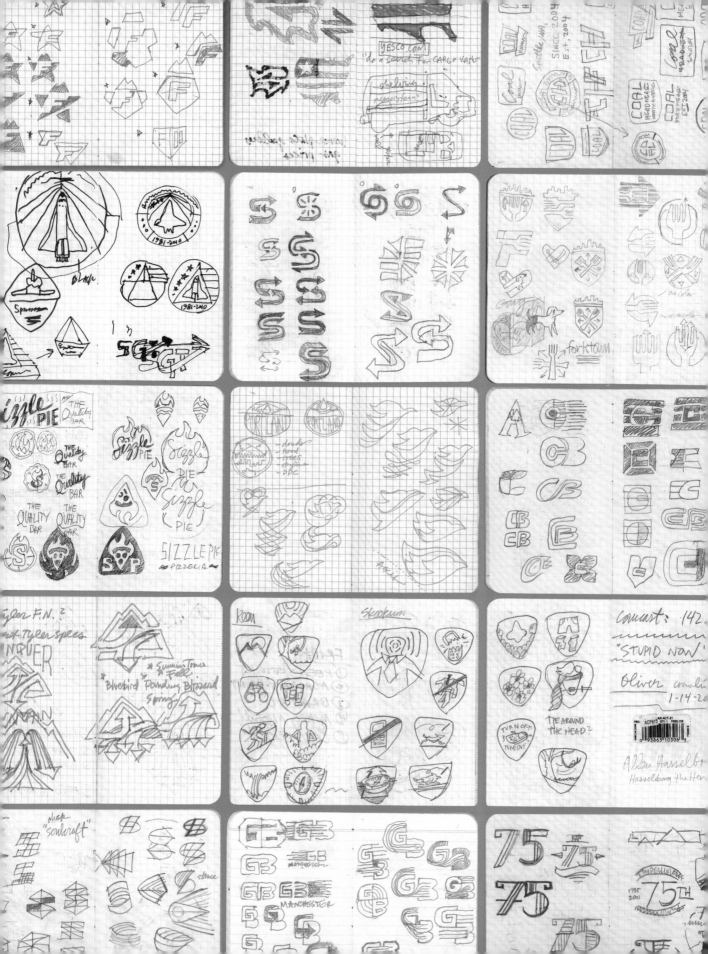

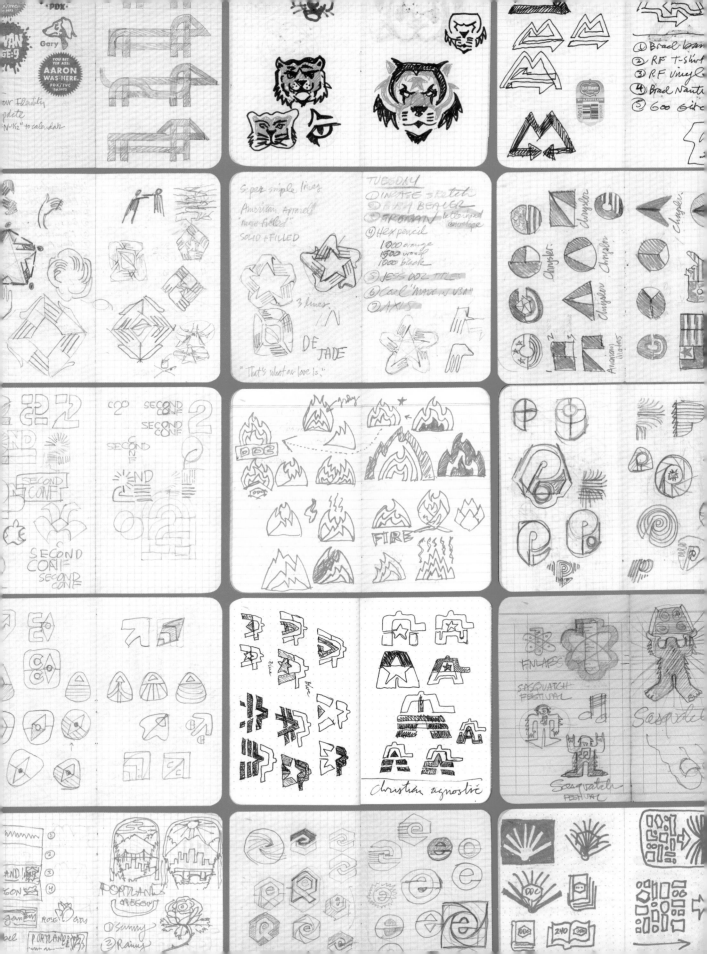

Logos

Field & Stream Mouse Icon. 2011.

Ten Years of the Union Binding Co. 2014.

Anthony Lakes. 2014.

MOB Distribution. 2006.

SecondConf. 2011.

Safari Flow. 2013.

Mama's Sauce Love Letters. 2013.

Nike Paul Rodriguez. 2009.

Institute of Possibility. 2013.

Junk Boys. 2010.

Made Right Here. 2014.

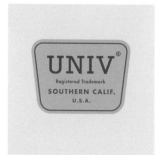

UNIV. 2008.

Nike Stefan Janoski. 2008.

Prairie Electric. 2014.

GB Manchester. 2014.

AOL Autos: EPA Challenge. 2010.

Panic Transmit 4. 2010.

Healthy Living Market & Café. 2015.

Search Discovery. 2013.

Octopus. 2010.

Draplin
Design Co.

Pretty Much
Everything

Aaron James
Draplin

File Under:
Proud Little Bursts

134
135

Brewery Outfitters. 2011.

Burnside Digital. 2012.

Grenade Options. 2007.

Assembly. 2014.

eRolling. 2010.

Finex Cast Iron Cookware Co. 2014.

Wesley Clark for President. 2004.

Editorially. 2012.

Coal Headwear. 2012.

Ten7. 2011.

South American Snow Sessions. 2006.

Snowboard Mag. 2004.

Jax. 2010.

Public Good Software. 2013.

Patagonia. 2010.

Southern Skies Coffee Roasters. 2010.

Rumblefish. 2015.

Abe Froman Productions. 2005.

Condé Nast Ideactive. 2011.

Tactics Boardshop. 2006.

Favorite Logos

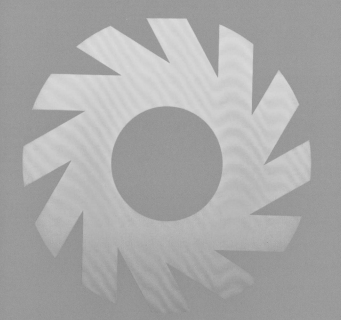

DDC Summer Sun. 2013.

Lookout. 2011.

Shelter Sales Co. 2014.

United Pixelworkers. 2011.

DDC

Draplin
Design Co.

Pretty Much
Everything

Aaron James
Draplin

File Under:
Favorite Logos

136
137

Cobra Dogs. 2008.

Vectors Are Free!

Here's a "pro tip" for the youngsters out there. When tuning a logo, be careful not to tune the same logo, "writing over" the previous version. Simply dupe the thing to the left or right, and then tune it. And do it again and again and again. And you'll have this "vector trail" of variations. I learned this lesson the hard way the first time a client wanted to revisit stuff from the previous rounds. After having to rebuild a handful of logos from memory, it hit me: Vectors are free. They aren't the same kind of heavy lifting like pixels. Be smart about it, and organize your workboard to capture all the variations you came up with along the way. Just like you do in your Field Notes.

◫◫◫

Draplin
Design Co.

Pretty Much
Everything

Aaron James
Draplin

File Under:
Option-Drag

138
139

Logos That Didn't Make Me a Cent

In a lot of ways, I tricked graphic design into hiring me. Yeah, sure, it didn't take too much of the "classic design conundrum" to freak me out, and get my ass into gear. You know, that pickle you find yourself in, where you can't get a job without any jobs to show? So I just started making my own stuff. I let design be a hobby first, and a job second. This came very natural to me. I've always enjoyed making things and being creative in all aspects of my life. Design offered a weird little buzz—and logos, they were these fun, concise things that could pack a big punch.

Make Your Own Stuff

Kids will ask me the age-old question each time I fill out their monotonous questionairre for whatever school project they are squirreling through: "How do you get to do what you do?" And I always try to break it down for them: "You need to get busy making stuff. And don't worry if it's real or just for fun. 'Real' being for a client. And then, show that stuff freely."

People hang up on that. When I got going, this stuff was simply for fun. I had my rent covered with pizza jobs, and learned how to do this stuff through projects for myself or buddies. I feel so thankful for that. I learned to love making logos first, before some turd client or boss ruined it for me. And then viciously applied it all to my little world.

Subversive Quality

My favorite thing about making logos is how—when done right—they'll elevate a little brand, band or idea up to their peers' perceived status instantly, and sort of level the playing field. I've made a lot of logos for people who had but one shot at getting going, and I like to think that I made them a logo that would help them along, something they wouldn't have to think about. I hear this one all the time: "We make great stuff, but don't look at our logo." And humor aside, it always hurts. It's the first thing people see a lot of times out there, and it has to be solid.

There's Always Time

It's funny how many new logo gigs I've gotten and people reference something they saw and like—and it'll be from my "made it for free" category. And I'd wager, it's because the spirit was right.

But let me clarify that a bit. I've had some turkeys come down on for me "diluting the design field" and "making it okay for people to ask for less and less." Yawn. But what about when it's for a buddy? Or you just like the idea behind something? Or it sounds like it's fun to make? What, you are supposed to pass those up? No. Not me. Opportunities, all of them.

I've built a career out of taking on gigs for friends, or folks in a pinch. There's always time for this stuff. And I'm always amazed at how a little bit of my time on something, sometimes, can have a big effect of a budding brand or idea. That's pretty intoxicating stuff. Be open to fun, freebie and weirdo gigs. There's gold there.

Cobra Dogs. 2006.

Bonehook. 2010.

Gary. 2005.

Herpetology Society. 2011.

Gary Longdog. 2007.

DDC Freight Div. 2011.

Robin. 2006.

Mike Basher Photography. 2011.

DDC Open Road Div. 2009.

Understanding Campaign. 2010.

MDP Bassworks. 2010.

Minneapolis Narwhals. 2009.

Draplin
Design Co.

Pretty Much
Everything

Aaron James
Draplin

File Under:
Centless Apprentice

140
141

The Jennings Hotel. 2015.

DDC Color Correcting Div. 2003.

Babe the Blue Ox. 2010.

Cove Cabin. 2012.

Beaver. 2010.

International Design Workers Federation. 2010.

Design Matters Podcast. 2012.

Peak Oil Records. 2012.

Forktown Food Tours. 2010.

Philly Liberty Bell. 2011.

DDC August. 2012.

Hoss. Hoss & Hoss. 2002.

Santa Jim. 2010.

Champion. 2007.

Ellis Designs. 2013.

BP Rogue Design. 2010.

State Plates Project: Oregon. 2014.

DDC Spectrum Excitement Div. 2013.

Action Cap. 2013.

50 and 50: The State Mottos: Oregon. 2011.

One Dinner, Sketching Logos

I vividly remember working on this one! It was the summer of 2010, and I was back in Traverse City for a couple weeks, visiting the homestead. We went to dinner at North Peak Brewing Company, and, sitting on the deck waiting for the food, I got to work on sketches for Jim Hutchins's "Serious Electronics" logo project. Jim was from Los Angeles and had hit me up to help out on a logo for a new division of his business. The bulk of their work was in the form of commercials, but doing more and more special effects stuff. Hence the S and E of Serious Electronics, boiled down to one electrified S.

And that's what you are seeing here. As we were waiting for dinner to be delivered, I was sketching along, and by the time the meal was done, I was finishing up those last couple pages and had a couple contenders to start vectoring up. That quick.

That's the magic of this stuff. Your hand is that much freer than a digital cursor on a screen. I start logos on paper. I sketch, sketch and sketch, and will try a ton of variations until something feels good. It's odd to me how things will be revealed through this process, or how things will sort of materialize. I'll be stumped on the screen and will hop over to my Field Notes, and in no time will have some new ideas.

In this case, I had to explore all the geometric opportunities of the "S." Outlines, bits, pieces, weird connections, spatial similarities, etc. Adobe Illustrator won't show you that stuff as quick as a pencil and paper will.

On the next spread, you'll see where we landed. Luckily, Jim was feeling the first couple pieces I showed him. That's not how this stuff usually goes. Sometimes, no matter how hard I'm hitting in that first round, people will push me further. And so it goes. The important thing is to be able to constantly push the stuff, and fast, in the client's best interest. And hell, with respect to the process, I like inventing stuff, and sometimes, that can take a mountain of sketching, thinking and refining on paper.

ODC

Draplin
Design Co.

Pretty Much
Everything

Aaron James
Draplin

File Under:
Supper Sketching

142
143

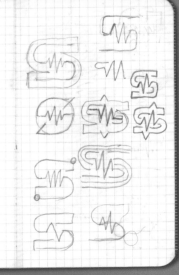

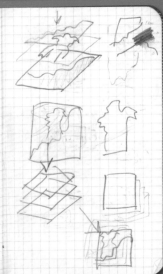

From Sketch To Vector Presentation

Sometimes, things go quick! In the previous spread, you see my sketching process. Here's what it looks like for the "first round" PDF presentation.

In "Round 1" on the facing page, you'll see me vectoring up my sketches and then offering up quick variations on each direction. Just to show the client the range of possibilities. Process-wise, "we are in this together." Meaning, as much as I am guiding the clients with options, I challenge and engage them to guide me with their feedback. In the end, it's theirs.

So it's my job to make them love it, and, have ownership along the way.

I have a hard time listening to people bitching about how "the client picked the shitty one" at the last second. I hear it all the time. It's our job to show options, get them excited to be in the space and then capitalize and make them something cool. I just want people to feel like they are a part of it. I've tried the Paul Rand approach a couple times where you hammer, refine and show up with a couple succinct, final options. And it worked

a couple times, and fell flat too many times. People just felt too surprised and on the spot to have pick one. That's too jarring, for both of us. I like working up to something, together. In the end, they are the one who wake up with it each day.

You'll see where the yellow is introduced in the second round. That was Jim's request. Done! Make the change and keep moving. His recommendation was perfect. You have to be open to you client's instinct. I put a lot of trust in them, as they are closest to their brand, you know?

Final mark.

DDC

Draplin
Design Co.

Pretty Much
Everything

Aaron James
Draplin

File Under:
Jim Hutchins, CA

144
145

Round 1 presentation.

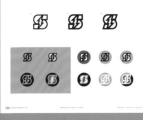

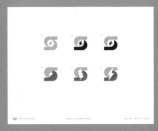

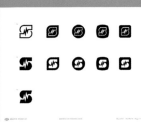

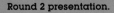

Round 2 presentation.

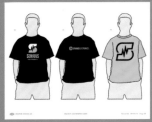

Round 3 presentation.

Pretty Much Everything Posters

I did my first "Pretty Much Everything" poster in May of 2009 for an art show at Office in Portland. Two-color "Dachshund Nose Black" and "Orange 021" on the biggest sheet of uncoated "house white" paper they could get out of the press. It weighed in at 24" × 39", pushing the trim to the limit on those 28" × 40" sheets!

That first poster had 1,112 things on it. That could be a logo, a buried detail from a project, a tribute to a buddy, or something experimental from my file archives. I like the idea of filling up a page. Being frugal real estate and making the most out of actually taking the time to print them. These become a game. What things rise to the top? Bright spots? Zones that need more "oomph"? Big puzzles.

How the percentages break down on the posters: Ninety percent of the stuff shown is for "fun"; the rest actually made me a buck. I am proud to show it all. I'm amazed at how much stuff I make will never see the light of day again. Logo comps will go by the wayside, buried forever in PDFs. But those are off-limits. When something is for a client, out of respect, I'll only show things that became real and in the world. These are really just celebrations of what I've been able to pull off. Each little

piece means something, and if I kept it laying around, then it "made the cut." Simple as that. And why not show it?

Seven years after the 2009 poster, that guy has become a little time capsule. It documented my output up to a certain time. When I did my 2013 and 2015 updates, it was tough to edit. I wanted to keep everything in. Making the jump to process color allowed for so much more fun stuff.

For the first poster, I made a key to tell each item's story. I think building the poster took me about forty hours. To find the stuff, collect it, and curate it into the puzzle. And let me tell you, those damn keys took more time than the actual posters. But the one time I saw the whole set framed in a guy's office? That made the hours completely worth it.

Plus, press checks are fun. I forgot. I miss going to them regularly. More and more, the work I do is uploaded somewhere to be printed somewhere far away, and often never seen again, unless I track it down. That's just weird. Big machines, safety glasses, weird smells, and fidgety operators? All good stuff. I love being close to the process and seeing the piece come

flying out. Such a technological marvel when you really think about it.

Be a good citizen on press checks. I try to be as respectful as possible with the press operators. Get on their good side and you'll notice they'll go the extra distance for you. One time in Tennessee, I ordered pizzas for the guys making our magazine. They were blown away. I've been in the situations where they were treated like dirt, and I'll NEVER be "that guy"—freaking out, huffing and puffing about some infinitesimal color shift. If I've learned anything on press, hitting 95 percent is pretty damn good, too. Done.

I remember seeing the "make ready" from the first run. It might've been more than my whole run. That messed with me. I wanted them, too. Damaged copies are always kept for future use. These things make great "on the spot" booth dressing. I've lined many floors with these things, creating a world of orange under customers' feet. Simple, quick, and putting each one to use.

I've shipped these posters all over the world! All the way to Kuala Lumpur, Rome, São Paulo, Tokyo, London and Branson. We'll ship anywhere, readers! Try us!

Making friends with Brad and Greg at CENVEO in Portland.

Stacks of these things.

Precious cargo!

Tasting the paper while print rep Mike Scherba looks on, confused. We have our methods; you have yours.

Approved!

DDC

Draplin
Design Co.

Pretty Much
Everything

Aaron James
Draplin

File Under:
Pretty Much Everything

146
147

Pretty Much Everything Up To May 27th, 2009
Draplin Design Co.

Pretty Much Everything Up To May 27th, 2009. 2-color. 24" x 39". 2009.

Pretty Much Everything Up To January 9, 2015
Draplin Design Co.

Pretty Much Everything Up To January. Process color. 24" x 36". 2015.

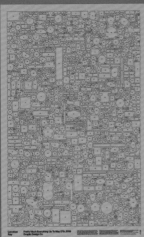

PME poster logos key. 2009.

PME poster explanations key. 2009.

1,112 things.

Hopefully it's not too dark to mention this, but, this is the last shot I took with my dad.
We were signing posters in Minneapolis, shooting the shit. Look how tired he looks?
He was feeling rough that day, and it shows here. October 11, 2013. Come back, Dad.

A Vectorized Protest: Warcons

This is a weird one. Leading up to the frenzied invasion of Iraq in the spring of 2003, I couldn't help but be transfixed by the television. "Live real time" war television, and, as disgusting as that was, I was gripped by it. I'm pretty sure that was the deal for all of America.

I'd work my day at Cinco and then head home to do my late shift and listen to the TV all night. Pissed, freaked out and scared, I started making these little icons just from the stuff I was hearing from the talking heads on the networks. Peculiar little phrases, quips and buzzwords.

And yet, in some weird way, trivializing these horrific things into cute, bite-size bits made them something I could wrap my head around. And I know that's not a good thing. If anything, that scared me, and made me look at what I was doing with my time on the job, and off. It made

the media frenzy surrounding the Iraq war shameful to me. They sold it to us. One little news flash and slick graphic at a time. As did a not-so-savvy president and his hawkish cabinet.

I posted some on my website and got some nasty e-mails from warmonger trolls. On a nerdy design site? That surprised me. This was the first time I spoke up. Frustrated with the pompous, folky quality of George Bush, I went off the rails a bit. I had no problem throwing the guy under the bus on my site or in graphics. I'm still embarrassed to have had him as my president for those eight years.

A wise friend back in the Midwest—oddly close to the Bush administration—put it best about the guy: "He's a good man for the most part. But not a good president. He'd make a good manager of a Target or something." Hmmm.

Embarrassed by the war, I never really did anything official with this project through DDC channels. They did show up on Travis Rice's Lib Tech model in 2007. We also did a naughty version called the "Skin Flute" that showcased every bad word ever, as well as every last little bit of cheeky, sexual slang. Dumb, sure, but still fun to see as a graphic texture, all flesh-colored and gross.

These little "warcons" came out of my disgust and fear at the events unfolding. I still don't understand their purpose, if any. It's just a weird time capsule, of sorts, for that scary spring of 2003.

A decade later, we know the rush to war was based on faulty intelligence and manufactured paranoia. And that breaks my heart. All those soldiers we lost. On both sides. All those families affected. On both sides. What a waste.

We protest the war.

Warcons
Icons protesting the war.
A tool designed by the Draplin Design Co.

Statement.
Build yer own poster.
Poster Gallery.
Contribute.
Links.
Contact.

An early web comp, in hopes of offering them to people to use freely. March 2013.

EMBEDDED MEDIA | "THANK YOU AMERICA. WE LOVE AMERICA." | EXPLOSIONS | KNIFE FIGHT IN A PHONE BOOTH | ALLOWED TO FILM | PRETTY MUCH | ANYTHING AND EVERYTHING | SMOKE 'EM OUT | GROUND FORCES | TOMMY FRANKS | PMD PENCILS OF MASS DESTRUCTIONS | MAN | BLEED RED | HEARTS FOREVER | AMERICA BRAVES

" | HEY, | LET'S FACE IT: | HE TRIED TO KILL MY FATHER. | " | MANY UNKNOWNS | BELIEVE. | GET RUN OVER | XMD X-ACTORS OF MASS DESTRUCTIONS | BROWN MAN | WE ALL BLEED RED | CITIZENS FEELING FREE | THE ULTIMA PRICE

WITHOUT ELECTRICITY | SISTER | HOUSE TO HOUSE | LAW-LESS-NESS | BRAVE MEN AND WOMEN | PEOPLE ARE DYING | SWIFT ACTION | MOTHER | VERY PROUD | BMD BAGELS OF MASS DESTRUCTIONS | RED MAN | WE ALL BLEED RED | HARD FACTS | ARM

BIOLOGICAL WEAPONS | WAR | THE GOOD | THE BAD | & | THE UGLY | "MOST-WANTED" DECK OF CARDS | YELLOW MAN | WE ALL BLEED RED | NAV

CAMO | SURFACE TO AIR | WART HOGS | FOOD AND AID | COMMANDER IN CHIEF | "FIGHT OR DIE" | DEVIL'S GARDEN | SPECIALLY-TRAINED DOLPHINS | MRE's | DROPPING LARGE ORDINATES | IN COUNTRY | PRESIDENTIAL PALACE | AIR FORC

OIL | PRESERVING NATURAL RESOURCES | BLACK GOLD | RED CROSS | EYE FOR AN EYE | PLAYED OUT AGAIN AND AGAIN | FRIENDLY FIRE | MAIM | GETTING SHOT AT ISN'T SO BAD... | GETTING HIT IS. | PLAYING POSSUM | ARMORED DIVSION | MARIN

LIKE THE REST OF THE WORLD | 9/10 | WE'VE HAD IT GOOD FOR A LONG TIME | BURNING OIL WELLS | CIA | HERO | GRIM AND GRAVE | LOTS OF FEAR | SURVIVAL | CONFIDENT SOLDIERS | SWEATY IRAQIS | COAS GUAR

FUEL | $4.62 $4.92 $5.22 | ? | MARTIAN RED | DRINK LOTS OF WATER | FEDA YEEN | PAIN | LIFE | FEAR FEAR FEAR | DEATH | INFIDEL | DOGS OF WAR | UDAY | BOY SCOU

FAIR PRICES | GAS WARS | ABOUT TIME | LIES | EMBRACING THE IRAQI PEOPLE | WHILE | CONFRONTING THE IRAQI REGIME | COLD AND HUNGRY | THE END | KILLER INSTINCT | THOSE IN THE AIR | SNIPERS | EXTREMELY LOYAL | WOMEN AND CHILDREN | GIR SCOU

BLACK GOLD | BLOOD MONEY | LIES | LIES | FBI | CUZ AT LEAST I KNOW I'M FREE | GOD BLESS AMERICA | LAND OF THE FREE | PLAYING POSSUM | BLOOD | DIRTY LOOKS | BAD PEOPLE | TERROR | BROTHER | SHRINE

TEXAS T | LIES | LIES | TRUTH | LIES | LIES | DOG TAGS | P.O.W. SITUATION | FUCK BUSH | BAD POLICY | BAD TIMES | BAD THINGS | THE KOOKS OUT ON THE STREETS | PULVERIZING THEM | SOFTE THEM

OIL THAT IS | TAKING POT SHOTS | LIES | LIES | LIES | UNCLE SAM | PLAY BY PLAY | TAKRIT | SEVERE | TERROR ALERT | WE'RE FUCKED | GO SHOPPING | BLOCK A HIGHWAY | HUMAN SHIELDS | LOVED ONES | FOO WATER AND MEDICIN

RAIN | BOOBY TRAPS | PROUD TO BE AN AMERICAN | LIES | ARMCHAIR WARRIOR | $$$ | BODY PARTS | HIGH | TERROR ALERT | MASS PARANOIA | ANTI WAR | US | GOOD GUYS | WM WEAPONS OF MASS DESTRUC

SNOW | GOOD | MARTYRS | LOOTING | BOMBS OVER BAGDHAD | DON'T | NO | THE ENEMY MIXED IN WITH VILLAGERS | ELEVATED | TERROR ALERT | HEAVY DRINKING | POWER | A "WAKE-UP CALL" | THEM

POW POW | HEROES | EVIL | AIR SUPERIORITY | TEXTBOOK OPERATION | BULLSHIT | STOP | WE DON'T APPROVE | GUARDED | TERROR ALERT | TAKIN' NAMES | HISS | COURAGE | BAD GUYS

SUN | BRING THEM HOME | WAR OF WORDS | ★ | BAD | EMERGENCY SPENDING PACKAGE | SUPPORT OUR TROOPS | LOW | TERROR ALERT | PICNICS | DARING | WE WILL NEVER FORGET | RIDDING THE WORLD OF THIS CANCER | AMERICA'S BRAVEST

BLUE SKY | AMERICANS ARE LOVING PEOPLE | HATE | BUY NOW | I'LL SEE YOU IN HEAVEN | HEAVEN | RESIST | CRYING MOTHERS | AMERICAN'S TEARS | IRAQI TEARS | CRYING FATHERS | VALOR | WIFE | PULVERIZ THEA

TREES | MIXING HUMANITY AND WARFARE | 43 | WHAM | WHAT-EVER | LIMBO | TOUGH DAYS AHEAD | FEAR | HEAVEN'S GATE | WHO SAYS YER GOD IS THE ONLY ONE? | BENNY HINN | OPERATION COMPLETE BULLSHIT | CHANTING PROTESTERS | MEDIA SLUT | BUSINES OWNER PROTECTING THEIR PROP FROM LOO

LEAVES | HOARD | BAD IRAQI MUSTACHES | WE'RE ALL GOING TO HELL | HELL | SATAN | VS. | ALLAH | GOD | JESUS | BRING THEM HOME | SCARED EYES | MY MOMMY | THIC SMO

DIRT | MAJOR SQUIRMISHS | EYE FOR AN EYE | PROTEST | LOCKING HORNS | TOOK A WRONG TURN | TELLING THE TRUTH | GHANDI | BUDDHA | ELVIS | TWIN TOWERS | UNITED NATIONS | QUESTION EVERY THING | DON'T BELIVE EVERYTHING YOU READ. | SHO EXECUTI STYL

BE LIEVE. | SERVING THEIR COUNTRY | MINOR SQUIRMISHS | "AMBUSH ALLEY" | SO, | RAT-A TAT-TAT | DIRTY BOMBS | PUSH FORWARD | PLASTIC SURGERY | THE PURSUIT OF AMERICAN BEAUTY | BUT HEY, MAN, | IT'S WHAT'S ON THE INSIDE THAT COUNTS. | RIGHT? | SADDA GOO

HARM | SAFETY | BOOM | OSAMA BIN LADEN | ANTI WAR SENTIMENT | WHAT WE ARE SAYING: | IS | GIVE PEACE A CHANCE | FAKE BOOBS | SMALL POX | BIOLOGICAL WEAPONS | $25,000 FOR SUIC BOMBER FAMILIE

ON THE ROAD AGAIN | REAL TIME WAR | BUT WAIT, WHAT "IT" ARE YOU TALKING ABOUT, EXACTLY? | ENJOY IT WHILE IT LASTS. | HEADS WILL ROLL | MY BABY | NO WAR | FACE LIFT | FALLOUT | GAS MASK | GERM WARFARE | NUCLEAR WEAPONS | OUTSKIRTS OF BAGHD

SEEIN' PLACES I'VE | STEALING FROM | UP TO THE MINUTE | GRAY AREA | SCARED FACES | CIVILIAN LOOTING | WMD | FAKE | NUCLEAR WINTER

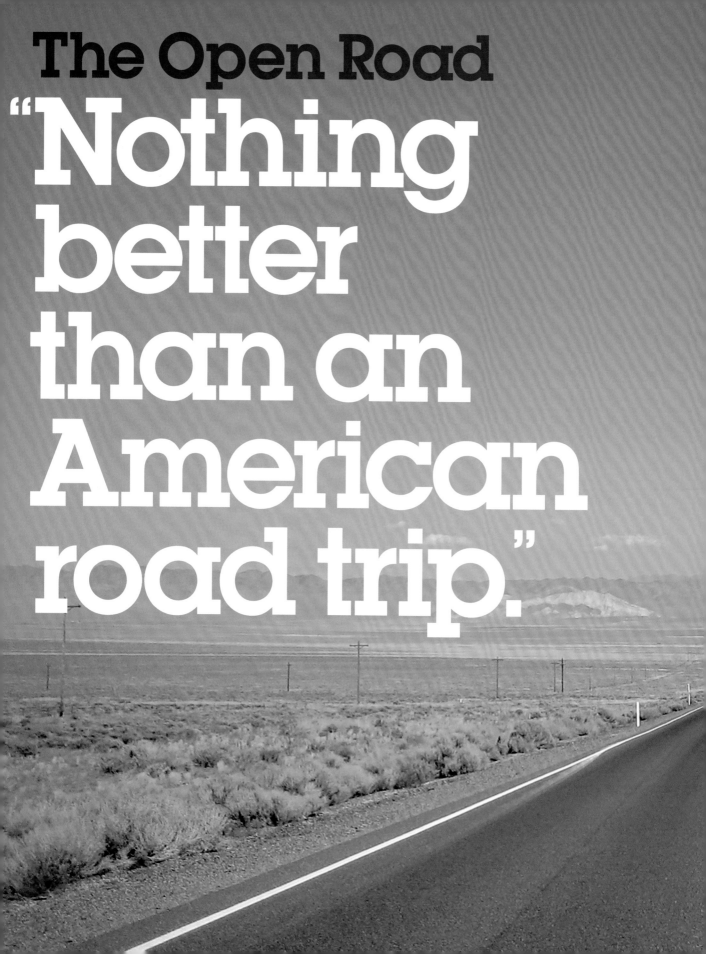

The Open Road

"Nothing better than an American road trip."

Along the Extraterrestial Highway, Route 50 Nevada.

Hitting the Road

I've lived far from home over half of my life. And it's weird. My Italian brother Martino told me one time, "Americans live too far from their homes." Which made me think hard about it. When we left, we left for adventure, snow and new opportunities. We felt like we had to. The distance from home to all the way out west was vast. A whole continent. And with each state, you notice a change in what it looks like and feels like. From that first road trip with Bry all the way to Bend, I was hooked.

Nothing beats a road trip. The freedom, wanderlust, lowbrow chow, new faces, places and spaces all packed into eight days across the nation. That's an aspect of America I cherish. The ability to jump in a car and drive as far as you can.

One of my greatest road trips was during the Indian summer of 1995. I was coming off a fun but fiscally unsound summer up at Mount Hood. I painted futon covers in Bend for a month to make some cash and then hit the road a couple weeks into September. Down along the coast, to Yosemite, down across Death Valley, into Navajo country, up into Fort Collins to see Rod Snell and then getting a wild hair and driving home in one shot from Colorado. But what I remember the most is driving through the desert one night, blasting the new Flaming Lips' *Clouds Taste Metallic* album as loud as Al the Minivan's speakers would go. I was just twenty-one years old. Completely on my own, driving across the American West! The world felt so big. I was sleeping in the van at night, on a budget next to nothing. That's the

most free I've ever been. Sure, I had a plan, but I could've gone in any direction I'd wanted. I'm so thankful I experienced that sense of freedom at that age.

When I got myself free from the clutches of the dayjob in 2004, I could draw up plans of what I wanted to do each month. And I started hitting the road each fall. I'd go on these monster road trips across the nation. I'd leave Oregon with my laptop, cords, a couple guitars, a bag of clothes and shit, and I went and saw America! I did this each fall from 2004 to 2008.

The whole time I always had a camera on the seat, ready to go. I took countless photos of landscapes, dead signs or kitschy roadside attractions. And I shared them on my website, blogging them up each night.

On big road trips with buddies, I'd be a slave to the monster I created with my site, sort of chained to a desk each night. They'd make fun of me because I would be "in the hotel room uploading shit" while they were at whatever horseshit watering hole they could find in the town we rolled into. Duty calls, all you slack-jawed mouthbreathers.

I feel like I've lived in a handful of cities because of those road trips. I'd roll into a town, find a cheap, safe hotel to set up shop and sort of take up residence for a week to ten days. I've done that in Louisville, St. Louis, Kansas City, Nashville, Memphis, Denver, Salt Lake City, Cleveland, Chicago, Cincinnati, Pittsburgh and Omaha. It allows you to get to know

the city a bit, the styles, the lingo and the highs and lows of a place.

I'd explore the town by day, enjoying the fall weather, junking, record shopping and generally lurking. By night, I'd be in the hotel room, hammering on projects, shipping rounds back and forth to keep the clients at bay. Often, those turkeys didn't even know I was out there, lost. As long as the work was showing up each morning, progressing along to completion, everything was cool.

The big Internet is everywhere now. But a percentage of you will remember the "pre-Internet road trip" era. Rolling into a town and having to find a culture paper to see what bands were playing that night. A complete crapshoot. I remember being in Iowa City in 1996 and so bummed out, having missing the Cows by one night. These days, all the mystery is gone. All the info is one finger swipe away, and so it goes.

When I hit the road, Wi-Fi was spotty at best. Some hotels were connected, like all of them are now. I'd check on their strength of their signal while checking in. No connection? Not interested in a room, then. And on down the road I would go. So here's a pro tip: If you are on the road and in a pinch and need to get some Internet on your laptop to download stuff, pull over and find a McDonald's. They always have strong Wi-Fi blasting! Pull up as close to the building as possible and tune in. Sure, stay away from the Big Macs, but, man, that hellhole has rescued me many a time.

DDC Open Road Div. 2009.

Testing our DDC-057 Open Road Tire Checker.

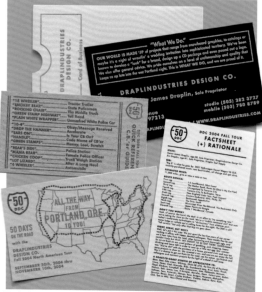

The business card set I made for my 2004 fall tour. Gocco print on shop scraps.

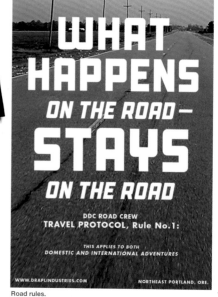

WHAT HAPPENS ON THE ROAD — STAYS ON THE ROAD

DDC ROAD CREW
TRAVEL PROTOCOL, Rule No. 1:

THIS APPLIES TO BOTH
DOMESTIC AND INTERNATIONAL ADVENTURES

WWW.DRAPLINDUSTRIES.COM   NORTHEAST PORTLAND, ORE.

Road rules.

Route 66

Dates: September 20–29, 2004.

Length: 2,451 miles.

States: California, Arizona, New Mexico, Texas, Oklahoma, Kansas, Missouri and Illinois.

My most cherished road trip is when Dad and I did the entire length of Route 66. Now, as the story goes, the initial travelers left the doldrums of the Midwest to end up in California, or "paradise." Dad and I flipped it. We started in Santa Monica and ended in Chicago. I'm so thankful I got to take him on the Mother Road in 2004. We took photos at every step, and I sent Dad a leather-bound photo album a month later. Mom said he choked up when he unwrapped it. The coolest.

Daily Website Tags From our Road Trips

"50 DAYS ON THE ROAD WITH THE DDC"

- DAY 01: PUSHING OFF
- DAY 02: DAD RETRIEVAL/SF
- DAY 03: INLAND EMPIRE!
- DAY 04: THE MOTHER ROAD
- DAY 05: RAISING ARIZONA
- DAY 06: NEW MEXICO'D
- DAY 07: TEX-ASS AND OKIES
- DAY 08: MISSOURAH...
- DAY 09: LAND OF LINCOLN
- DAY 10: REGROUPING
- DAY 11: EASTERN CANADA
- DAY 12: VERMONTERS
- DAY 13: VERMONTERS
- DAY 14: LEAVING VERMONT
- DAY 15: CHROMALAND
- DAY 16: NEW YORK, NY
- DAY 17: 50 IMAGES 4 Y'ALL
- DAY 18: WHITNEY IN DC
- DAY 19: SMITHSONIAN!
- DAY 20: MORE MUSEUMS
- DAY 21: FUN IN THE SUN
- DAY 22: VIRGINIA IS FOR...
- DAY 23: CAROLINA BOOGIE
- DAY 24: THE CALE COMPOUND
- DAY 25: GEORGIA, GEORGIA
- DAY 26: 'BAMA BIRTHDAY
- DAY 27: THAT BIG EASY
- DAY 28: BIG RIVER, NORTH.
- DAY 29: JUKE JOINTS.
- DAY 30: UNCLE TUPELO TOUR
- DAY 31: BIG SHOULDERS
- DAY 32: AH, MINNEAPOLIS.
- DAY 33: WET MINNEAPOLIS.
- DAY 34: BYE, MINNEAPOLIS.
- DAY 35: THE HOMELANDS.
- DAY 36: DOING NOTHING.
- DAY 37: SENT MY VOTE IN!
- DAY 38: ELKSTER OFFICE.
- DAY 39–43: PAGE LAYOUT!
- DAY 44: GOODBYE, GEORGE.
- DAY 45: REAL SAD.
- DAY 46: DEVASTATED.
- DAY 47: TRYING TO FORGET.
- DAY 48: UNCLE JESS
- DAY 49: DETROIT CITY TOUR
- DAY 50: HEADING HOME

BACK HOME: 13,919 MILES.
TIRED BIG. TIRED DOC. REAL GLAD TO BE AT BEST.

Snowing Lots,
Home-Cooked Meals,
Sleeping In,
Little Sisters,
Mom and Dad,
Real Good.™

"GARY ACROSS AMERICA"
NORTH AMERICAN FALL TOUR of "60 DAYS ON THE ROAD WITH THE DDC"

- DAY 01: PUSHING OFF — SOUTH OUTTA PORTLAND AND DOWN TO THOSE MAJESTIC REDWOODS
- DAY 02: NOR CAL — DOWN TO THE REDWOODS, ACROSS NOR CAL AND DOWN TO RENO
- DAY 03: HIGHWAY 50 — ACROSS NEVADA ON THE LONELIEST HIGHWAY IN AMERICA AND IN TO UTAH
- DAY 04: MOAB MORNING — BIG, ORANGE ROCKS OF SOUTHEASTERN UTAH, AND UP OVER THOSE ROCKIES
- DAY 05: PRAIRIE BOOGIE — DENVER MORNING, AND THEN OUT ACROSS THAT KANSAS PRAIRIE
- DAY 06: AND ON HOME... — TOPEKA, LAWRENCE, KC, ST. LOUIS, CHICAGO, GARY, HOLLAND AND TRAVERSE CITY
- DAY 07: TC RECHARGE — RECHARGING THE ENGINES, GARY TIME AND SUPPER WITH MOM AND DAD
- DAY 08: OVER TO MILAN — THE ITALY OFFICES OF THE UNION BINDING CO. CALL UPON ON OUR SERVICES
- DAY 09: JETLAGGIO — WAKING UP IN THE MIDDLE OF THE DAY
- DAY 10: ITALIAN STYLE! — WEIRD LITTLE POCKETS ON THE KNEE, OR SOMETHING
- DAY 11: LAKE COMO DAYS — TRANSLATE THIS, MOTHERFUCKER: WE GOT NO WEB CONNECTION!
- DAY 12: UNPLUGGED. — DEBATING SOME SORT OF "SMOKE SIGNAL" METHOD OF TRANSMITTING DATA HOME
- DAY 13: COLICO STAIRS — THE STAIRS OF COLICO, IN OUR BOOK, ARE THE EIGHTH WONDER OF THE WORLD
- DAY 14: WRAPPIN' IT UP — MY PAPERS FOR "ITALIAN CITIZENSHIP" WERE DECLINED, SO I MIGHT GO UP
- DAY 15: AMSTER-DAMN! — LAYOVER DYNAMICS: THREE HOURS HOOFING IT AROUND DOWNTOWN AMSTERDAM
- DAY 16: STATESIDE! — SO GOOD TO BE HOME, DEEP IN THE NORTHERN MICHIGAN WOODS
- DAY 17: RECHARGING. — HOME IS WHERE THE COUCH IS. MOM AND DAD ARE NURSING ME BACK TO HEALTH
- DAY 18: PORTLAND — WE HAD BIG DREAMS. WE THOUGHT WE COULD DO THIS FROM AFAR. WE WERE WRONG.
- DAY 19: PRE-GAME PAGES — GETTING READY FOR ISSUE THREE. BRING ON THE DUDES.
- DAY 20: SLAYING PAGES — ONE PAGE AT A TIME, THAT'S HOW WE DO IT. TAKE NO PRISONERS.
- DAY 21: PAGE PROGRESS — WITH BAKER AND NUNEZ HERE, SHIT HITS THE FAN AND PAGES GET BUILT
- DAY 22: THE MEAN GREEN — PANTONE 356, ALL DAY LONG. SOON TO BE RENAMED, "SNOWBOARD MAD GREEN"
- DAY 23: TUNES, MAN. — THIS IS WHAT WE ARE LISTENING TO, AS WE FIGHT THIS GOOD FIGHT.
- DAY 24: MISSING GARY. — I REALLY DO, I MISS THE LITTLE MAN. HE'S IN GOOD HANDS, THOUGH.
- DAY 25: LUNCH WITH FAZ. — THAT'S THE ONLY THING WORTH TALKING ABOUT. REALLY.
- DAY 26: ONE FINAL PUSH. — WE'RE SO CLOSE, WE CAN SMELL MID. WAIT, THAT'S JUST THE "DUDE FASS."
- DAY 27: BACK HOME. — FIRST CLASS, MAN. FIRST CLASS. GLAD TO BE BACK IN THE MIDWEST.
- DAY 28: HAMMERING. — SPENT THE DAY FEVERISHLY TRYING TO GET THE FUCKIN' MAG DONE.
- DAY 29: BURNING DISCS. — BURN BABY, BURN. SO CLOSE, SO CLOSE...
- DAY 30: EASY LIVING. — WAS GONNA HIT THE ROAD TODAY, BUT... WELL... IT'S JUST "TOO NICE" HERE.
- DAY 31: DOWN TO DETROIT. — NORTHERN MICHIGAN, MID-MICHIGAN AND SOUTHEASTERN MICHIGAN
- DAY 32: OHIO BIRTHDAY. — TURNING 32 AND 327 COINCIDENCE? OF COURSE IT IS, MAN.
- DAY 33: RIVER STRADDLE. — WORKED MY WAY DOWN TO LOUISVILLE, WITH THE OHIO RIVER AS MY GUIDE.
- DAY 34: LOUISVILLE'D. — HEATED CALLS TO IDAHO, BIG BATS AND BRAND NEW MARTIN 0-35 GEE-TAR.
- DAY 35: KENTUCKY-FRIED. — OUT OF LOUISVILLE AND INTO THE COUNTRY, AND THEN BLOWN AWAY IN UNO.
- DAY 36: NASHVILLE TOWN. — GOT LOST ALL OVER THE CITY, AWAITING THE ARRIVAL THE ONE THEY CALL "RYNO"
- DAY 37: N'VILLE TOURISTS. — HATCH, RYMAN AND DOWN TO ALABAMA AND OXFORD, MISSISSIPPI.
- DAY 38: NEW ORLEANS. — DOWN TO THE BIG EASY IN RECORD TIME, WHERE TIME SORTA STANDS STILL.
- DAY 39: UP HIGHWAY 61... — VICKSBURG TO CLARKSDALE TO MEMPHIS: EVERYONE 'GOT THE BLUES.
- DAY 40: UP HIGHWAY 61... — MEMPHIS TO DYESS TO ST. GENEVIEVE TO FESTUS TO ST. LOUIS
- DAY 41: UP HIGHWAY 61... — ST. LOUIS TO HANNIBAL TO DAVENPORT TO REDWING TO MINNEAPOLIS
- DAY 42: MINNEAPOLIS — GETTING BACK IN TOUCH WITH REALITY, AS WELL AS SOME FIRED-UP CLIENTS
- DAY 43: MINNEAPOLIS — CATCHING UP ON STUFF, ALL OF THE GRAPHIC DESIGN CATEGORY.
- DAY 44: MINNE-NO-PLACE — CAT GOT BLUES. PICKING AND STRUMMING. OUT AND ABOUT, SORTA.
- DAY 45: MARK TWAIN'D — WATCHED THE MOST AMAZING KEN BURNS DOCUMENTARY ABOUT SAMUEL CLEMENS.
- DAY 46: OLD STAMPS. — THINGS WE LIKE: PERFORATED EDGES, ODD MARKINGS AND WEIRD LANGUAGES.
- DAY 47: CANNON FALLS, MN. — WENT JUNKIN' FOR THE BETTER PART OF THE AFTERNOON, SOUTH OF TOWN.
- DAY 48: HALLOWEENAGE — SLAVE TO THE GRIND. DIDN'T GO SHIT TODAY OTHER THAN MAKE PAGES.
- DAY 49: ONE LAST DAY... — MORE PAGFS, SOME LOGO DESIGN, MISSING GARY AND GETTING READY FOR PDX.
- DAY 50: BACK TO PDX. — GOTTA MAKE ANOTHER MAG. HAD TO FLY BACK TO DO SO.
- DAY 51: PAGE-BUILDIN' — BAKER AND NUNEZ ARE HERE, AND MAN, WE ARE KICKING SOME ASS.
- DAY 52: BULLDOG VISIT — PROOF THAT "SOMETHING BIGGER IS AT WORK" IN THE FORM OF THREE LITTLE FRIENDS
- DAY 53: LARRY'S GIFT — WITH VERY LITTLE HOPE ON THE DDC FACTORY FLOOR, LARRY COMES THROUGH.
- DAY 54: 800th POST. — CELEBRATED BY "TRYING LIKE HELL" TO GET THE MAG DONE AND SEND TO DISCS.
- DAY 55: WRAP 'ER UP! — AFTER MUCH DEBATE, BATTLE AND CARNAGE, WE WRAPPED UP ISSUE FOUR.
- DAY 56: BACK TO MINNE... — WOKE UP, BURNT SOME DISCS, DROPPED THEM OFF AT FEDEX THEN HOPPED A JET PLANE.
- DAY 57: MPLS MORNING... — ...AND THEN ALL THE WAY BACK TO TRAVERSE CITY...ALL 700 MILES OF IT.
- DAY 58: MOM AND DAD'S. — THERE'S JUST NOTHING BETTER ABOUT COMING HOME.
- DAY 59: GARY TIME. — GETTING TO KNOW THE LITTLE RASCAL AGAIN, AS WELL AS HAMMERING ON PROJECTS.
- DAY 60: ONE LAST DAY. — READYING THE BIG, EATING GOOD MEALS, SENDING OFF COMPS AND SLEEPING.
- DAY 61: OVERTIME! — SO MUCH FOR 60 DAYS! UP INTO CANADA AND THEN WESTWARD ON HIGHWAY 17.
- DAY 62: LAKE SUPERIOR... — SNAILING ALONG THE NORTH SHORE OF THE GREAT LAKE SUPERIOR, TO THUNDER BAY.
- DAY 63: WINTER UP HERE! — WILD CANADIAN HIGHWAYS COVERED WITH A COUPLE INCHES OF ICE. "FALL," EH?
- DAY 64: SASKATCH-A-WHO? — HEARD SOME GUY TALKING ABOUT THE "STORM OF THE CENTURY" OR SOMETHING...
- DAY 65: ALBERTA CLIPPER. — FINALLY THREW IN THE TOWEL AFTER SO MANY LIFE-THREATENING KILOMETERS.
- DAY 66: COMING HOME. — DOWN THROUGH MONTANA, THE PANHANDLE OF IDAHO, WASHINGTON AND INTO OREGON.

"EIGHT CITIES EIGHT WEEKS" — DDC FALL TOUR

INDY · CHICAGO · IOWA · KANSAS CITY · ST. LOUIS · NOWHERE, USA · PORTLAND · TRAVERSE CITY · CINCINNATI · PITTSBURGH · NYC · WESTBOUND

Fourth Annual — Draplin Design Co. — North American Fall Tour

- Day 01 — Pushing Off — Portland, Ore.
- Day 02 — A Long Haul — Dallas to Salt Lake
- Day 03 — Treacherous Terrain — SLC to Avett Bros.
- Day 04 — Setting Up Shop — Boulder
- Day 05 — Slaying Pages — Boulder
- Day 06 — Hammer Down — Boulder to Des Moines
- Day 07 — Summit Meeting — Iowa, Chicago & Home
- Day 08 — Back Home — Traverse City
- Day 09 — Back Home — Traverse City
- Day 10 — Back Home — Traverse City
- Day 11 — Back Home — Traverse City
- Day 12 — Hammertime — Lake Ann
- Day 13 — Hammertime, Still — Lake Ann
- Day 14 — Conclusion — Lake Ann
- Day 15 — Westernizing — Lake Ann
- Day 16 — Sunday, Sunday — Lake Ann
- Day 17 — Monday Marauder — Downtown TC
- Day 18 — Kansas City or Bust — TC & Southbound
- Day 19 — Some Lips — Lake Ann
- Day 21 — Back Home — Traverse City, Mich.
- Day 22 — Saturday — Lake Ann, Michigan
- Day 23 — My Hometown — Central Lake, Mich.
- Day 24 — Salutation: Monday — Backwoods, Lake Ann
- Day 25 — Chipping Away — Lake Ann, Michigan
- Day 27 — Required Things — Lake Ann, Michigan
- Day 28 — Required Things — Lake Ann, Michigan
- Day 29 — Fridayville — Lake Ann, Michigan
- Day 30 — Relaxation Station — Lake Ann, Michigan
- Day 31 — Full Steam Ahead — Backwoods, Mich.
- Day 32 — Retooling The Plan — Backwoods, Mich.
- Day 33 — Matchbox Minutiae — Backwoods, Mich.
- Day 34 — Cabin Fever — Backwoods, Mich.
- Day 35 — Back On The Road — Michigan, Etc.
- Day 36 — Southbound — Towards Toledo, Ohio
- Day 37 — Lips Night — Mistake By The Lake
- Day 38 — Heading Back — Retracing Routes
- Day 39 — Making Pages — Lake Ann, Michigan
- Day 40 — Making Pages — Lake Ann, Michigan
- Day 41 — Enough Already — Defeated, Michigan
- Day 42 — Magazine Pages — Lake Ann, Michigan
- Day 43 — Completionism — Lake Ann, Michigan
- Day 44 — Cabinterventon — Backwoods, Michigan
- Day 45 — DDC Consumerism! — Shipping Everywhere!
- Day 46 — Autumn T-shirts... — Shipping Everywhere!
- Day 47 — Filling Orders — Shipping Everywhere!
- Day 48 — Southwestin' — Santa Fe, New Mexico
- Day 49 — Southwestin' — Santa Fe, New Mexico
- Day 50 — Southwestin' — Santa Fe, New Mexico
- Day 51 — Heading Home — Santa Fe, New Mexico
- Day 52 — Situation: Mid 30s — North America
- Day 53 — Back To Grinding — Lake Ann, Michigan
- Day 54 — Making Progress — Lake Ann, Michigan
- Day 55 — For Leigh — Mackinac Island, Mich.
- Day 56 — For Dad — Traverse City, Mich.
- Day 57 — Readying Things — Traverse City, Mich.
- Day 58 — Donkey Kong'd — Traverse City, Mich.
- Day 59 — Into the Windy City — Chicago, Illinois
- Day 60 — Back To Ryno — Madison to Minot
- Day 61 — Downrunning — Mississippi, Minn.
- Day 62 — The Prairie — MN > IA > SD > NE > ND
- Day 63 — Straight Shot — North Pacific to Boulder
- Day 64 — Weekending Magic — Boulder, Colorado
- Day 65 — Still Making Magic — Boulder, Colorado
- Day 66 — Still Making Magic — Boulder, Colorado
- Day 67 — Driving All Day — Salt Lake to Portland

Rescue Efforts

"Goin' junkin'"

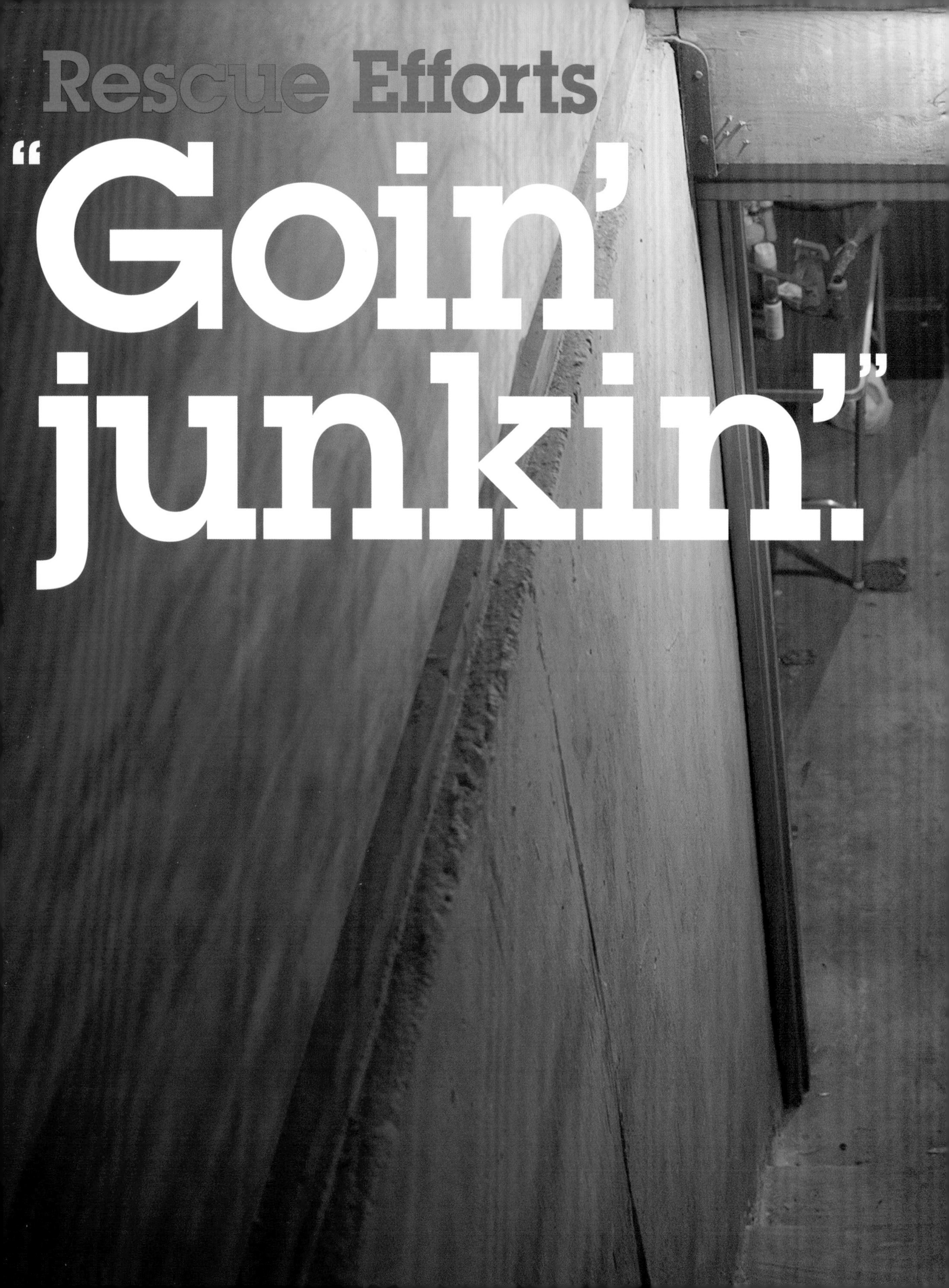

DDC

Draplin
Design Co.

Pretty Much
Everything

Aaron James
Draplin

File Under:
Hey, Ya Never Know

158
159

Into the depths we go. Some estate sale in Spokane, Washington. 2009.

All I Wanna Do Is Junk

When I dug into design in the mid-'90s, I found inspiration from the big design annuals at Powell's Books. I couldn't afford them, but would flip through them and make notes about stuff to check out. The record store was a big spot, too. I'd check out all the record art to see new cover designs. Remember, this is before that big ol' Internet exploded. I would write in to House Industries, CSA, Emigre and T-26 to get on their mailing lists. As each piece would show up, I'd devour it, hungry for new material. But where did my heroes find this stuff? As a kid raised on garage sales, it didn't take long for me to get dirty and start collecting dead, beautiful junk.

My dad taught me the beauty of junking. When I was growing up, we'd hit a lot of garage sales under the wide-reaching mantra of "Ya never know." Dad would needle me, and entice me with the things I was pining for. "This garage sale, punk… this is going to be the one with…a box full of skateboard decks!" Or insert "Lego," "*Stars Wars* stuff," or whatever I was into at the time. And, hell, I never did find any of that shit.

Until a couple summers ago. Dad and I were driving back out to their house on Cedar Run. Right pass the bend where the Strait Road turnoff is, there's a little house that always has a garage sale going. Dad started in: "This could be the one! C'mon, c'mon, cmon, C'MON!" We pulled into the drive, walked up and Dad saw a stack of records. "Hey punk… records!" He was pointing at the stack as he went in deeper. I walked up to the stack and, sure as shit, on the very top was *The Freewheelin' Bob Dylan*! A mint mono

pressing! That's a $50 record. Dad gave me a snide, sideways glance and I ate a big plate of crow.

I feel a weird responsibility with this old stuff. I just don't want it to go away, you know? When I'm at an estate sale, and I walk up with my little pile of junk, nine out of ten times the cashier lady will say, "Honey, just take it." And in my hands, that's a weird little chunk of American design there. And the idea of cleaning it up and sharing it with the world? There's something cool about that. Think about this one for a second: As a designer, if you know how to look at the world, that's a pretty special thing. That's not how shit goes down in insurance sales.

I've been at this stuff a long time. But I didn't really start to focus and document the shit until I was on my own, free from the daily-job rigor. I started documenting stuff around 2000, kicking into high gear by 2004, sharing photos on my site. When Flickr hit, I went whole hog and uploaded a ton of shots.

Photos are free. Don't like the prices at whatever overpriced antiques mall you are at? Take a photo of the stuff. But be warned. "Proprietors" love to get on your case about the "Please ask to take photos" thing. If I notice they are eyeballing me as I come into their booth or shop, there's the "Hey, my dad's a big collector of [whatever you are trying get a shot of]. Do you mind if I snap a shot to show this to him?" Now, in their minds, this could lead to a sale, so of course they are going to let you do it. A couple months back, at the Portland Antique Expo, I walked in, saw a cool little logo and without thinking,

took a shot. The guy quickly came over and started in on me. "And why are you taking photos?" he said. I went into my "I collect dead logos" spiel. He wasn't having it, and went on to tell me how his booth is like a museum. Sure, a museum filled with shit you got from people who died, and now you make a buck off of. Fun museum, bud. I looked at him wryly and said, "Really? No problem. Sorry." But I still got the shot.

Junking has been in the American spotlight for some time now. Goofy, scripted TV shows and hopefuls trying to hit pay dirt on *Antiques Roadshow*. One time, we saw a film crew at the World's Longest Yard Sale, with a camera crew and the caked-on makeup on the "funky" host. So eclectic! Get the fuck out of my way, Guy Holding a Boom. (For the record, the DDC does not use the word "funky," ever.)

And let's get something very, very clear: I don't want to go back to 1950. America was a nastier place then. Intolerance, subjugation and exploitation written into the laws. I've been connected to some pretty rough, heavy rhetoric, and rather unfairly. For the record, I do not champion the olden days' wicked ways. Just because I revel in the dead, forgotten forms, by no means do I condone the hateful, ignorant, backwoods, horrific ways of generations before us. We clear on that? There you go.

Don't let this stuff die. When you see something cool, snap a pic of it and share it. If you don't, we'll all be at the mercy of lackluster memes, trite fads and fuckin' *Star Wars* remix posters. Yawnsville. Now get out there and help me rescue the treasures of the American underbelly!

Junk's Ten Commandments:

01 All prices are negotiable. Never forget this.

02 Always turn shit over. Hidden treasure awaits.

03 Never ask the price on something. Ask the price on something next to the something you are interested in.

04 There's no fuckin' science to this stuff.

05 Understand precisely this: Someone died, and that's how these turds have this stuff in their booth.

06 For the bigger flea markets, get a wheeled cart. Can't tell you how many times I had to lug some sign or stainless-steel shelf around.

07 When scouting, beware: The more colorful the spread, the better the chance it's what we fear most— baby clothes.

08 Always be mindful to look at the thing that's holding the thing. Those metal bins and containers are gold!

09 Dress the part. Remember, these proprietors are sizing you up the moment they see you. Dale always made sure to tap into his Kentucky roots, and some twangy accent would appear. Me, I like the cutoffs game, and a little butt crack when crouching down goes a long way.

10 Take no mercy. All's fair in love, war, record collecting, emissions testing, jury duty, client relations and junkin'.

Junking Hit List:

Impko stickers, first day covers, patches, Decoral decals, political buttons, festival buttons, one-color key chains, bullet pencils, Stenso stencil kits, Press Kal decals, match booklets, milk bottle caps, license plates, ticket stubs, stamps, stamp booklets, ration booklets, 7-inch sleeves, spent Letraset transfer sheets, tool logos, Bicentennial items, rusty tools, beer coasters, beer cans, military manuals, *Popular Mechanics* periodicals, trashy smut/star mags from the early '60s, beat-up tape measures, encyclopedias, roll-down educational maps, memo backs, nameplates, feed-and-seed memo books, bric, brac and bric-a-brac.

Words to the Wise:

I'm seeing a lot of spirited junkers sharing stuff out there, which is great for design. The more shit we rescue, the better. But if you are going to do it, here's a couple tips:

01 Make sure the shit is in focus.

02 Don't bore us to death with a hundred images. Five choice shots is enough. Then take a break, you bandwidth hog.

03 Take the time to straighten the damn things up in Photoshop. I try to shoot things as straight on as possible, eliminating frenzied tinkering later on.

Junking Sources:

01 Estate Sales. My absolute favorite.

02 Antiques Malls. Tricky.

03 Storage Unit Sales. Sad as hell.

04 Garage Sales. The most volatile. Too many times I've walked up on some god-awful spread of "bullshit they bought at Target a couple years ago." Don't say we didn't warn you, bud.

05 Junk Stores. The dirtier the better. Tread lightly.

06 Auctions. Be prepared to be strong-willed. There's just something about going to battle with some old-timer hayseed. Those guys don't fuck around.

07 Some old guy who finally said, "Fuck it," and opened his barn for the world to decimate.

Junking Events:

01 Brimfield Antique Show, Brimfield, MA.

02 World's Longest Yard Sale, Highway 127, OH to AL.

03 First Monday Trade Days, Canton, TX.

04 Portland Antique Expo, Portland, OR.

05 Rose Bowl Flea Market, Pasadena, CA.

Draplin
Design Co.

Pretty Much
Everything

Aaron James
Draplin

File Under:
Dead Things

160
161

Our "Dead Stuff Collage" from things found on the ground.
Six years' worth. Always remember to look down. 2002-2008.

ER·PRICE® mily ⓐ Fran

AL CINEMA

FARMERS ELEVATOR
YUMA — HYDE — SCHRAMM
Grain — Feed — Service

For copper wire only.
For use only in 3-wire gr
systems.

GENERAL ⓖⓔ ELECTRIC

4 LBS-NET

Hi·Q

FOR 1000 USES
23 ITEMS
of Quality
MASONITE
Presdwood
The LEADING Hardb

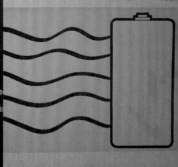

© 1965, HEMISFAIR '68 ®

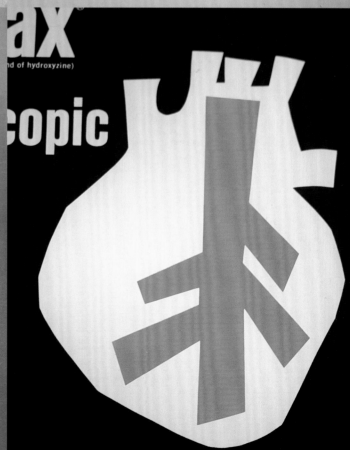

aX®
(nd of hydroxyzine)

copic

T. M. REG. U. S. PAT. OFF

YOUR PROTECT

34

for all fan
and V-belts

NET WT. 4½ OZ.

SNO BRONCO

f the Union

COIN HERE

HOMOGENIZED MILK

HALF GALLON

DIE QUALITÄTSMARKE

SL
SULO

R

Herman Melville

Moby Dick
United States 6

RETAIL STORE

262

S.E. MASS. FISH & GAME ASSN.
1952
"BROCKTON, MASS."

FAMILY FIRST AID

EMERGENCY
FALLOUT KIT

BEAM-O-LITE B 550

U.S. PAT. APPL'D. FOR—REG. U.S. PATENT APPL'D. FOR
MADE BY BEAM-O-LITE SIGN CO. NEW YORK, N.Y.

DISTRIBUTORS
DISPLAY
LIGHTING CORP.
L.A. & S.F. CALIF.

GENERAL ELECTRIC
PUSH BUTTON STATION

BICYCLE
LICENSE
3134
TRAVERSE
CITY

HISPANO
WITH CHAPMA
FUSE
THE CHAPMA
INDIAN

STEEL		ALUMINUM
STRIP		SHEET
SPRING		COILS
SHIM	AM 2-6700 DA 8-3000	BARS
BARS		RODS
FLAT WIRE	STEEL &	WIRE
TIN PLATE	ALUMINUM	TUBING
FEELER GAUGE		PLATES
ELEC. GALV. STRIP		EXTRUSIONS

DECIMAL EQUIVALENTS

KORHUMEL STEEL & ALUMINUM CO.
2424 OAKTON ST.   EVANSTON, ILL.

KROEHLER
—MADE—
CHICAGO   NEW YORK   SAN FRANCISCO
LOS ANGELES   DALLAS   STRATFORD CAN.

MICROPHONE 1

4   5   6
3   7
2   8
1   9
0   10

X PRESS 956   YARWAY   SERIAL 244
RANGE HI-LO GRAPH   CONTROLLER
YARNALL - WARING CO.   PHILA 18 PA.
PATENT APPLIED FOR

WIRE ROPE CO.
OF AMERICA

TRACTION

	PREFORMED	NON-P
STRENGTH		
6X19	IN LBS. 6X19	
3/8	8200	
7/16	11000	
1/2	14500	
9/16	18500	
5/8	23000	
3/4	32000	

ROPES INSTALL
HAUGHTON EL
DIV. OF TOLEDO

KNOX-HUTCHINS
FURNITURE
COMPANY

GOLD SEAL
USED WHEREVER
TICKETS ARE SOLD
THE MARK OF PERFECTION
AUTOMATICKET

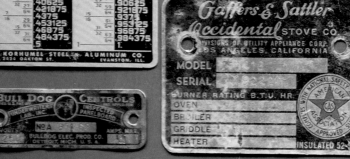

Gaffers & Sattler
Occidental STOVE CO.
DIVISIONS OF UTILITY APPLIANCE CORP.
LOS ANGELES, CALIFORNIA

MODEL
SERIAL
BURNER RATING B.T.U. HR.
OVEN
BROILER
GRIDDLE
HEATER

AMERICAN
STANDARD SAFETY REQUIREMENTS
APPROVED

INSULATED 52

BULL DOG CONTROLS

UNDERWRITER
INSPECTED PANELBOARD

No. A
VOLTS   250
BULLDOG ELEC. PROD. CO.
DETROIT, MICH. U.S.A.
AMPS. MAX.

TYPE LC2 P DELTA
AMPS VOLTS WIRE
15   240   3 L.H.
SANGAMO ELECTRIC COMPANY
15 AMPS.
240

Kb 7-2
AMPS. VOLTS WIRE
R.H. 15   240   2
SPRINGFIELD, ILLINOIS, U.S.A.
TWO ELEMENT

SERIAL NO.
SIZE & TYPE
STAGES   R.P.M.
G.P.M.   HEAD

PORTLAND ORE. SHREVEPORT LA. VANCOUVER B.C.

HOBART
ALTERNATING CURRENT MILL
MADE BY
THE HOBART ELECTRIC MFG CO
TROY O USA
No. 40871
VOLTS 110 SPEED 1750
H.P. 1/4 PHASE 1
CLASS 7342 RD CYCLES 60
MOTOR 338966
PATENTED

The Magnavox Company FORT WAYNE, IND

MODEL	CP241M	STYLE	P213-81	VO
WATTS	90	CYCLES	60	SERIAL NO.

GLADIATOR PUMP
PROTECTO MFG. CO.
351 EAST BURNSIDE ST.
PORTLAND, ORE.
SIZE   NO.
PATENT NO. 14968
OTHER PATENTS PENDING

ECLIPSE MOTOR GENERATOR

TYPE	MODEL	DWG NO	STYLE
D.C. INPUT		AMPS	R.P.M	PHASE
	VOLTS		FREQ.	
A.C. OUTPUT	VOLTS	AMPS	FREQ.	PHASE

BENDIX AVIATION CORPORATION
ECLIPSE-PIONEER DIVISION
TETERBORO N.J.   MADE IN U.S.A.

SUITAB
SERIES

POTTER ELECTRIC SIGNAL CO.
ST. LOUIS, MISSOURI

ELECTRIC PROTECTION

POTTER	MODEL	ST. LOUIS
	SCB	

SEA KING BOAT TRAILER

MODEL	SERIAL NO.
9064R	56X 76542

TRAILER CAPACITY 1000 LBS.
MONTGOMERY WARD & CO. U.S.A.
TIRE LOAD CAPACITIES VS INFLATION

REPUBLIC FLOW METERS CO.
CHICAGO, ILL. MADE IN U.S.A.
CHART NO.
GREEN PEN
RED PEN
BLUE PEN
SERIAL NO.
U.S. PATENTS

MODEL B-1
LIGHTING RELAY
CONTACT CAP. 15 AMPS.
CYCLES
SERIAL NO.
SOUTHERN SIGNAL COMPANY
LOUISVILLE, KY.
U.S.A.

WRIGHT CO
MADE IN ENGLAND

BB...D
...TO..UNIT
...SIZE
...E MFG. CO.
...MASS.

REPUBLIC FLOW METERS CO.
CHICAGO, ILL. MADE IN U.S.A.
CHART NO.
GREEN PEN FLOW
RED PEN
BLUE PEN
SERIAL NO.

TO DISCONNECT CURRENT OR TO REPLACE FUSES
LIFT COVER AND FOLLOW INSTRUCTIONS INSIDE

MURRAY
SERVICE EQUIPMENT

| CAT. NO. | 77-4N | | AMP. | 100 |
| VOLTS | 125-250 | | POLE | 3 |

Underwriters Laboratories
INSPECTED
SERVICE EQUIPMENT
FORM 31-196
ISSUE 7-60
METROPOLITAN DEVICE CORP., BROOKLYN, N.Y.

CLIMAX ELECTRIC WORKS,
NEW SALEM, MASS.
MOTOR No.

Tucker COFFEE
TUCKER-EMMRICH CO.
1499

CHEMICAL WARFARE SERVICE U.S.A.
COLLECTIVE PROTECTOR M1A1
RIGHT HAND
U.S.A.W.CO. SERIAL NO. M 856 LOT U.S.A.W.CO.
EDGEWOOD ARSENAL, MARYLAND

THE
Walsh
NO-BUCKLE HARNESS
JAMES M. WALSH CO.
LIMITED
TORONTO CANADA
STRENGTH PATENTS

6 X 30   462-34
TYPE CH PLAIN GRINDER
LANDIS TOOL COMPANY
WAYNESBORO, PA., U.S.A.

CAUTION
DO NOT RUN
PUNCH INTO DIE
SEE INSTRUCTION CARD

STATE
AUTO INSURANCE
ASS'N
INSURED
INDIANAPOLIS

ENCLOSED   ON
SAFETY SWITCH ↑
WALKER
ELECTRICAL CO., INC.
ATLANTA, GA.   OFF

ERLA
TB POWER
OPERATE ON A.C.
CYCLE A.C. SUPPLY
105 TO 125 VOLTS
Electrical Research
Laboratories

PHILLIPS PUMP & TANK CO.
CINCINNATI, OHIO
MADE IN U.S.A.
MODEL
SERIAL

PUSH
ON
BULL DOG
Trip-Breck
SAFETY SWITCH
EQUIPPED WITH
"Clampmatic"
CONTACTS
TYPE   BOS.
CAT.NO.   14321 ⓜ
AMPS   30
VOLTS   240 A C   3
MAX. H.P.
MAX. H.P.
PUSH
OFF
THROW SWITCH OFF
BEFORE OPENING DOOR
BULLDOG ELECTRIC PRODUCTS DIVISION
I-T-E CIRCUIT BREAKER COMPANY
DETROIT   MICHIGAN   U.S.A.

FABRICATED BY
▲ AMERICAN
AMERICAN.
SHEET METAL WORKS, Inc.
PORTLAND, OREGON

The *Selectie*
PAT. PENDING
T.R. JENKINS CO.—CHICAGO, ILL.

ATR
RECTIFIER
POWER SUPPLY
...MANUFACTURING CO., INC.
MADE IN U.S.

ELECTRICAL   EQUIPMENT
Ⓖ
GENERAL
GENERAL
SWITCH CORP.
BROOKLYN 11, N.Y.
U.S.A.

...ED
...WITCH
...825 1L
SERVICE EQUIPMENT
ON
↑
...PANY
...ES
OFF
...VOLTS
...2   ...H.P.
MADE

LINCOLN
AIRLINE LUBRIGUN
SERIAL NO.   PUMP NO.
81864
LINCOLN ENGINEERING CO.
ST. LOUIS, MO.

James Draplin

TELETYPE
REG. U.S. PAT. OFF.
MANUFACTURED BY
TELETYPE CORPORATION
CHICAGO, U.S.A.

CAUTION
KEEP THIS SIDE UP
DO NOT BLOCK ANY
VENTILATING OPENINGS
ATR MANUFACTURING CO., INC.
SAINT PAUL, MINNESOTA U.S.A.

Firestone
AIR CHIEF

MANUFACTURED AND GUARANTEED BY
...ED SOUND & SIGNAL COMPANY, INC.
COLUMBIA   PENNSYLVANIA
...P. F-1.2 REFRIGERANT ...OZ. 7½ AMPS.
...ON 115v 60 CYCLE ALTERNATING CURRENT
MODEL
W-J D
SERIAL NO.

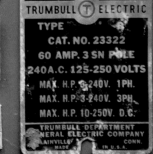
TRUMBULL Ⓣ ELECTRIC
TYPE
CAT. NO. 23322
60 AMP. 3 SN POLE
240 A.C. 125-250 VOLTS
MAX. H.P. 5-240V. 1PH.
MAX. H.P. 3-240V. 3PH.
MAX. H.P. 10-250V. D.C.
TRUMBULL DEPARTMENT
GENERAL ELECTRIC COMPANY
PLAINVILLE   CONN.
MADE IN U.S.A.

AUTOPULSE
FUEL-LIFTER
FULLY PATENTED
MODEL SH-1...
110 V.A.C. 60 CYCLE .5 AMP.
AUTOPULSE CORPORATION
LUDINGTON, MICH., U.S.A.
INSTRUCTIONS
TO RESTART PUMP
AFTER CURRENT FAIL-
URE, OR TANK BECOMING
EMPTY, PRESS BUTTON
INDICATED BY ARROW
UNTIL FUEL STOPS
POUR OIL
SLOWLY INTO
COMPARTMENT
MARKED
"PRIME HERE"
UNTIL OIL
STOPS RISING.
CONNECT 110
VOLT 60 CYCLE
ACROSS TWO
TERMINALS BE-
NEATH THIS
INSTRUCTION.

CONSTANT VOLTAGE
TRANSFORMER

MODEL
80   **SKIL DRILL**   CAP.
1/2
VOLTS AMP. R.P.M. SERIAL NO.
115 4.6 450
SKILSAW, INC.   CHICAGO
MADE IN U.S.A.

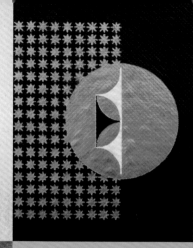

ROCKWOOD'S **R** CHOCOLATE

CLO
U.S.A

decca

Energy
80's

INDUSTRIAL
DISTRIBUTOR

BURND
BURND
BURND
BURND
BURND
BURND
BURND

7-786-2211   DINING

rland Golf C
iston, Michigan 49

KOKUSAI

camino real

san salvador

ELECTRIC
APPLIANCE
Repair and
Servicing

— MANLY

FISH
BAIT

toilet seat

Araban®

COFFEE OF COFFEES

FIREBIRD

PRESTIGE

utah

GM Assembly

MINNESOTA

TEREX

IBH

DETROIT TIGERS

FOUR WHEELER

AMERICAN REVOLUTION BICENTENNIAL 1776-1976

DAC

HALLMARK

SPACE SHUTTLE

Grain Belt

PETRO

BLITZ The Beer Here WEINH

Hawaii

CALIFORNIA

EQUIPMENT SERVICES

philadel

DYNA SYS

PICKERING

OMSI

WOOLRICH

Bud's BAR
JEFFERSON, SD

GOD BLESS
AMERICA

THE ATHLETICS
CONGRESS
TAC
USA

OCEAN
DYNAMICS

CO OP

Job Corps

CAT
LIFT TRUCKS

Marilyn

grizzly

O.H. KRUSE
Perfection
BRAND FEED

CAMP HIWELA

Montréal 1976

MANITOBA
SCOUTS CANADA

R
RYDER

GARST

rovral
FUNGICIDE

CAL CUSTOM

AMERICAN REVOLUTION BICENTENNIAL
1776-1976

"YOUR S

MOORE ®

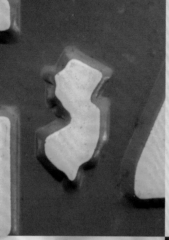

QUADRADISC
CD4 CHANNEL DISCRETE

Hillary

CHREST

CULLO

Delav

USA
200

MPOEXPG 7/ G

nd to 12th JUNE 1971

BRAND

MICRO-METAL

SPACE NAVIGATOR

GALAXY®

SATURN

Leigh

FAR OUT

CAPRICORN

VOCAL
CAP-22523-MO
ASCAP
C-8021
Time: 3:39

© 1971

EMMA

JONATHAN EDWARDS

Produced by Peter Casperson for
North Country Productions, Ltd.
From Capricorn LP 007

SLEEVE MANUFACTURED BY: FAR OUT PRODUCTIONS, INC. 7417 SUNSET BLVD., LOS ANGELES, CALIF. 90046

FAR OUT PRODUCTIONS, INC. PRINTED IN U.S.A.

AMAHA GOLD CUP
MOTORCYCLE RACES
ARLINGTON PARK
SEPTEMBER 10 8PM

professional riders. AMA sanctioned. Box seats $6.
served seats $5. General Admission $4. Now on
at Ticketron, Sears Chicagoland stores, and
gton Park Towers Hotel. For information
special group call
) 354-6339 or (312) 394-0349. Parking
0,000 cars. Rain date Sept. 11, 1 P.M.

71

VEMBER 1973 75c

CSP

LOSE-UP OF
SMALL TOWN

IDWESTERN FAMILY

715

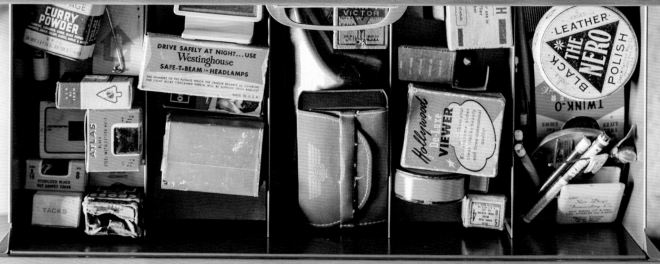

DDC

Draplin
Design Co.

Pretty Much
Everything

Aaron James
Draplin

File Under:
Timeless Treasures

178
177

"Things We Love" State/City Posters

I've been able to go to so many incredible places on my speaking tour. And for each of these gigs, I tried to make a poster for that state or city. The event would be the launch of it, and then once the dust settled, the poster would go into the general population on our DDC merch roster.

The posters combine my love for lore, slang, regional heroes, bands and dead logos. Logos that were redesigned at some point—often for political purposes—which would ruin the originals. So I'll dig them up and get them locked in there.

People always ask me, "How long do the 'Things We Love' posters take to make?" Depending on the "everythingelseness" (my logos/merch/Field Notes/tour gigs workload at any given time), if I can focus, it's about eighteen to twenty hours for each one. A couple hours to get going, digging stuff out of my photo archives, combing through old eBay auctions, Etsy examples, and then tuning up the logos to be print-ready, into vectors. Like little rescue missions, bringing them back to life.

Keeping the posters in stock has been quite a battle. All it takes is one well-placed link on some "Krazy for Kansas" Facebook page and I'll move a cool 125 posters. Now, at editions of 250 per poster, that's 125 posters combined with however many I sold at the show and any orders that trickled in up to that point. I could be down to five to ten prints. Danger! So then I have to get another order going, begging my screenprinters for open printing slots.

A couple years back, Uncrate put a link to the posters on their site. It was the day after Obama's second election. The link said something along the lines of "Feeling patriotic? Grab a couple of Draplin state posters." A buddy who understood the gravity of a link on Uncrate wrote to me. "Dude, you are going to be demolished. Did you see the link that went up? Congrats." I didn't understand what he meant. Then I checked my inbox and saw the first string of orders come flying in. *Ding! Ding! Ding!*

That first day, there were some three hundred orders that came in. Uh-oh. Cool, but trouble for a one-man band who had to finagle his girlfriend into handling our merch order onslaught.

And it stayed that way from November 7 right up to December 22, or whatever our "Christmas shipping cutoff" was that year.

We averaged 100 to 150 orders a day for fifty days. Absolutely bonkers.

In no time, we were out of our popular posters. Ohio, Colorado and Iowa. We got reorders in right away, but due to the meticulous nature of indie screenprinting, things move a bit slow. It's an Amazon.com world, and people are conditioned to expect minute-by-minute updates, confirmations and parcel tracking. Myself included. We had none of this going for us. Our primitive shipping methods were scrapped and Leigh modernized things with an Endicia system with printed address tags, tracking numbers and shipping notifications. Technology! Thank you to our buddies at Uncrate for believing in us!

And, holy shit, the biggest, hairiest thanks to Leigh for answering the call and handling all those orders that holiday season of 2012. And for dealing with those horrific holiday post office lines. A fate worse than death. One tough lady, that Leigh.

As this book goes to print, we're up to forty-two posters. Virginia, Wyoming and New Mexico are the next ones I'll be tearing into. Thanks to everyone who bought one!

Getting in close on our "Oregon, Oh Yeah!" poster, 4-color on "Way White" uncoated stock. 2013.

DDC

Draplin
Design Co.

Pretty Much
Everything

Aaron James
Draplin

File Under:
Michigan Blood

178
179

Say yes to Michigan! Finally pulled off a "Magnificent Michigan" poster in the Fall of 2014!

MONTANA

NORTH DAKOTA

idaho
usa

Washington State, Pacific Northwest, **USA**

SOUTH DAKOTA

IOWAUS

OREGONUSA

NEVADA

UTAH

COLORADOUSA

NEBRASK

CALIFORNIA
CALIFORNIA
CALIFORNIA
CALIFORNIA
CALIFORNIA

ARIZONA

KANSA

OKLAHO

DDC

Draplin
Design Co.

Pretty Much
Everything

Aaron James
Draplin

File Under:
Signed & Numbered

180
181

Multiple Impressions

"Going sorta viral."

Draplin
Design Co.

Pretty Much
Everything

Aaron James
Draplin

File Under:
Medicine Ball Head

182
183

Is this shot to scale? So gross. Medicine ball head.

That Damn Sign

The Internet is weird. And it can bite back. Here's a little something about the first time I "went viral." I was back in Michigan, spending some summer time with Mom and Dad. 2007. A couple nights before I headed back out to Oregon, I was on eBay screwing around. And found a big sign for sale. It just so happens, I was a little tipsy from a night out with buddies. And I'm not all that much of a drinker. Never have been.

So there I was, under the influence, digging around on eBay. "Drunk eBaying" is a dangerous thing, people. So I put a bid in on the sign, hit the sack and woke up to discover that I'd won it! For, like, $300. And the thing was twenty-eight feet high!

The sign was from a little hotel in Sedalia, Missouri, that were upgrading to a new sign. They were bringing the old one down. It was beautiful. A couple of the classic arrows and stars and two big panels that read SUNSET and MOTEL. I remember telling Dad, "I bought a sign!" And he sort of freaked out on me. "What do you mean, you bought a sign? Do you know how big twenty-eight feet is? Do you know what it takes to bring something like that down? How are you going to haul it out of there?"

And of course, I didn't really have any answers for the old man. I was just sort of going for it. I called down to Sedalia ahead of time, and spoke to some people from the motel. Their English was pretty minimal, but somehow we agreed on a time for me to come and get it. So I arranged the removal with a local Sedalia sign company and got my shit in order to head down to Missouri the next day.

Gary and I drove down in my old Passat wagon. Left Michigan and headed down to Sedalia. I think we did it in a long day. We got to Sedalia, found the sign at the Sunset Motel and were floored how big the thing was in the flesh. I met the motel owners with a couple awkward handshakes. From there I went to the sign company to pay for the removal, and to pick up the loose pieces that had already been taken down.

I remember some kid running my credit card. He could've cared less about some out-of-town yahoo carrying on about this American relic. He was as uninterested as the next guy. I remember that.

I pulled behind the sign company and found all the parts laid out for me. I didn't have a lot of room in my Passat wagon, but was able to secure the pointer arrow to the top. And then get the orange arrow into the back. The stars were too big. The sunset and motel signs? There was no way to get those out of there. Hell, they were still up in the air.

After grabbing the arrows, I headed back to the motel to take some shots of the sign that I had to leave behind. And in the process of meeting the owners, the wife mentioned a new sign that was slated to go up. Curious, I asked her if I could see it. She took me into the motel's lobby and dug behind the counter to pull out a three-ring binder. She let me flip through it and, a couple pages in, I was staring at the new, updated design from the sign company.

My heart broke. I was staring at this half-assed CorelDraw gradient sign, complete with clunky Blippo Bold type and monoweight "birds" in the sunset. I kept going through the binder, hoping this was just a comp. Nope, that was the design. And then I saw the invoice. It was for ten or fifteen thousand or something. And sure, I get it. That stuff isn't cheap. All that steel and electrical this-n-that. And the installation. And the removal of the old one. All of it adds up to a pretty big price tag. But the actual design part of it? I'm sure there was also a big price tag for that.

Frankly, the design was phoned in— embarrassingly lackluster without so much as one thought about the heritage of the place, or how it might look on the strip in between all the big-box stores and fast-food joints. It was stripped of all the charm the old sign had going for it. This little motel wasn't the Hampton Inn or whatever corporate competitor down the way. This was a mom-and-pop joint, and that's still a special thing in America. But with this new sign, it was just one more nail in the coffin on the place. I was pissed and saddened, and drove away stinging.

Because, sadly, no matter how you look at it, that's just how things go in America. New stuff goes up and it's always worth a shit. Whatever was cool about something is gone, lost forever. And yet, they still paid the big prices for it. Thinking about that sign company still bums me out. Who am I to say one fucking thing about the job they do? Sure, the product is sound and I'm sure they build beautiful sign products. But for fuck's sake, please hire a capable designer. It's one thing to update the landscape with state-of-the-art signage, but it's another thing when it's some piss-poor design that's gonna pollute the landscape for the next couple of decades. Heartbreaking.

And Then Jess Filmed It

A couple years later, my filmmaker buddy Jess Gibson approached me about a project he was working up around Portland, featuring local designers and how they work. I knew some of the guys he was talking about and agreed to give it a shot. Pretty simple stuff: Point the camera at me and see what happens? A first for me.

He came to the shop and got at it for a couple hours. We covered all the basics. And then he hit me with this one: Tell me about something that bummed you out. I tell the Sunset Motel story, go apeshit and we call it a wrap. Jess packs up his gear, and the next time we talk about it, he's showing me the clip where I talk about "drunk eBaying the sign." It's funny to me, and yet just biting enough. So Jess puts it up as a bit of a teaser, for the upcoming "Draplin Project." Suddenly he's working on a documentary about me? Sure. And that little video explodes.

Rethinking the Whole Thing

You know, in all honesty, eight years later, I feel a little bad about the whole thing. Sure, it hit a half million views and had a thousand supportive e-mails thanking me for having the balls to say something. It opened many doors for me—speaking gigs, documentary spots and all sorts of other fun stuff.

But I have to tell you, to see something go big like that? It's freaky. When Jess put it up, I never really thought about the impact it would have, or how it might affect the people/person who did the work. I know what it's like to get nasty e-mails from people who don't like what I do. And as thick-skinned as I try to be, that stuff still haunts me. So the idea of the person who made that shitty sign design being affected by the video? That makes me feel a little bad. And no matter how many times people still tell me, "I wouldn't feel bad one bit," I realize that they are in the easy spot. They aren't the ones in the video.

So yeah, I still feel a little bad about the whole thing. And I'll take this opportunity to apologize to whoever made the sign. I can't and won't accept the shitty design, though. There's just no excuse for that. As designers, we are privileged with making things the whole world will see. Or maybe just in Sedalia. But still, it's our job to make good stuff and honor the client's wishes. And maybe add a little something special to the American landscape.

DDC

Draplin
Design Co.

Pretty Much
Everything

Aaron James
Draplin

File Under:
Heartland Heartbreak

184
185

Scenes from that afternoon in Sedalia, MO. April 2007.

Vans Shoot

It's easy to get cynical about people pointing cameras at you. You are freaked out by how you look or sound. It's not like it's any secret, I'm a man mountain and talk like an asshole, but to see it on a screen? Always surreal. When my buddy Jared Eberhardt approached me about doing a little documentary about what I do, of course I hesitated. I'd been down that road with Jess Gibson and Adobe, and was still freaked out by the random comments that "experts" would weigh in with. But Jared

promised me he'd do it right, and show a fun snapshot of my mess. I wore Vans as a kid skateboarding, so there's no way I could say no to being a part of it.

The funnest part of the ordeal was being able to lay all my shit out on this big studio floor. Assembling all the stuff, you get nervous you won't have enough shit to show. And all that freak out, money spent, rented space, production assistants and shit will be let down, you know? But fuck

if I didn't fill up the entire zone that Jared had taped off for his shot. And standing back, it was overwhelming. All that stuff. So many years in one massive shot. And it all being work I was proud of!

I'm so thankful for the life I've had in design, the opportunity to document it and all the eyeballs checking it out. If you haven't seen Jared's series for Vans, please go and check them out. Cody Hudson's and Nikki Lane's are required viewing, too!

Putting the finishing touches on the 666 items! 2014.

Assorted screen grabs from the films. 2014.

Media Saturation? You Bet!

I haven't turned down too many interviews or podcasts. It's always fun to chew the fat with new people, and, on whatever brand-building level, it's always been good to get my story out there. But you have to understand, that's not a strategic thing. Every single request or invite is an opportunity to share. To just sort of wing it. Plain and simple. And damn, I can talk. I think my podcast record for one answer is like eight minutes. Who the hell talks for eight minutes straight? I get going and can't stop. By the end of my diatribe, I can't even remember the question. That's just weird. Cracks me up.

Some of my greatest hits have been the interview with fellow Michigander people of *The Great Discontent*, Mark Brickey's *Adventures in Design* podcast, telling my story on *FPK After Dark* with Sean Cannon, Steven Kurutz's feature on me for the *New York Times* style section, the recent *HOW* magazine cover and the time Debbie Millman gave me a shot on her *Design Matters* podcast. Kids still ask me about these all the time. Which is a testament to the power of these blasts going out. But those were the big ones, and you sorta know they are going to carry some weight. I'm proud to have made time for all the small stuff, too. From podcasts to interviews to blog contributions to the humdrum Q&A's from kids about to get out of school. How cool is it that we get to share this stuff with each other? That's what it's like in the pharmaceutical industry, too? I'm betting that's not the case.

Here's a little pro tip: This is the kind of stuff that burns up time on a flight. Flying is weird enough, and I'll save the question-naires until I'm up in the air. Then I knock them out and, before I know it, I'm landing. That's where I catch up on a lot of this stuff. To everyone who's given me a shot on the airwaves, in pixels, or on the printed page, thank you. Always proud to do it.

Maron vs. Aaron

I've been a fan of Marc Maron for a couple years now. I flew into Los Angeles in 2013 for Adobe MAX, grabbed my bags and there he was. I slowly walked up to him, introduced myself and got a quick shot with Marc. He was nice enough to handle this man mountain. That sold me on the guy. Jump to a couple years later, and I'm hooked on the podcast. I go into Mondays excited to see who he'll have on next. I've had a couple moments with the guy, listening to him talk about his dad or old friends. He puts it out there, and aside from the neurotic shtick, that's admirable and is the side of Marc I love the most.

Watching his tweets, you'll see new stand-up shows pop up, then the posters that people made for him and sold at the shows. I thought I'd reach out to see if I could do a poster for Marc. I called on my new buddy Coop to put a good word in for me. I've been a fan of Coop's work since 1994! I recently met him on a street corner in Austin for a quick handshake. I tweeted out to Coop, Coop tweeted out to Marc, and that got his attention. Marc tweets at me, we set up a call, we talk about the poster and how to pull it off, and then he says, "Hey, man, I want to put you on the podcast." I about shit. Huh?! On the podcast? I was already high as hell just being able to do the poster. We agreed to do it when he came to Portland to do his comedy shows. I was blown away and completely freaked out.

By the time this book goes to print, my Maron podcast will be up. We just recorded it yesterday, and I'm nervous as hell I didn't do a good job. I'm lucky to do a lot of podcasts, but it's one thing when its going out to fellow artists and design nerds. But Marc Maron's audience? That's a big one. I was scared shitless recording that chat. Trying to tell jokes to a comedian? Ha! I totally psyched myself out, then recorded it to be played for a half million people. Totally crying about Dad, and then embarrassed. I was there to talk about design, right? I mean, why was I even on there?! I still can't believe he was interested in my mess. I still listen each week. A fan first, it's gonna be so fun to be on there. Hope it sounds good! So honored to be on my favorite podcast. Thanks for giving me a shot, Marc.

This is what it looks like a minute before Marc Maron interviews you. He might've been battling trolls on Twitter?

Sharing the Mess

"Getting stuff up on the wall."

In January 2015, I was invited by Jeff Van Kleeck from Cal Poly University in San Luis Obispo to do an exhibition of my work and my "Tall Tales From A Large Man" speaking fiasco. We filled a 37' x 11' wall with a ton of my work. That big, blank wall was pretty foreboding when we started. In no time we had that thing just full! We used something like 1,000 metal pushpins! Special thanks to Jeff and Charmaine Van Cleeck for such a great visit.

Draplin
Design Co.

Pretty Much
Everything

Aaron James
Draplin

File Under
Radical Real Estate

190
191

Art Shows

I love art shows. And I hate how I'm always busy and it's hard to find the time to contribute. Same old shit, and I've had to pass some up. But when it comes to benefits, I'm here to tell you we can always find the time to make art to raise some loot. I'm so proud of the contributions I've made to help raise needed funds for skateboard parks, dogs shelters, arts programs, or the chance to help kick the shit out of my buddy Kevin's testicular cancer. This kind of collective community spirit is good for all us. And powerful.

I'm always inspired by fellow designers who find the time for this stuff. Seeing their work outside of the normal client humdrum reminds me of why we're in this shit in the first place: We enjoy making stuff, and it's fun to see it all come together. And if it can help someone? The best.

Or just a chance to fill up a big wall with a ton of work? Such a cool, surreal thing. I've had three big art shows so far. Co Exhibitions in Minneapolis, the Dennos Museum Center in Traverse City and Cal

Poly University in San Luis Obispo, California, were chances to blast a ton of work up on the wall. Very proud of those walls. To pause everything and contribute to a cool art show? A weird, little treat when things are going bonkers. Another reason to love design at large.

It's always fun to get out there and bump elbows with the community. Even with my nightmarish workload, I've been able to make time for some pretty cool blogs, fund-raisers and exhibitions.

"Oregon"
Fifty and Fifty: The State Mottos.
June 2011. Online.

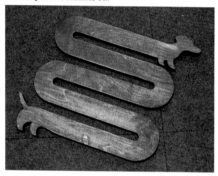

"The Dachshund: A Really Long Breed"
Wurstminster Dog Show.
February 2007. Portland, OR.

"GaryMobile"
PDX Pinewood Classic at Nemo Design.
May 6–May 31, 2008. Portland, OR.

"My Bend Years"
Push Skatedeck Art Show.
February 2008. Bend, OR.

"Mountain Town"
Push Skatedeck Art Show.
February 2011. Bend, OR.

"Denver: 5280 Feet"
Bordo Bello Fundraiser.
September 2011. Denver, CO.

"Thick Line Valley"
Ride On PDX.
November 2014. Portland, OR.

"Michigan"
Sideways, Dennos Museum,
Summer 2015. Traverse City, MI.

DDC

| Draplin | Pretty Much | Aaron James | File Under: | 192 |
| Design Co. | Everything | Draplin | Priced To Move | 193 |

"DDC 'Lifetime Achievement' / 'Completely Despicable' Award Wheel"

The Awards Show. Reading Frenzy. May 6-May 31, 2010. Portland, OR.

Six of the absolute best. Six of the absolute, rock-bottom worst.

"Aaron James Draplin Art Show"

Office. May 27-June 20, 2009. Portland, OR.

Collage No. 05, "White."

Collage No. 06, "Field Notes."

Collage No. 07, "Orange."

Collage No. 08, "Red."

Collage No. 05, "Green."

Collage No. 06, "Blue."

Collage No. 07, "USA."

Collage No. 08, "Black."

Website advertisement.

Plywood logos.

One of the Coolest Nights of My Life

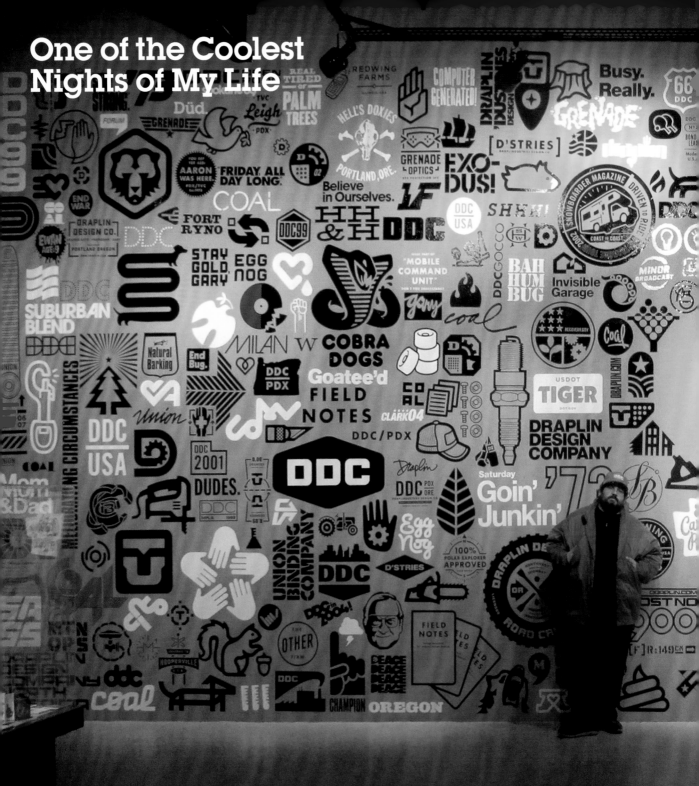

This spread shows the final moment of one of the coolest nights of my whole life. In October 2010, I got to do an art show at the Co Exhibitions gallery in Minneapolis, in partnership with Burlesque of North America. The show was called *Thanks MPLS*, as an ode to the town I loved and learned so much from. Head curator Joe Belk was shutting the place down for the night and we had a couple minutes

to get one final shot. I went and stood up against the wall and Leigh snapped it. We almost forgot to.

I had four hundred logos readied for the wall, and we got 'em all up there in three days and nights. All that hustle, freak out and all-nighters…and the opening was just four hours long. It was over in a flash. So many people from the Minneapolis

design community came to check it out. Jon Baugh, Scott Thares and Derek Schille came by. Hell, Leah and Lee Crane were even there, and they live in California!? My old MCAD buddy Jason Miller's band, the Evening Rig, played a set! I met so many cool people that night and we all stared up at that big orange wall together.

And then it was done. We had to fly back

to Portland the next morning. I didn't want to leave that big wall behind. I had this dipshit idea of building a new wall in the gallery. With dimensions of "however wide I am" away from the big wall. And then that would be my "Minneapolis Office"! An office two feet wide, sixteen feet tall and forty feet long. A little door at the end and a tiny little desk at the other end with me sitting there pecking away at files.

Still sad that big wall ever came down. I think about that night and how cool it was to see all those logos in one spot, so big, orange and wild.

Thanks to Joe, Mike Davis, Wes Winship, Jodi Milbert and Ben LaFond for the opportunity. The hero of the event was Nate Johannes, who showed up with his mobile vinyl plotter! And of course, the army of "die-cut vinyl smasher-downers": Ted Quinn, Ben Ellis, Adam Burchard and Ryno Simonson. It was one thing to plot the logo and weed out all the negative pieces. It was another to get the logo up on the wall and make it stick. Painstaking, inch-by-inch burnishing went down for each piece. A triumph of spirit and vinyl! I'm still blown away it ever happened in the first place. That was one cool wall.

"Keeping those lines thick."

DDC

Draplin
Design Co.

Pretty Much
Everything

Aaron James
Draplin

File Under:
Lick Thines

196
197

Thick Lines

Why is simplicity refreshing? And on some weird, metaphysical level, can simple lines evoke some kind of positive response? I've got some half-witted theories on these musings. Maybe it's because the world is moving so fast? And always seems to be speeding up? When you reduce this wild world down to its simplest of elements, there's something refreshing there. And it still feels "new" to me. In a design world of more and more complex techniques and styles, this stuff still gets me. So I started to explore it for fun, and the jobs started coming in shortly after. I sort of stumbled into this style in Adobe Illustrator, out of desperation. I was working on the All Tiny Creatures record for Hometapes in 2011, and experimenting with simple vector shapes, all lined with a consistent thick line. So rudimentary, but when done with a little consideration, pretty powerful. There was this odd uniformity to it all that was striking, almost Utopian in the feel.

These designs used to line the landscape. Seymour Chwast, Milton Glaser and Peter Max come to mind. Or Keith Haring. What happened? Where'd it go? Universal art forms, with this global, ubiquitous quality. Modern, yet playful and accessible. Lighthearted, but breathtakingly complex. Dead stuff that I find out there junkin' reminded me of this. Maybe we forgot? Let this page of goodies be a reminder of the power of reductionism. There's a big word for ya!

Perfect Valley. 2014.

Sub Pop Records. 2014.

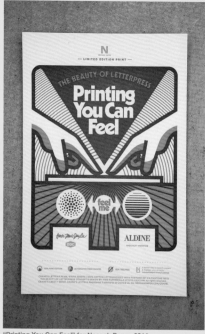

"Printing You Can Feel" for Neenah Paper. 2014.

Inch x Inch buttons. 2015.

Thick Lines Valley. 2014.

Kevin Nimick Benefit. 2013.

"Big Jim" for Culture of Cult art show. 2014.

DDC

Draplin
Design Co.

Pretty Much
Everything

Aaron James
Draplin

File Under:
Valley of Love

198
199

Thick Lines Poster Series

Here's another one of those "frustration projects" where I made something because I couldn't find it out in the world.

Big canvases. Simple, geometric designs. Sunsets. I don't even know what to call the ones I remember as a kid. Wall art? Fabric panels? From the '70s, the big, stretched fabric art stuff. Verner Panton did the coolest stuff in the genre. Smooth, undulating lines and shapes. Simple, analogous color spectrums.

I was at a cool, little midcentury boutique in Portland, and asked the proprietor, "Do you have any of the stretched fabric pop art thick lines…uh, fabric panels?"

Blank stares from the workers. No one knew what I was asking about. I tried to explain, going into detail about ones I remember seeing as a kid or ones I'd seen in other shops. And the guy kept giving me that blank stare. Experts, with no idea about some of the greatest pieces from the era. Impeccable customer service!

And then you find one in some shop. Nothing sucks more than seeing one of the originals for $1,000 or whatever. Don't get me wrong, I love that stuff as much as the next guy and have popped for many pieces. I have a beautiful Danish credenza I snagged for a pretty penny back in 2006. I'll have that thing for the rest of my life.

So I'd keep an eye out when I was junking. And my number just wouldn't come up. Or when it did, it would be so much money, it would just sour the whole discovery.

Frustrated, I made my own little series of screenprinted posters. These are $35, shipping included. Simple color and design for everyone, you know? Design for coolest of offices, and for dorm rooms. And, there's something fun about stripping the vintage hounds of their power!

Each poster is signed and editioned. Lovingly screenprinted by the good people of Seizure Palace, the Half & Half and Vahalla. Shipping forever!

Getting lucky at the Portland Expo with a Hiroshi Awatsuji gem.

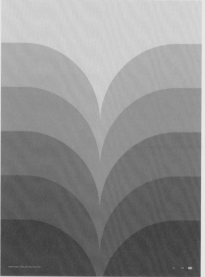

Thick Lines Poster Series No. 02 "Foliage." 6-color. 2014.

Thick Lines Poster Series No. 03 "Peaks." 6-color. 2014.

Thick Lines Poster Series No. 04 "Clouds." 5-color. 2014.

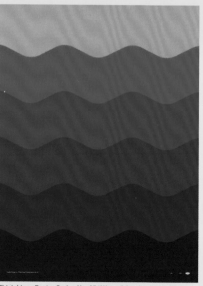

Thick Lines Poster Series No. 05 "Water." 6-color. 2014.

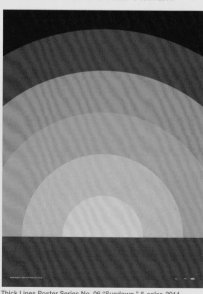

Thick Lines Poster Series No. 06 "Sundown." 6-color. 2014.

DDC

Draplin
Design Co.

Pretty Much
Everything

Aaron James
Draplin

File Under:
Thick Lines

200
201

Thick Lines Playing Card Set

Damn, this just might be my favorite thing I've ever been lucky enough to make. I was contacted by Andrew Gibbs from the Dieline about making a set of cards for the HOW Design Live Conference in Boston. I quickly accepted and got all the templates tuned up and ready to go. I tore into it with an idea of doing a simple, thick-lined set, completely boiled down, stripped of the decorative filigree and excessive detail of the playing card landscape. (Stuff we love, of course!) There was an opportunity to strip these of all of that stuff. I remember being freaked

out when I did a little search to see what other card sets were being released. Beautiful examples with foils, exquisite packages, and, most important, that classic, authentic fit, finish and feel.

So when Andrew hit me up, I couldn't say no. When I started digging into the design of the card pips, I did the first "Single Thick Line" version, and that exploded into multiple lines, then gradients, and so on. I kept going and going and had settled on the "Thick Lines" version you see below. The cards informed the

packaging—bright and vibrant. They just felt odd and new enough, considering the card landscape. And, after seeing all the incredible sets in circulation, I quickly moved past the idea of doing traditional red and black pip colors into the warm sunset palette. All the face cards? I had to make my own. The templates you get sent have the classic design we all grew up on. That just wasn't gonna cut it.

We sold out of these way too fast. Damn. I'm saving for another production run, on my own terms. Coming soon, cardsharks!

Single Thick Line   Thick Lines   Gradient Thick Lines   Core Colors   Half and Half   Final Pip Designs

Space Shuttle Tribute Series

I'm still a little bummed they called it quits on the space shuttle program. Growing up, it gave me something to believe in. For that last mission, there was a final patch made. And if I remember correctly, it was a contest where anyone could submit a design. I was alerted after they had picked the winning design from the painful array of crayon drawings,

wonky freehand tributes and crude but well-meaning patch designs. Nightmarish. And of course, the one they picked was terrible. And that was that? It was. So that afternoon—pissed off—I made my own space shuttle graphic. Monday morning quarterbacking, sure, but I wish I could've submitted something to that contest. I think I could have had a shot!

Our little shuttle graphic has had quite a run. That first run I did with those Space Coast orbiters at Mama's Sauce sold out fast! So we printed them again. Two years later, we're up to our ninth edition, along with decals, T-shirts, Tattly tattoos and action caps. Plus some fun placements in unfun TV shows and movies, namely *The Goldbergs* and *Aloha*. Liftoff!

Second Edition. 2014.

Third Edition. 2014.

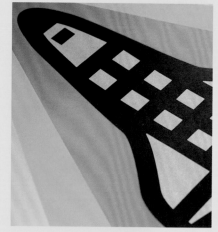

Sixth Edition. 2015.

Seventh Edition. 2015.

On the wall in *The Goldbergs*.

Launching Soon!

Fourth Edition. 2014.

Eighth Edition. 2015.

Ninth Edition. 2015.

LIFT-OFF!

DDC-093
Space Shuttle Tribute Action Cap

DDC

Draplin
Design Co.

Pretty Much
Everything

Aaron James
Draplin

File Under:
Rocket Boosters

204
205

Space Shuttle

1981

2011

A TRIBUTE TO THE AMERICAN SPACE SHUTTLE ERA, BY THE DRAPLIN DESIGN CO.

VERY LIMITED EDITION.   001/150   DDC

DDC Factory Floor

"Around the shop."

Shop Tour

DDC Social Media Nightmare

I always take to the new stuff a little slowly. It's always been that way for me. I waited a couple months on the iPod. And then when the iPhone hit, I remember being shamed into a purchase by my buddy Jared Eberhardt with this poke to the ribs: "Draplin, Helvetica never looked so good."

Social media took a bit of time for me, too. When Twitter came out, I just sort of watched how people were using it for a while. Short, throwaway bursts of data, often lacking any context, misspelled and just sort of half-witted. But a couple people were creative with it and that caught my eye. It was Jim Coudal who laid into me about its benefits. And that's when I jumped in.

But I wanted them to mean something. Seeing the vaporlike quality of shitty little tweets with no meaning, no context or confusing conversation threads? Seemed a little haphazard, lazy and scattered. So I tried to make each one count. I started numbering them. My first tweet was on June 13, 2009: "DDC/T—No. 0001: Hitting a Kinko's, then heading across the river to see Shellac with Mark and Dale."

Pretty serious shit! The "DDC/T—No. 0001" proved to be a pain in the ass to type on the little keyboard with my meatfingers. That was refined down to "DDC000" with this tweet: "DDC074: I've been instructed by someone smarter than me to shave my twit'n naming convention down. I'll take that advice. More real estate." I've numbered them ever since. And I'm always asked, "Why do you number your tweets?" So here's the reply: "Because each tweet matters." There's something to be said for being creative with the limited 140-character thing. And spelling properly and using appropriate punctuation. Have a little pride in your output, you know?

Each tweet feels special to me. Particular. After seeing confusing conversations and monosyllabic replies and whatnot, I was determined to think about each one just a little bit, and use them as effectively as possible. And, hell, what do I know? Am I using it the wrong way? Jury's still out on that one. These things are tools. I was taught to use each tool with skill. Or what about being creative with your hashtags? Such a fun way to make sense of this stuff, or completely fuck with it all.

Here's some of my favorites over the years:
#thicklines = thick lines
#morecolor = color spectrums
#goddammit = frustration
#largemaninasmallseat = airline travel
#largemaninalargeseat = first-class upgrade

Instagram made sense right out of the gate. Such is a concise way to share dead stuff I'll come across junking as well as funny/weird/cool moments. Always fun to post.

It's easy to get sidetracked by the yahoos out there. Anonymous voices. Cheap shots. All too often, it's just a bunch of windbags spewing nasty and hateful comments. Anonymous. But that just goes with the territory. Or just posting a little "too much." That gets my goat, too. For the record, on DDC channels, we pledge posting nothing to do with sports, cats or fucking coffee. That's just bandwidth abuse.

If you use it right, social media can be powerful, positive and add an interesting "real time" or "behind the scenes" quality to your overall voice. I've tried to do a good job with my bandwidth, and thank all the folks for giving my mess a shot.

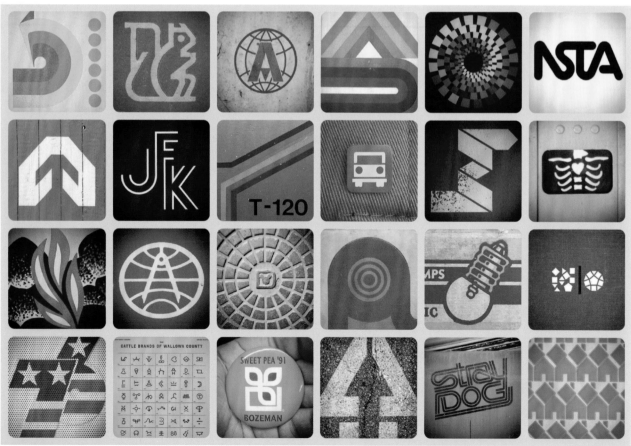

A selection of our favorite Instagram offerings. 2010-2015.

aplin Design Co.
C6208: Sometimes, we wait
do our Tweeting at night,
en the bandwidth is
MPING, and "can
" bullshit shit is fast
ep.

aplin Design Co.
C6239: To all the expecting
ents out there: Please
sider "Gary" for possible
names. No one names
r kid "Gary" anymore.
ary

aplin Design Co.
C6274: Yes!
nptymiddleseat

aplin Design Co.
C6348: For our "Daily
vement Module" we went
into the stuffy San Antonio
ht and walked around the
mo block six times.
mins

aplin Design Co.
C6430: This show is
dicated to Mom, Dad,
eighola and even Ryno!
ey'll be out in the crowd
EBALLING me, hard.
ingforbroke #ddc

aplin Design Co.
C6432: This one is for the
eatest dad a kid ever knew.
e funny, honorable and wild
mes Patrick Draplin,
43-2013. #dad #forever

aplin Design Co.
C6433: I miss my dad so
ch already.

aplin Design Co.
C6443: Heading over to the
WhiteOwlSocial for an
DISCLOSED SOMETHING-
-OTHER? #mysteryvibes
xcitement #buddies #40
rmydad #happy

aplin Design Co.
C6447: The video montage
s my favorite part! Buddies
m high school, or who
ved away, from the road,
m design circles and…

aplin Design Co.
C6448: …with
waynecoyne serenading
? What?!!! I about died.
d David Yow? My weirdo
ie rock uncles? Thank you,
ck and roll. #40

aplin Design Co.
C6465: Sent Dad off today
th jokes, tears, chicken
arsala, hugs, smiles,
emories, retellings, pumpkin
and waves of laffs. #fordad

raplin Design Co.
DC6500: Another road
mains, it provides no more.
can only take us away.
uthbound, you can taste the
ather. It feels like home.
V

raplin Design Co.
DC6523: As part of our DDC
l Tales pre-game ritual, we
e currently "Crying in our
tel room." The show will go
. #threadcountblues

raplin Design Co.
DC6558: I talk to Dad daily.
eam about him too. Been
nelling his jacket we have
m that day. My hope is he is
ERYWHERE, all at once.

raplin Design Co.
DC6649: Mom: "You don't
e the Nevilles?" Kid: "Their
og's a ball-sniffer."

Dad. That one's gonna hurt for a long time. Thinking about him. #jimdraplin #dad

Draplin Design Co.
DDC6693: Went for the middle, but got sidetracked. #routes

Draplin Design Co.
DDC6746: Nothing a little "Greetings from Asbury Park, N.J." wouldn't fix. #theboss

Draplin Design Co.
DDC6793: We stay busy. One part "survival," another part "sickness." We can't say "No" and CONTINUE to stike while the IRON IS HOT. #clank

Draplin Design Co.
DDC6802: Been on "tarantula watch" the WHOLE TIME I've been on the ground here in Tucson. Don't cross me, arachnid. #300poundsofamericanbeef

Draplin Design Co.
DDC6822: Can feel my hair growing. #caffeinegreenhorn @stumptowncoffee

Draplin Design Co.
DDC6859: Horses sure are beautiful. #horses

Draplin Design Co.
DDC6915: As soon as I got into the room, I whipped all the "accessory pillows" off the bed at the ceiling. Hate that shit. #ddcroadshowrules

Draplin Design Co.
DDC6965: This place is all, "Conch this, and conch that..." #keywest #conch

Draplin Design Co.
DDC7000: Our 7000th DDC TwitFeed™ tweet goes to Dad, whom we hope is EVERYWHERE AT ONCE, inside me, and you...making the universe laugh. #dad

Draplin Design Co.
DDC7090: We're flying over Billings right now. Which means, the airspace we just whipped through was where we lost Dad. #dad #jimdraplin

Draplin Design Co.
DDC7118: URGENT. [stop] ON THE GROUND IN SASKATOON. [stop] NEED DIRECTIONS TO U.S. EMBASSY. [stop] SURROUNDED BY CANADIANS. [stop] #DDCvsYXE

Draplin Design Co.
DDC7120: When ya think about it, having to go down the hall to get a bottle of water is stupid. Tonight, we drink out of the toilet! #hotel

Draplin Design Co.
DDC7216: "MAN OF SIZE" TRAVEL PRO TIP: Aisle arm rests! Run finger along bottom side of arm rest, find button, press and lift up. #moreroom

Draplin Design Co.
DDC7240: Right about now, Dad would walk and ask, "Whatcha watching?" I'd answer and he'd walk away saying, "...the book was better." #dad

Draplin Design Co.
DDC7277: Listen up, @Signalnoise: BLARING Barenaked Ladies at this hour is your idea of a good time? Trying to get some shut-eye over here.

Draplin Design Co.
DDC7286: "Man of Size" Travel Tip: Seat 11F on Delta 737s are my preferred sardine slot. Window for shoulder room, big belt & meatfoot room.

Draplin Design Co.
DDC7330: We're doing our part to rescue American design from it's own bad self. We've been fighting back. This Friday, you will to. #howlive

Draplin Design Co.
DDC7386: HOUSTON, WE HAVE A DRINKING PROBLEM: The 4th edition of our Space Tribute poster is now shipping: bit.ly/RbpKc9 #liftoff

Draplin Design Co.
DDC7405: For Massimo Vignelli.

Draplin Design Co.
DDC7478: Already sweating. #charleston @GiantConf

Draplin Design Co.
DDC7491: If you've still got yer dad, call him. Go have some lunch. Spend a night. And damn, make sure you throw yer arms around him. #dads

Draplin Design Co.
DDC7518: These AM Gold tunes remind me of Mom driving to the beach in that big Oldsmobile. Hot seats. Picnic lunch. Mask. Snorkel. #summer

Draplin Design Co.
DDC7565: The DDC factory floor is OFFICIALLY CLOSED. We'll flick the switch back on around July 6th! Now, we head to the American Southwest!

Draplin Design Co.
DDC7594: Monument Valley was great. Whipped through it too fast, though. Made it up to Cortez, where we secured a flophouse for the night.

Draplin Design Co.
DDC7605: "Grand Canyon" is my favorite song off @drivebytruckers's "English Oceans." About their merch guy who died: bit.ly/TNcwn3

Draplin Design Co.
DDC7698: With my work done, it's time to retreat to the dining room table to KICK THE LIVING TAR out of my Mom in Scrabble™. #blankfeelers

Draplin Design Co.
DDC7730: One wrong word or sideways glance, and I swear to Highway 127, I'll leave those fucks right there on the road. don't try me. #WLYS

Draplin Design Co.
DDC7740: For Robin Williams. What an original.

Draplin Design Co.
DDC7759: And I'll say this just once, Ohio: Anyone fucks with @JASONXSHULTS, know they fuck with the entire DDC. That's the policy.

Draplin Design Co.
DDC7780: I find myself thankful I found Fugazi. What if I only had the standard radio bullshit of 1989? That band make me AWARE. #thankful

Draplin Design Co.
DDC7792: Sleepless in Grand Island. Real tired, yet, amped up after all that prairie racing. Took backroads from Edina down here. #diagonal

DDC7820: AIRWAVES ALERT: @aprilbaer visited the DDC and put the thing on the radio! Proof: bit.ly/1lHJz9p #radioairwaves @OPBWonder

Draplin Design Co.
DDC7879: Landing in Boston, with a heavy heart. Little Otto of the @jaredeberhardt estate was taken by some dickhead coyotes. #forotto #sad

Draplin Design Co.
DDC7893: GOLDEN RAYS OF WASATCH LIGHT: Shining on this dog's ass. Got the first class upgrade from SLC to PDX! #relief #largemaninalargeseat

Draplin Design Co.
DDC7908: In my youth, I never understood my uncles' love for The Stones. Think I might get it now. #startmeup

Draplin Design Co.
DDC8000: Our 8,000th DDC TwitFeed tweet is dedicated to THE GOOD PEOPLE who made this leg of gigs happen. And all past gigs, too! #thankyou

Draplin Design Co.
DDC8047: I'm older now but still running against the wind. #segerbullshit

Draplin Design Co.
DDC8114: Damn, it's good to be in the Midwest. #home

Draplin Design Co.
DDC8153: Gonna go ahead and declare a "GOLD BOND WARNING" for the greater Jacksonville area. In effect THE MOMENT we get off the plane. #JAX

Draplin Design Co.
DDC8172: On the ground in Nashville. Screw graphic design—this just might be my chance to finally "cut that big country record." #nashville

Draplin Design Co.
DDC8220: Heavily considering some of those sweet gauges for my ears. Any tips you can share, @Dan_Cassaro? Or, a "nose-to-ear" chain thing.

Draplin Design Co.
DDC8221: Can't wait to tear into some pumpkin pie. #thanksgiving #thankful

Draplin Design Co.
DDC8237: For Bobby Keys.

Draplin Design Co.
DDC8284: Our little @lynda video has gone COMPLETELY APESHIT: vimeo.com/113751583 Up to 525,000 views!!! That's, like, all of Omaha? #wow

Draplin Design Co.
DDC8324: When I can't sleep, I think about going in one direction forever. #staggeringinsignificance Terrifying and beautiful. #getcosmic

Draplin Design Co.
DDC8386: Owe a debt of gratitude to Lawrence's Kill Creek. "Proving Winter Cruel" got me through a whole summer washing dishes. #alaska1996

Draplin Design Co.
DDC8424: 41 years old. And I'm starting to feel it. But I'll tell you this much: CAN STILL PISS ONE BEAUTIFUL ARC. #solidstreamhydraulics

Tommy Keene, Hooters, Outfield, Smithereens, dBs and Bill Lloyd. Love this stuff. #80spowerpop

Draplin Design Co.
DDC8450: Earshot "Traveling Cheerleader" names: Makayla, Makaylee, Makylee, Mackenzie, Maddie and Rylee, Rylie and Riley. #goddammit #spirit

Draplin Design Co.
DDC8451: Earshot "Traveling Cheerleader" conversation topics: "Glitter or Plain Ug Boots," "That Bitchy Spotter From..." and "Bangs." #fuck

Draplin Design Co.
DDC8452: Alright, who's got a copy of Bob Seger's "Brand New Morning" they'd like to unload? I know you are out there. #seger #rarerecords

Draplin Design Co.
DDC8502: "Interstellar" the second time around was just as moving. Might've been the altitude messing with me? I shed a couple tears. Again.

Draplin Design Co.
DDC8665: While driving tonight, we see a couple silhouettes on the horizon. Armadillos? Goats? Rabbits? Nope. 2 mini dachshunds. #seriously

Draplin Design Co.
DDC8669: @CoryGrove: @leighola was just talking about you! She was picking scabs off my back and said, "This mole...it reminds me of Cory."

Draplin Design Co.
DDC8702: I asked C.J., "You ever drive any big names around?" And he said, "What's that guy...Silver Bullet band...Bob Seger!" YES. #seger

Draplin Design Co.
DDC8720: @marcmaron: If you haven't locked in a poster for your Portland show, I'd love submit a bid. @ARTofCOOP, will ya vouch for me? #WTF

Draplin Design Co.
DDC8743: Waiting for the hotel shuttle, this just invaded my medicine ball head: "YOU ARE IN "WAFFLE HOUSE COUNTRY," PECKERWOOD." #hunger

Draplin Design Co.
DDC8783: RT: @tsoulichakib: Why do you add tweet count in your tweets? > We try to make each tweet count. Each one is special to us. #policy

Draplin Design Co.
DDC8792: I never met a "Larry" I didn't like. #larry

Draplin Design Co.
DDC8831: @aronharris: Which payment method do you prefer? Or does it just depend on what's in the burrito? > Burrito with $100 bills in it.

Draplin Design Co.
DDC8877: DDC Rule No. 231: "Treat the UPS Guy, Mail Lady and FedEx Humper like they are pure gold." That is, until they drop boxes and shit.

Draplin Design Co.
DDC8888: Our 8888th Tweet is for @leighola, who rolls, fills and ships our DDC merch with poise, precision and grace. #merchmistress #woosh

Draplin Design Co.
DDC8907: Rindfleischetikettierungsüberwachungsaufgabenübertragungsgesetz, Berlin! (Translation: "I need to bathe, Berlin!") #berlin #typo15

Draplin Design Co.
DDC8953: 34 planets aligned, while 34 stars shimmered in unison and that ball fell into the "34" slot—with a $100 bucks on it. #boom #vegas

Draplin Design Co.
DDC9004: What the fuck is biting me in this room? Tiny little gray striped things? Is that just my mind, or? #bite Having fun in Charleston.

Draplin Design Co.
DDC9047: So proud to see America inching forward. #lovewins

Draplin Design Co.
DDC9085: For Mrs. Perkins, my kindergarten teacher. Makes me sad to hear the news of her passing. A sweet, wonderful lady.

Draplin Design Co.
DDC9119: Big day here on the DDC factory floor. Possibly the biggest? Can't elaborate further. #bigdays #ddcfactoryfloor #saturdayshift

Draplin Design Co.
DDC9145: RT: @randompattern: Wanted to point out you're following 666 people. WHAT ARE YOU TRYING TO TELL US? > Keepin' our shit evil! #666

Draplin Design Co.
DDC9161: The amount of whiskers, fuzz, crumbs, dust, pebbles and grime on my desk never ceases to amaze. Shit just accumulates. #deskdebris

Draplin Design Co.
DDC9176: ARACHNID RIGHTS: Woke up wondering about Australian spiders. And what 300 pounds of American beef can do, in defense. #DDCvsOZ

Draplin Design Co.
DDC9202: WILDLIFE UPDATE: Kangaroos? No. Platypus? Nope. Bandicoots? Nope. Mouse spiders? Better not. No drop bears sightings. Yet. #DDCvsOZ

Draplin Design Co.
DDC9262: The chicken dish will pair nicely with the succulent scent of foot. Lady next to me just took her kicks off and chirped, "Woohoo!"

Draplin Design Co.
DDC9263: I'm jetlagged precisely to "Ireland Leprechuan Time". Ballyshannon or Kilmuckridge or Graiguenamanagh, but that's splitting hairs.

Draplin Design Co.
DDC9267: BOOM: We just hit "Delta Diamond Medallion" for 2016! #125000miles Gonna be a whole bunch of "DRA, A" in the upgrade list in 2016!

Draplin Design Co.
DDC9299: Dad, on car upkeep: "When something is wrong, the first thing I do is check to see if my license plate is on tight." #shitmydadsaid

Working with My Buddies in the Northwest

Some of my proudest work has been done for friends here in Portland. For the sheer fact that I use their stuff. Poler bags to lug gear back and forth from the coast, my Finex skillet to cook up a grilled cheese sandwich, and damn, there's nothing like a hot slice of Ace of Spades pizza from Sizzle Pie after midnight on the way home from the shop. These are guys who are making Portland the cool place it is. And the coolest part? They are my friends. There's something so gratifying about working with your buddies. There are bigger and better jobs in our town. Shoes, software and whatever else, and I've been able to cobble together a little career with friends. It's the same sort of stuff that allowed me to start up Field Notes. If you can't find what you want out there, fuck it, make your own version of it.

The last time Benji from Poler came by the shop, he left me an XL Poler Napsack. You oughta see me outfitted in it—I look like a goddamn camouflage water buffalo in the thing, warming up a slice of pizza in my Finex skillet. Thanks, fellas.

Poler

"Mountain Rainbow" T-shirt print, 2015.

"Snap Back D Patches." 2015.

"Thick Lines Cyclops" hoodie back print. 2015.

"TreePee" T-shirt print, 2015.

Sizzle Pie

The existing sign was paramount. The logo was designed around it. 2011.

OPEN LATE

HOME OF THE
"NAPALM BREATH"

SIZZLE PIE

624 E. BURNSIDE ST.
926 W. BURNSIDE ST.

503-234-PIES

OPEN HERE   OPEN HERE

The raddest pizza box in the Northwest! 2011.

Finex Cast Iron Cookware Co.

Here's another one of those "feels right from the first time you hear about it, so you say yes right away and take the job" sorts of jobs. Mike Whitehead is a funny guy. We go toe-to-toe with wisecracks and stories and don't get a goddamn thing done when he comes by the shop. That's how I know I like a guy—if he can hang with my mess. And Mike Whitehead can hang.

Mike was a product developer for Leupold out in the suburbs for a number of years, making high-tech scopes and binoculars. Intense stuff. Being a bit of a foodie, he designed an eight-sided skillet and needed help launching the brand. He came to the shop, we looked at drawings, flipped through some files and I got to work. The company was to be called Finex Cast Iron Cookware and would be carried in local shops in Portland and big stuff like Williams-Sonoma.

When you cast things in cast iron, it's a bit of an intense process. It's primordial, unpredictable and dangerous. So the logo and typography needed to take that tricky process into account. Simple forms, etc. We designed the logo around this. Uniform lines that could expand and contract, reduce well and work in some of the most rudimentary materials on the planet. And, to our relief, those first castings turned out amazing!

Molds aren't cheap. Mike mortgaged his house to get that first mold funded. This haunted me. But Mike's got this cool "mad scientist" quality to him that you trust and get inspired by instantly. I'm so proud to see Finex taking off. I knew it would. It's simple: If you make cool stuff, present it confidently and be consistent . . . things will take off. And they did! Job well done, Mike. Let's get a sandwich and scheme up the next project!

FINEX No. 10 Grillet. 2015.

Our first time designing for cast iron!
The FINEX No. 12 Skillet. 2013.
Following spread: A collage of the stuff that
we got to do for buddies, budding brands,
benefits, bands and Brad. 2000-2015.

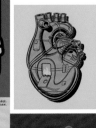

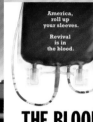

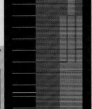

On the Clock for America

In my live talk I've got a little section called my "Tall Tales." My work for the Mode Project, who were commissioned by the Obama administration, just might be my tallest of tales.

It was late February 2009, just six weeks after Obama's inauguration. Leigh and I had gone to DC to see him sworn in. It was cold as hell that January day, and I remember all the people praying and singing and some even collapsing, overwhelmed by the history at hand. A charged, historic day. Mainly, I was just relieved to have that other turkey out of office. From the ages of twenty-six to thirty-four, I was afraid of my country. Not necessarily the policies, the blunders or the misinformation, just the president opening his mouth. That was enough for me. Good riddance, buddy. Go back to Texas and clear some brush.

On February 25, I get a call from Steve Juras from the Mode Project out of Chicago. These are the people who developed the incredible Obama campaign logo! I was such a fan of the work. If the new administration could pull off such a beautiful, smart logo and website, that seemed just the tip of the iceberg.

They had been commissioned by the Obama administration to develop two logos: one for the ARRA (American Recovery and Reinvestment Act) and TIGER (Transportation Investment Generating Economic Recovery) programs.

That first call from Steve was on a Wednesday morning. We discussed the direction, the brief, signed an NDA and got rolling. My Cincinnati buddy Chris Glass would be working on the project, too. Chris Glass! Hell of a photographer, graphic designer, maker and human being. Knows his way around a piece of meat loaf! I was relieved and honored to be working with a friend on this.

I remember Steve telling me that he might have to put me on hold, as "calls from Axelrod's people" were the highest priority. And then it happened, and I remember sitting there in silence, freaking out with this one thought: *Axelrod's people? Wait a second. If they are talking to Axelrod's people, uh, Axelrod talks to the president . . .*

And suddenly it hit me. This was big.

They wanted to see five comps by Thursday morning. I remember cleaning off my desk, calling Mom, Leigh, Dale and then Jess to come over and film it. Somewhere, we've got footage of the first couple hours, and me sending off that first batch of comps to Steve.

Here's a little something I never talk about in the telling of this tale. I went to Spokane that weekend on a junking mission with Dale and Jess. I wasn't gonna miss that trip! The first round of the TIGER logo was developed from the back of my Passat wagon while Dale drove. And then refined

that night from the hotel room once we got into town. I remember having to leave an estate sale to go find a Starbucks to work from, to make refinements for Steve. And there being no one in the place that morning and the bored barista woman looking over my shoulder and asking me what I was working on. "I'm making a logo for the president!" And the funny look she got on her face. She could care less. A fun memory.

We went back and forth. Chris and I would submit our stuff to Steve. They'd tune them up into presentations for the White House. At one point Steve e-mailed me and said, "They like it!" And I remember thinking, *Who is "they?"* Completely freaking out. The Joint Chiefs of Design?

The final logos were picked by Sunday, and unveiled Monday morning. President Obama, along with Vice President Joe Biden and Secretary of Transportation Ray LaHood, held a press conference detailing the stimulus package. Steve alerted us and I tuned in to C-SPAN online, watching it from my laptop at the shop. I'll never forget that moment: President Obama briefing the nation about the American Recovery Act, with Chris and my logos behind him. I sat there and cried, so proud to have helped out.

This wasn't just for the president—we got to work for America. Every time I see the signs out there I get goosebumps. And now and again, I'll stop to polish the logo.

American Recovery and Reinvestment Act. 2009.

TIGER, U.S. Department of Transportation. 2009.

President Obama addresses the nation. Photo by Pete Souza, courtesy of the White House.

Exploring period typefaces.

Studying the "Do Your Part" eagle.

Sketching initial ideas.

First vectors.

Refining.

Tinkering.

Explaining something important to Jess.

Stuff to start showing a couple hours in.

More tinkering.

Was careful to give red and blue equal play.

Explaining something profound. Or debating lunch options.

Just a couple hours in, and things were starting to take shape!

Getting rolling on TIGER.

Working in the back seat.

Initial TIGER iterations, made on the road.

Initial TIGER studies.

The star didn't last long. Replaced it with a T and sent it off.

Client meetings.

Found a sealed Flaming Lips "Transmissions" record in Spokane!

Shut-eye. Stayed up a little too late each night working.

Quick shot with road manager Dale Allen Dixon.

Farmer John

This tale starts with one e-mail from a John Hughes from Harvard, Illinois. April 2008. He discovered me through Field Notes, which led him to my website and work. He had a farm called Redwing Farms that bred rare sheep and cattle. He was looking for a logo that harkened back to the bold vernacular of classic farm equipment manufacturers. And then said something about how The Sea and Cake were a good choice. Sounded like a cool farmer.

I wrote him right back, and the next morning he gave me a ring. We quickly talked through the logo, with him telling me the current logo looked like a "bad winery from the early nineties." I'm usually pretty good with clients on the first call. I hear them out, can get them laughing and, most important, make them feel comfortable to work with me. Usually people are quick to get off the phone once the business is out of the way. But John and I went pretty deep and proceeded to chew the fat for four hours. Four hours?!

I remember the name John Hughes instantly ringing a bell, but, there was no way it could have been *that* John Hughes. A common name, I deduced, and focused and got to work on the logo.

The next bunch of calls, Farmer John and I talked about everything. Our Michigan roots. Our parents. His children and wife. My life in Portland. His life on the farm and around Chicago. How he loved my writing and work, and had been following my site for a couple years. I dug in and sent John the first logo presentation a couple days later. This stuff was right in my wheelhouse! After a couple rounds of presentations and daily calls, we quickly settled on a couple. He liked them all. And I liked John and sent him the whole mess. As I was sending him the final files, John said, "Watch for a FedEx coming with your check." That was odd. No one in my world pays that quick. Usually it's "30-60-90 days thing" and then the dreaded call to Phyllis in Accounts Payable to smooth-talk her into sending the check.

The FedEx showed up a day later, and when I opened it, there was an envelope with my check from Redwing Farms LLC, from an accounting firm in Chicago. So I started doing some Google searches. There was John Jr. and James, his sons he'd spoken about so much. There was Nancy, his wife he'd spoken about taking out for lunch. From *that* John Hughes. So I called John up and asked him point-blank, "Are you the John Hughes who made *Uncle Buck*?" He laughed and said, "It took you long enough, Aaron." And I freaked out inside: John was the quintessential '80s director! A Midwestern iconoclast. The guy who had put the Midwest on the map and gave teenagers a voice. As the story goes, I went and saw *Ferris Bueller's Day Off* like eight times the summer of 1986. *That* John Hughes.

See, up to that point, he hadn't told me he was *John Hughes*. I'm not a celebrity. And when you see a name like that, you just assume it's one of the many John Hugheses out there. I felt comfortable with the guy so asked him what it was like to be John Hughes. He told me he had to get out of California. "I'd wake up and there would be a new car in the driveway. A gift from the studio. What about the license plate and tags?!" He spoke about River Phoenix dying, and how that's when he knew he didn't want his boys to grow up in Hollywood. He moved his family back to the Midwest in 1993, after a rough experience with the movie *Curly Sue*. Hollywood can turn on you. I think it might've turned on John. He told me stories of going to bat for John Candy against persnickety Beverly Hills studio heads. So cool.

The second project I did for John was a logo for Consolidated Fiction, a fictional company for his writing. He had been writing all those years. We also talked about doing *Uncle Buck* flyers and stuff.

We'd miss each other's calls. One time, he said something about being at lunch with Vince Vaughn. And here I was at lunch with Dale. It just didn't add up. But you know what? The next time I'd talk with him, he'd make their interaction sound as normal as the next. I'd be staring up "celebrity mountain" each time, and John would bring me right back down to earth.

I was on the World's Longest Yard Sale when I first heard of John's death. My buddy Vin wrote me. He was one of the few friends I had told about meeting John. John warned me about talking about our friendship on my site. "They'll come after you, buddy." He explained I'd be inundated with interview requests.

That summer, I had kind of backed off bugging John. Leigh would say, "What if you are like a pet to him?" I mean, maybe he had twenty designers working for him? I just didn't want to waste his time. The final project I did for John was to make him business cards for his favorite characters: Buck Russell from *Uncle Buck* and Del Griffith from *Planes, Trains and Automobiles*. Quickie cards, that John would leave in "free lunch" fishbowls at diners or in the back seats of cabs. And after John passed that August, his son James wrote me and told me he passed out those cards to friends on the day of his dad's funeral. That shook me up pretty good. The idea of John's friends remembering him with those little cards I made? Pretty incredible.

Sadly, I didn't get to meet John in person. I'd be passing through Chicagoland, or whipping around the "Horn of Gary" on my way out west, and would call. He'd be on the road or something, and we'd talk of him coming to Portland. "Bring your dad and I'll bring my boys." Still sad that didn't happen. John was a sweet man who spoke so highly of his wife and his sons and their families. My first chat with John? Still my longest phone call, ever. I'll be a fan of his movies forever, and consider John a friend.

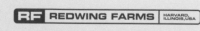

Redwing Farms logo kit. 2008.

| Draplin | Pretty Much | Aaron James | File Under: | 220 |
| Design Co. | Everything | Draplin | Moley Russell's Wart | 221 |

Consolidated Fiction logo kit. 2009.

Buck Russell's coffee-stained card of business. Go Cubs! 2009.

A whole career's worth of Del Griffith cards of business. 2009.

Tall Tales From a Large Man

"We'll go wherever they'll have us."

Let me lock this one in forever. I'm writing these words right this second, some thirty-five thousand feet over the Pacific Ocean, on my way to Australia for three shows in Brisbane, Melbourne and Sydney. Never in my wildest dreams did I think I'd be going as far as I have on the graphic design speaking circuit. And now to Australia? The coolest.

This whole "speaking fiasco" thing started in Santa Fe, New Mexico. Andrew Campo, an old *Snowboarder* magazine buddy, invited me to come and sit on a panel and talk about design. I was a little scared to get up in front of people, but there were six of us and a scant crowd. No big thing. Then I got an invite to come tell my story at AIGA Minnesota's Design Camp up in Nisswa. I lived in Minnesota for two years and remember people talking up Design Camp. I couldn't go. Couldn't afford that stuff on my nonexistent MCAD budget.

On the flight back to Minnesota, I put together my first presentation. It's basically the same thing I do these days. Where I'm from, my trajectory west, going back to school, first jobs, getting free, working on my own and then some of the weird stuff that has gone down. I remember going up on the stage in front of that four-hundred-strong Design Camp crowd. I totally seized up, gripped by fear, or just out of my element. All those eyes. All those people wondering what the hell just walked up to the podium. It was pretty surreal. I got my bearing, let the PDF guide me and gave my first real talk.

The kids loved it. I had dragged a mountain of merch to the camp with me, selling posters, T-shirts, Field Notes and DDC trinkets. I sold through EVERYTHING. Rich, I summoned my rotgut buddy Ryno up from The Cities and took him out for a night on the town. I treated him to the finest walleye dinner Nisswa offered. A magical night, so freaked out, just blown away I was even allowed into the conference.

I went to all the lectures at MCAD. If I remember correctly, they were taking attendance. I remember being thankful for so many cool chances to hear people tell us their stories. But a couple of them were turds. One group from London, man, they were pretty high on themselves. Terse answers, fidgeting, monotone delivery, snarky challenges from snarky professors. Just a bit too adversarial for my liking. I mean, shit, it was graphic design they were talking about. Not human rights. Or geopolitical policy. Posters and typefaces and shit. Simple show-and-tell, more or less. I remember thinking, *Shit, do you even like your job? Sure doesn't sound like it.* If you do, tell us why. So much hot air, and yet very little substance.

Shepard Fairey came to the Walker Art Center in 1999. I paid a good chunk to go see that show, and had to stand *allllll* the way at the back of the big, oversold crowd. Could barely see the guy, much less get a handshake at the end of the show. He was blowing up in the design world, and was quite the sensation around Minneapolis, having bombed the town with gigantic, awesome Obey posters. I was a fan and the show was cool. That stuck with me.

I probably shouldn't be putting this paragraph in here. Is there a statute of limitations for smuggling kids into shows? I'll just say this much: I've been pretty lucky to sell out a number of my shows. And then I'd hear from some kid who couldn't get a ticket. Or didn't go to the school where the exclusive event was being held. There's always room to squeeze some punk kid in. If someone reached out to me, I'd tell them to chill out, sit tight and be close to the event before I went on. And then I'd just walk out, grab the kid, usher him in and tell him, "Sit here. Don't touch anyone. Don't make a scene. Okay?" And then I'd hammer up to the stage and do the show. No harm done. My record for smuggling folks into a single event is nine guys! Into a big convention in a big city. Through a back door. Can't get into specifics.

When people come up to me after the show, I get thanked for being "authentic" and told how they actually hung on to every word through the talk. Which is always a bit weird. Of course, we hug it out and I'm always flattered by the admiration, but shit, what's that say about the other speakers they might've seen? And shit, I'll ask them, "Who else was fun?" Aside from Kate Bingaman-Burt, who the whole design world—and my little self—loves, I hear some pretty tricky reviews. Which hurts. People are paying for this stuff, design speakers! Kick that shit up a notch. And I don't mean you should get up there and go apeshit, but come on, what are people going to take home with them? The monotone, show-and-tell, "Then I did this, then I did that" shit only goes so far. Light the room up.

Or shit, don't, and keep making fidgety jokes about not having enough coffee, like every other turd out there.

I've spoken to some hard rooms. One that comes to mind is a luncheon in South Dakota. Sure, the organizers are always cool, and there's one table of peers who get it. But shit, when 130 of the 150 people are chomping on salad, things can get a little weird. Here's how Margie the Marketer from Nebraska tells you she didn't like your show: "My son would love this!"

I'm proud to write that I made time for EVERY kid who came up to me. I shook EVERY kid's hand. I mean, that's why we are out there doing this shit, right? To connect. For me, it goes a bit deeper. It's to show a kid they can make their own life be whatever they want it to be. Sure, it's gonna take work, but it means a lot to me to tell them dirtier paths exist, and sometimes, there's gold to find.

A couple months back, I did one of my biggest shows yet—the HOW Design Live conference in Chicago. Four thousand people or something. Amy and the HOW folks let me set up a booth and hock merch, shake hands and sign stuff. So for two full days, from ten A.M. until six P.M., I stood at that table and talked to every kid. Heard stories. Shared tips and tricks. Smiled for selfies. The whole deal. At the end of the first night, exhausted, I went up to the room and hit that big bed, dog-tired. And I jumped up and pushed myself off the bed, and noticed the smear of "handshake grime" on the white duvet.

I've crafted a couple other talks, too. "Graphic Treasures from the American Underbelly" gets into the the finer pints of junking. "The DDC 50 Point Plan to Ruin Your Career" speaks for itself. I try to change things up from show to show, updating new work and lofting out regional curveballs. Just trying to keep the shit fun.

For the record, my Portland buddy Eric Hillerns came up with the "Tall Tales from a Large Man" moniker. For my first sanctioned Portland event for the great Designspeaks series. It was 2009 and I was so proud to have my little sister Leah in the front row. I quickly hijacked Hillerns's title and the rest is some pretty ugly history. Thank you, buddy. And thanks to each and every one of you who came to the shows, bought some merch and came up to shoot the shit! Meant the world to me. All of it.

DDC

Draplin
Design Co.

Pretty Much
Everything

Aaron James
Draplin

File Under:
Poor Little Gary

224
225

TALL TALES
FROM A
LARGE MAN

DDC 2013
WINTER/SPRING TOUR

GOING WHEREVER
THEY'LL HAVE US

DDC MERCH ITEM NO. "DDC-074"

MEAN GREENS ON DEATH BLACK

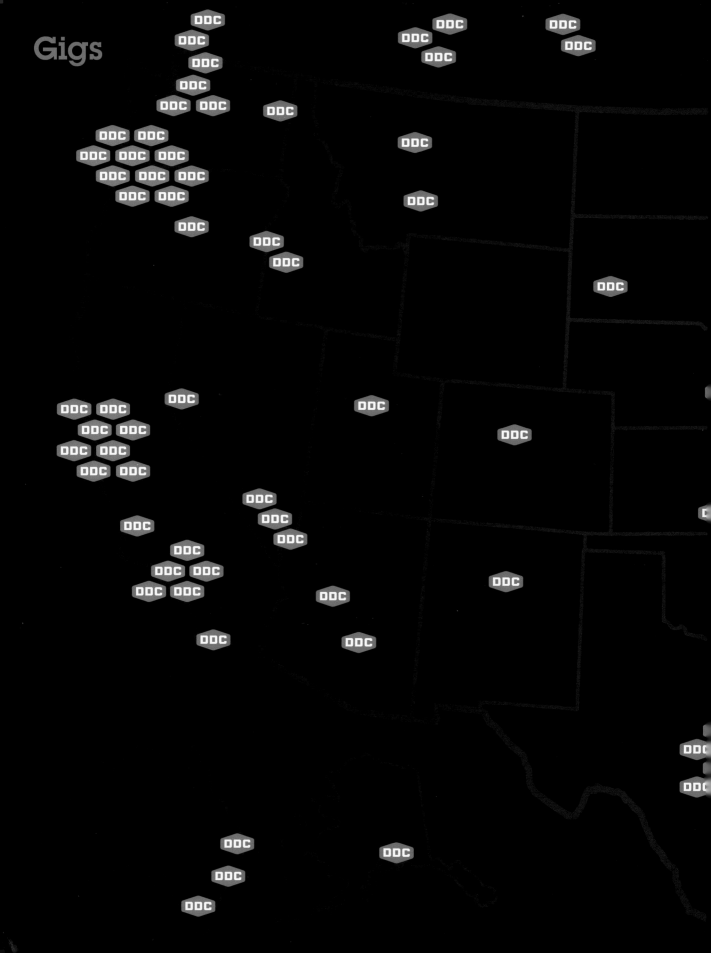

Gigs

Draplin
Design Co.

Pretty Much
Everything

Aaron James
Draplin

File Under:
Orange Proliferation

226
227

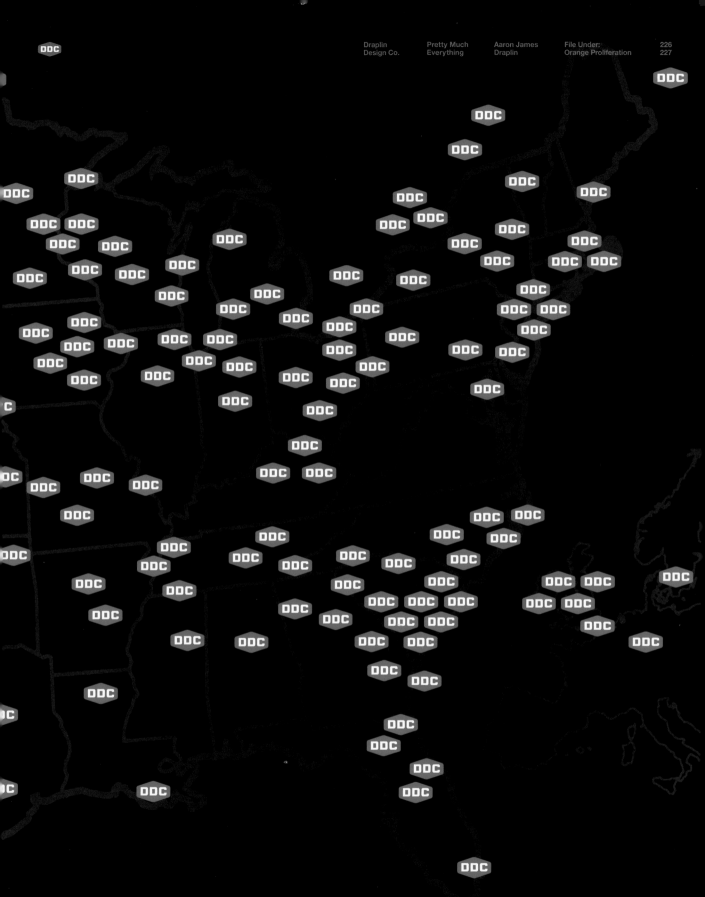

Gig List

2007
001 Santa Fe Design Week, Santa Fe, NM

2008
002 AIGA Seattle "The Hills Have Eyes," Seattle, WA

2009
003 Jason Resch's Branding Class, PNCA, Portland, OR
004 Cut & Paste judge, Portland, OR
005 AIGA Minnesota Design Camp, Nisswa, MN
006 Geekend Conference, Savannah, GA
007 Dallas Visual Communication Society, Dallas, TX
008 Designspeaks, Portland, OR

2010
009 Show and Tell, PSU, Portland, OR
010 AAF New Mexico judge, Albuquerque, NM
011 Richmond Ad Club judge, Richmond, VA
012 Valencia Community College, Orlando, FL
013 AAF Minnesota judge, Minneapolis, MN
014 AIGA Detroit and Team Detroit, Detroit, MI
015 Minnesota State University, Mankato, MN

2011
016 AIGA Alaska, Anchorage, AK
017 AIGA Mizzou, Columbia, MO
018 Futura play lecture, Portland Center Stage, OR
019 AIGA San Diego Spark Conference, San Diego, CA
020 Creative Worker's Union, Austin, TX
021 AIGA Kansas City "Design 360," Kansas City, MO
022 AIGA Kansas City "Design 360" judge, Kansas City, MO
023 AAF Lincoln, Lincoln, NE
024 Weapons of Mass Creation Conference, Cleveland, OH
025 Art Directors Association of Iowa, Des Moines, IA
026 Target "Spark" Lecture Series, Minneapolis, MN
027 Draplin Does Philly, Philadephia, PA
028 Always Summer Kick-Off, Jacksonville, FL
029 Designspeaks "Spit Swap," Seattle, WA
030 Keri Newman Design Events, London, UK
031 Beep Industries, Manchester, UK

2012
032 AIGA Arizona, Tempe, AZ
033 AAF Central Oregon, Bend, OR
034 Walker Arts Center, Minneapolis, MN
035 Creative Mornings, Show 1, Portland, OR
036 Creative Mornings, Show 2, Portland, OR
037 AIGA South Carolina, Columbia, SC
038 AIGA South Carolina, Charleston, SC
039 Ottawa Creative Collective, Ottawa, ON
040 FITC Conference, Toronto, ON
041 FITC Conference & Influxis VooDoo, Toronto, ON
042 FITC Conference panelist, Toronto, ON
043 GDC BC Mainland, Vancouver, BC
044 Signal Kitchen & Shavemart Ent., Burlington, VT
045 AAF Spokane, Spokane, WA
046 LGDA Louisville, Louisville, KY

047 HOW Design Live Conference, Boston, MA
048 Somerville Library, Somerville, MA
049 AIGA Las Vegas, Morioka, Beeler, Las Vegas, NV
050 Inter-Agency Coalition, Calgary, AB
051 Portland Digital Experience/MFNW, Portland, OR
052 Brand New Conference, New York, NY
053 AIGA Salt Lake City, Salt Lake City, UT
054 Brooks Museum, Tall Tales, Memphis, TN
055 Brooks Museum, 27-Point Plan, Memphis, TN
056 AIGA Nashville, Nashville, TN
057 University of Iowa, Iowa City, IA
058 Cedar Rapids/Iowa City AAF, Cedar Rapids, IA
059 Cedar Valley AAF, Cedar Valley, IA
060 Dubuque AAF, Cedar Dubuque, IA
061 Brooklyn Beta Conference, Brooklyn, NY
062 Advertising Club of Buffalo, Buffalo, NY
063 SketchXChange, Portland, OR
064 Build Conference, Belfast, IE
065 Yay Festival, Stockholm, SE
066 AAF Black Hills, Rapid City, SD
067 AIGA San Francisco, San Francisco, CA
068 Citrix, San Jose, CA
069 AAF Portland, Portland, OR
070 LEGO Christmas Party, Enfield, CT

2013
071 AIGA DC, Washington, DC
072 Type Directors Club, New York, NY
073 Type Directors Club judge, New York, NY
074 AAF Boise, Boise, ID
075 SCAD, Savannah, GA
076 InControl Conference, Orlando, FL
077 AIGA University of Texas Arlington, Arlington, TX
078 Montana State University, Bozeman, MT
079 OTA Sessions, Sioux Falls, SD
080 AAF North Dakota, Fargo, ND
081 Screenland Hackathon, KS City, MO
082 AIGA Reno/Tahoe, Reno, NV
083 New School of Architecture + Design, San Diego, CA
084 AIGA Los Angeles, Los Angeles, CA
085 AAF Omaha, Omaha, NE
086 AIGA Nebraska, Omaha, NE
087 AAF South Dakota, Sioux Falls, SD
088 FITC Conference, Toronto, ON
089 RIT Design Program, Rochester, NY
090 ConvergeSE Conference, Columbia, SC
091 Creative South Conference, Columbus, GA
092 AIGA Maine, Portland, ME
093 Made By Few Conference, Little Rock, AR
094 Adobe MAX Conference, Los Angeles, CA
095 AIGA Knoxville, Knoxville, TN
096 AAF Lexington, Lexington, KY
097 AIGA Charlotte, Charlotte, NC
098 Mail Chimp private event, Atlanta, GA
099 AIGA Wichita, Wichita, KS
100 Interlink Conference, Vancouver, BC
101 Hand-Eye Supply, Portland, OR

SETTLE DOWN, TRUCKERS:
WE'RE EXPERIENCING
TECHNICAL DIFFICULTIES

SOME TRUTH:
I'M SCARED SHITLESS
BEING UP HERE IN FRONT OF ALL OF YOU

OUR VERY OWN BRAND OF "DUMB"

A SPEAKING FIASCO TESTED THE WORLD OVE

TALL TALES FROM A LARGE MAN

```
<there>WON'T BE</any>
<fucking>CODE TALK</in this>
<half-ass>SPEAKING FIASCO</so>
<deal>WITH</it>
<goto>CODE SCHMODE</kill me>
<uh>BEEPBOOPHONK</fart>
<end>
```

HELLO, TULSA!

SPECIAL DEUTSCHE AUSGABE!

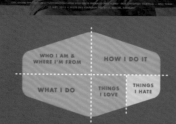

WHO I AM & WHERE I'M FROM | HOW I DO IT

WHAT I DO | THINGS I LOVE | THINGS I HATE

HALLO BERLIN

DEFY THE FUCKIN' ODDS

01. I SHOULDN'T BE UP HERE.
02. HAVE NO CREDENTIALS.
03. NO PROFESSIONAL ACCOLADES.
04. HAVE NEVER WON AN AWARD.
05. DON'T HAVE A BOOK TO SELL.
06. USUALLY DON'T WEAR PANTS.

1974

BEHIND THE ORANGE CURTAIN
2000

SCIENTIFIC PROOF:
PRECISELY 84 LEGITIMATE ITEMS OF BONAFIDE GRAPHIC ARTS

LONG DRIVES; LOUD OCTAVES; CONSPIRACY
VAZ & RABBITS
EXPECT THE WÜRST
HEAD FOR THE WEST

MISSING DIGIT
MISSING DIGIT
MISSING DIGIT

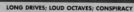

HOW WE DO IT

"United States and Canada"

THANK YOU FOR BELIEVING IN FIELD NOTE.

R **DC** **5** **C** **E**

DDC VS. DULUTH – P.S.A. NO. 01

MONUMENT CREST MFG T.P.W. MONARCH

WOW.

★★★★★

SORRY, THAT'S A

MATTER OF NATIONAL SECURITY

★★★★★

REDWING FARMS

REDWING FARMS
ILLINOIS, USA

BUCK RUSSELL

AMERICAN LIGHT & FIXTURE

FIELD NOTES

STANDARD ISSUE
DDC FACTORY FLOOR
MEMO BOOK

EXCEL MACHINE TOOLS

TEN FOR A SOME-WHAT **FAIL-PROOF EXISTENCE***

POINTERS

WE'RE HERE TO HELP. Our best literary foot forward, we offer up a range of loose pointers that aim to save you from a life of embarrassment, clogged e-mail pipelines, imprisonment, lumbering files, loneliness, shame, data loss, contempt for society, isolation, wheezing complaints, lackluster results, deepair, ridicule, and/or financial ruin. Seriously.

*IN THE
GRAPHIC
ARTS,
AND OTHER
PLACES

A. DRAPLIN
Graphic Artist
Amateur Article Writer

FULL DETAILS BELOW

KEEP READING. ROLL THE DICE. NEW LIFE AWAITS.

Enclosed find $1, Send postpaid.
Send C.O.D. I will pay postage $1 plus postage
$1 refund if un-delighted.

DRAPLIN DESIGN CO., NORTH AMERICA

DRAPLIN.COM

Dept. "A-72"
Portland, Ore.

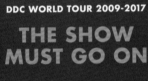

DDC

AARON JAMES DRAPLIN / DRAPLIN DESIGN CO.

DDC WORLD TOUR 2009–2017

THE SHOW MUST GO ON

DDC VS. NOW DESIGN LIVE 2012 – "FULL TALES FROM A LARGE MAN" SPEAKING VIDEO
MAY 8, 2012 · 91857 BUCKLEY BASEMENT, CHICAGO, ILL, U.S.A.

BOOK DEAL!

AARON JAMES DRAPLIN / DRAPLIN DESIGN CO.

C WORLD TOUR 2009–2017

20. MANCHESTER
21. RENO
22. MINNEAPOLIS
23. DENVER
24. PORTLAND
25. COLUMBIA
26. CHARLESTON
27. OTTAWA
28. TORONTO
29. WATERLOO
30. VANCOUVER
31. BURLINGTON
32. SPOKANE
33. BOSTON HOW
34. SOMERVILLE
35. CALGARY
36. LAS VEGAS

39. PORTLAND
40. BRAND NEW NYC
41. SALT LAKE CITY
42. MEMPHIS
43. NASHVILLE
44. IOWA CITY
45. CEDAR RAPIDS
46. WATERLOO
47. BROOKLYN
48. BUFFALO
49. WATERLOO
50. CHICAGO
51. MAILCHIMP
52. BELFAST
53. STOCKHOLM
54. RAPID CITY
55. SAN FRANCISCO
56. SAN JOSE
57. BROOKLYN

58. GREAT FALLS
59. SEATTLE
60. SAN ANTONIO
61. HOUSTON
62. AUSTIN
63. KETTERING
64. CINCINNATI
65. ST. CLOUD
66. MINNEAPOLIS
67. MCAD
68. PITTSBURGH
69. NEW YORK
70. CHATTANOOGA
71. FORT WAYNE
72. DEKALB
73. OKLAHOMA CITY
74. YOUR TOWN
75. ANYWHERE
76. EVERYWHERE

FROM A

JOEY FROM CALEXICO

KIP

FROM
POLEON DYNAMITE

MY FAMILY

LEGOS

SWEATPANTS

AND THEN

12"/12"

KNOW THE DIFFERENCE

SAY YES

MAYBE A LITTLE MORE
THAN YOU SAY NO.

BUY SOME MERCH!

WORK HARD

AND LOVE THIS SHIT.

THANK YOU BIRMINGHAM!!!

FOR DAD

1943–2013

DDC!

"TALL TALES FROM A LARGE MAN"
AARON DRAPLIN

Draplin
Design co.

Pretty Much
Everything

Aaron James
Draplin

File Under:
DDC Gig Posters

232
233

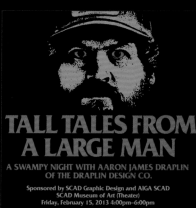

TALL TALES FROM A LARGE MAN

A SWAMPY NIGHT WITH AARON JAMES DRAPLIN
OF THE DRAPLIN DESIGN CO.

Sponsored by SCAD Graphic Design and AIGA SCAD
SCAD Museum of Art (Theater)
Friday, February 15, 2013 4:00pm–6:00pm

DDC!

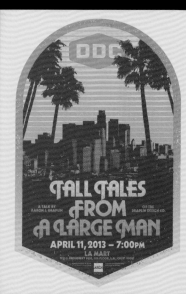

DDC!

DDC!

Michael Zavacky!

DDC!

Invisible Creature!

DDC!

DDC!

Chris Avantaggio!

DDC!

DDC!

Thanks to All Who Came Out to the Show!

St. Cloud, MN. 2013.

Akron, OH. 2015.

Lancaster, PA. 2013.

Springfield, MO. 2015.

Boise, ID. 2013.

Toronto, ON. 2012.

Vancouver, BC. 2013.

St. Louis, MO. 2013.

Columbus, OH. 2013.

Menlo Park, CA. 2013.

DDC

Draplin
Design Co.

Pretty Much
Everything

Aaron James
Draplin

File Under:
Settle Down Truckers

234
236

East Lansing, MI. 2014.

Memphis, TN. 2014.

Boston, MA. 2014.

Los Angeles, CA. 2014.

Denver, CO. 2012.

Grand Rapids, MI. 2014.

Birmingham, AL. 2014.

Chicago, IL. 2014.

Baltimore, MD. 2014.

DDC Merch Table

Of course I'm gonna have a merch table. Just like a band, right? Right.

The night before each gig, the last thing I'll do before leaving the shop is assemble all the merch into travel-ready boxes and Filson bags. It's quite a mess of boxes and bags.

And by "travel-ready" I specifically mean "Able to take a beating on the plane." And even more specifically, able to take the inspection the concerned TSA agents will hand over, as well as the thrashing the baggage handlers will certainly administer.

SIDE NOTE: I'd like to extend a gigantic "Fuck off" to all the half-assed, lazy baggage handler bros I've watched over the years from my seat—helpless—as they throw my bag around like it's a dead sack of potatoes. No finesse. No care. Just hucking shit and listening to things break. Have a little pride in yer work, you know?

Just a little. I'm not saying it's all of you turds, but it's a good chunk of ya. Thanks for nothing. Please get sucked into a plane engine.

Okay, where were we? Yeah, getting the merch ready to travel. Once I have it in boxes and bags, I'll load out of the shop down to the Volvo. That's always the last step. And in the morning when the cab comes to get me, that's how I remember to lock the Volvo when I leave. By grabbing the merch out of the back of it. That one always works. Pretty impressive, eh?

So, say the gig is at seven P.M. In the best-case scenario, I'll be there a couple hours ahead of time, unloading the boxes and bags and setting up the merch table. First it's the posters. Then the T-shirts and hats. Then all the small stuff. Then the price tags are applied based on whatever town I'm in. I'll keep the same prices that I have on my site in the big cities. But in

small towns? Hell, I'll reduce the price of everything just because. Once the table is set up, the sales start. Open for business!

And, most important, if I notice some rat kid digging through his wallet, fretting the price or not having enough, then I'll motion him over and tell him, "Hey, man, what do you want?" And I'll simply give it to him. See, that's what happened to me when I was growing up. I remember a couple of times being a little short at the merch table of whatever band I was seeing, the roadie noticing it, and cutting me a deal, or simply handing me the record I couldn't buy. That blew my mind and made me love, hell, the Jon Spencer Blues Explosion that much more.

Same policy at the DDC merch table. And if you are reading this and know what I'm talking about, well, thanks for coming to the show and I hope you enjoyed your merch purchase!

The closest thing we'll get to "set lists."

DDC MERCH
1. POSTER............$10
2. T-SHIRTS.........$15
3. HAT...............$20
4. BEANIE...........$10
5. FIELDNOTES......$7
6. STENO BOOK......$6
7. COIN PURSE.......$2
8. PENCIL SET.......$4
9. PENS, PENCILS....$1
STOCK UP!

MERCH LIST: DDC
1. VERMONT POSTER...$20
2. T-SHIRT...........$15
3. NATIONAL CROP SET...$12
4. FIELD NOTES (THREE PACK)...$7
5. STENO BOOK........$7
6. BEANIES...........$10
7. PENCIL SET........$5
8. COIN PURSE........$2
9. EVERYTHING ELSE
   PENS, PENCILS, ETC......$1
CASH / CREDIT CARD!

DDC/801 DDC73

DDC MERCH
SPECIAL "IDAHO-ONLY" PRICES

01. "IDAHO ALL THE WAY" POSTER................$20.00
Everything we love about the "gem state." Four color printed on beefy stock, made just for Idaho! 16" x 24". Big!

02. DDC "ACTION CAP"................................$20.00
Absolutely fuckin' MADE IN THE U.S.A.! Finally back in stock. Spirited colors. Will brave the element. Modern fit.

03. FIELD NOTES THREEPACKS......................$8.00
Special "Idaho" edition! Durable. Pocket-friendly. Graph Paper. Serious real estate. Made in U.S.A. Fun for all.

04. FIELD NOTES "STENO BOOK"...................$8.00
My mom helped make these. Big and beefy, with tons of pages. Just like the old ones. Toughest chipboard cover, ever.

05. DDC "SHIPPING DOCK BEANIE"................$10.00
I know Iowa gets colder than a mother-in-law's love? Fight off frostbite. Made in the U.S.A. by COAL Headwear!

06. HEX PENCIL 6-PACKS.............................$5.00
Hot off the presses! Made in America. Value Pack!

07. COMB, COIN PURSE or EVISCERATOR.........$3.00
C'mon people. This is the shit you need. Seriously. Proud items to survive that swamp-ass lifestyle you guys love so much.

08. PENS, PENCILS and LITTLE STUFF.............$2.00
C'mon people. This is the shit you need. Seriously. Proud items to survive that swamp-ass lifestyle you guys love so much.

WE GLADLY ACCEPTS:
COLD, HARD CASH / DEBIT CARD / CREDIT CARD
Thank You For Yer Business.

"IF WE DON'T HAVE IT, YOU DON'T NEED IT."
DRAPLIN DESIGN CO., MERCH DEPT., ROAD SHOW DIV.

Charles S. Anderson and Scott Thares!

Chip Kidd!

Kim Deal!

Louie Anderson!

Steve Turner, Superfuzz Bigmuff!

Mike Watt!

Todd Piper-Hauswirth!

Thanking Wayne for the 14th time!

Our favorite Jick: Mike Clark!

David Yow and Henry Owings two-fer!

Backstage with Debbie Millman!

Pressed up against Chris Ware. Poor guy!

Taking Gary Hustwit's last book off him!

Talking Ragnarok with John Hodgman!

Meat Puppet Kirk Curtwood and Chad!

Greg Gourdet from *Top Chef* with Leigh!

No, Erik Spiekermann, we aren't hiring!

Steve "The Colonel" Cropper!

J from Dinosaur Jr! O from Fluf!

Kevin Parker from Tame Impala!

Napoleon Dynamite's Aaron "Kip" Ruell!

Marc Maron at LAX!

Making Art Chantry sign records!

Patrick Keeler of those Greenhornes!

Richard Simmons bear hug!

Making Friends With Heroes

With all the places I've been going to, there's been a lot of downtime in airports all over the nation. And it's a chance to see people walking by who you might recognize. And if I see someone, I'll go up to them, slowly of course. I'll introduce myself and thank them for what I love about them. Simple stuff, and on some level, a bit of a test. If they'll be cool about it, all the better.

I didn't do that with Joan Rivers. Or Gene Simmons. Or Vanilla Ice that one time waiting to catch a flight out of Florida. No thanks. What you'll see here are characters I look up to. Some from the rock world, TV and design world.

Now I get kids coming up to me. And they'll be super nervous, fumbling words. "Uh, are you Aaron Draplin?" And I'll laugh and say, "Hope no else looks like this!" And we'll hug it out and become buddies. As simple as that. We're all just people in the end. My heroes represent uncompromised creativity, freedom and fuckery. The econo living of Mike Watt, the growl/humor/ball sack of David Yow and the cosmic frequencies of Wayne Coyne. Fringe motherfuckers, sure, but always the coolest.

Tricky Renderings

A buddy once told me, "You know you've made it when they start drawing pictures of you." Maybe, maybe not? I do know this much: One of the coolest parts about taking my mess on the road has been the interactions with people who come to the shows, and every now and again kids will come up and show me their Field Notes with a portrait they did of me! Such cool moments. Or one'll show up in my e-mail a couple days later. Or on some kid's Instagram. Fan art? Maybe I just have a weird head that's fun to draw? Sometimes it's just a buddy messing with me, more or less reminding me of the gourd that sits on my shoulders. My favorites involve the creator shaving fifty pounds off me! Mighty nice of you. I've collected all of them, always freaked out, humbled and entertained by what people are coming up with. Here's a collection of my favorites from over the years, starting with my very favorite one from one Mike Gaughan on this page right here. Check out the little flying Gary! I still don't know what to do with this thing. Frame it? Crop it down to Gary? So fun, and so surreal. I love me some Mike Gaughan. Or the one Ryno did of me playing guitar with no pants on? The stuff of fuckin' nightmares.

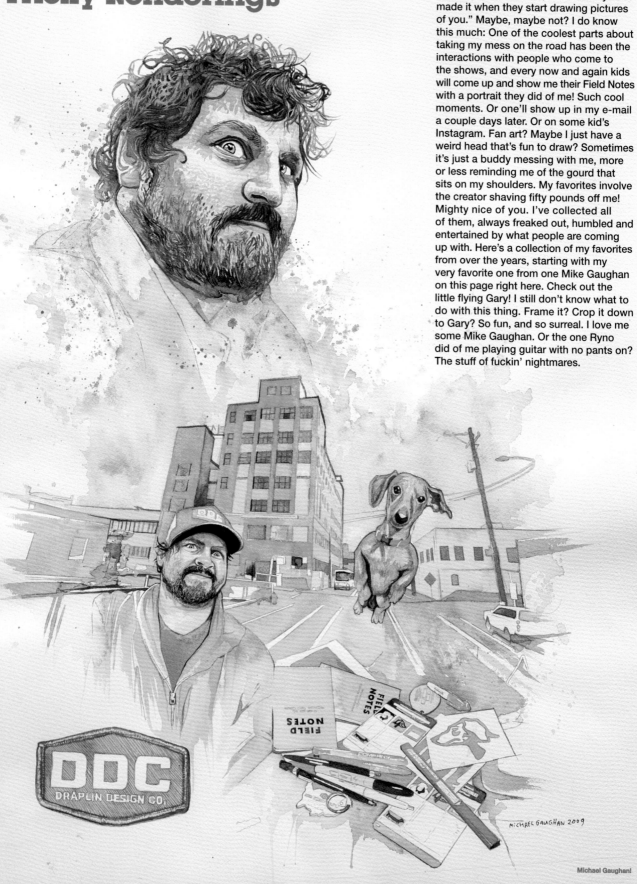

Michael Gaughan

Any one has a roast beef sandwich? Anyone?

AARON DRAPLIN DDC

Hue Pham!

Draplin Design Co.

Pretty Much Everything
DDC

Aaron James Draplin

File Under:
Uncanny Likenesses

238
239

David Sizemore!

Martin Lebrun!

Nate Uteschl!

Dan Cassaro!

Dana Lechtenberg!

Carl Fox!

Ryno Simonson!

DDC

Dennis Cortes!

THICK LINES

MUTHA FUCKA!

Kimberly Day!

Tricky Renderings

John Hammer!

Frank Chimero!

Dan Rood

Lydia Nichols!

Daniel Duplex!

James Kamo!

Dan Christofferson!

Travis Millard of The Other Fudge!

AARON DRAPLIN

James White of Signalnoise!

P.J. Chmiel!

Draplin
Design Co.

Pretty Much
Everything

Aaron James
Draplin

File Under: 240
Tricky Subject Matter   241

Tim Boelaars!

Jordi Sanchez!

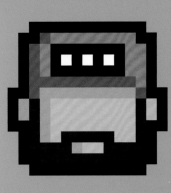

Andy J. Miller!

Ray Scarborough!

erms Lanningham!

Jacob Ashley!

Luke Naff!

Rocky Roark!

Robert Generette III!

Testimony, Tips, Tricks and a Couple Turds

Things We Love

001 Mom.
002 Dad.
003 Little Sister Sarah.
004 Little Sister Leah.
005 Nephew Oliver James.
006 Almost-Brother-in-Law Jacob.
007 Little Gary.
008 Girlfriend Leigh.
009 Super Teenager Ewan.
010 Field Notes.
011 The gang at Coudal Partners.
012 "Al" the Dodge panel van.
013 "Red" the minivan.
014 "Big S" the Passat wagon.
015 Our 2011 Volvo XC70 station wagon.
016 The DDC Factory Floor.
017 A small Craftsman on NE 67th Avenue.
018 Our backyard.
019 The Open Road.
020 Fall foliage.
021 The month of Octobrrr.
022 Cool summer nights.
023 That Flat Midwest.
024 The Wet Northwest.
025 Making an honest living with design.
026 Staying outta the red.
027 Acoustic guitars.
028 Electric guitars.
029 Bass guitars.
030 Walls of sound.
031 Helvetica.
032 Futura Bold.
033 Trade Gothic.
034 Lubalin Graph.
035 Lego.
036 Bad wildlife art.
037 Thick paper with a good tooth to it.
038 My beat-up Carhartt jacket.
039 Levi's 501s.
040 Saucony Jazz & Shadow 5000 kicks.
041 Gold Toe socks.
042 A new pair of socks.
043 Adobe Illustrator.
044 Adobe Photoshop.
045 Adobe InDesign.
046 Adobe Bridge.
047 Being straight with Uncle Sam.
048 Being a good citizen/being a bad citizen.
049 Standing up to shit that "isn't right."
050 The stars in the summer night sky.
051 A cold Coke.
052 Vignelli oversize calendars.
053 Compact discs.
054 iTunes.
055 iPhones, iPads & iPods.
056 Apple products—essential and brilliant.
057 My big wall of books.
058 Corner rounders.
059 Flat files.
060 A disc on the player.
061 A stack of records from the record store.
062 Checks showing up in the mail.
063 Midwestern accents.
064 Girl hands.
065 Hitting that "34" on the roulette wheel!
066 Clean sheets.
067 Down comforters.
068 Cold water.
069 Hot water.
070 A hot shave.
071 A tall glass of ice-cold water.
072 Mom's spaghetti.
073 Dad's "killer pizza."
074 Club sandwiches.
075 The Ideal Diner in Minneapolis.
076 The hard day's work.
077 Untucked shirts.
078 Autobiographical tattoos.
079 Impko stickers.
080 Cards of business.
081 Spot UVs.
082 Ikea.
083 Old postcards with "scalloped edges."
084 Just about everything Minneapolis.
085 Route 66.
086 Leaving Southern California.
087 Schaedler rulers.
088 Aluminum items.
089 A vanilla milkshake.
090 The goddamn Flaming Lips.
091 Making lists.
092 And checking everything off.
093 Feeling "complete" after paying bills.
094 Jackalopes.
095 Bigfoot.
096 Nessie.
097 Skunk apes.
098 Flying home to Mom and Dad.
099 Old Penguin psychology book covers.
100 A Gary "twofer"; pissin' and shittin'.
101 Ham radio cards.
102 Bose speakers.
103 Bose noise-canceling headphones.
104 Rainsqualls.
105 Fall breezes.
106 Spring rain showers in Portland.
107 Mowing the grass.
108 The color orange.
109 Pantone Orange 021.
110 Pantone books.
111 One-inch rocker buttons.
112 Those bridges of Madison County.
113 Kentucky's rolling hills.
114 Appalachia.
115 Universal icons.
116 A western straightaway.
117 Business loops off the highway.
118 Neon "OFFICE" signs.
119 Going home.
120 Mom's French toast.
121 Dad's vegetable beef soup.
122 The hills of eastern Oregon.
123 A full tank of gas.
124 Flat-screen TVs.
125 Dual monitors.
126 Old dime stores filled with dead stock.
127 Considered hierarchy in typography.
128 Brick buildings.
129 The houses of Louisville.
130 Shotgun houses in Louisville.
131 A nice piece of Alaskan halibut.
132 Uncle Ben's wild rice.
133 Chicken fried rice.
134 Pad Kee Mao from Cha'ba Thai.
135 Beans and rice, Dominican-style, off the J.
136 Punjabi, late-night, on Houston in NYC.
137 Water chestnuts.
138 Baby corn.
139 Green beans.
140 Asparagus.
141 Utah's license plates.
142 Moab.
143 Those badlands of South Dakota.
144 Gary gallops, hops and endos.
145 Getting home after a long road trip.
146 Writing things down.
147 Practicing our penmanship.
148 Harmonicas.
149 That Dm7 chord.
150 Pilot Butte.
151 Old Santa Cruz skateboard stickers.
152 Good grammar and punctuation.
153 Apsco pencil sharpeners.
154 Boxer shorts.
155 Pesto.
156 Old warehouse buildings.
157 Dogs who lay on their sides.
158 Bullet pencils.
159 Old maps.
160 Thunderbolt data copying speed.
161 Dogs jumping from bed to bed in a hotel.
162 Ford Econoline vans.
163 Scandinavian flatware.
164 '70s textile wall art by Verner Panton.
165 Heartart textiles by Hiroshi Awatsuji.
166 '60s and '70s political campaign buttons.
167 Union pinbacks.
168 Golden books.
169 Golden guides.
170 Having Marc Maron in the shop.
171 Spaghetti Westerns.
172 Volvo station wagon typography.
173 Orange iPhone protective cases.
174 Strawberries.
175 Bananas.
176 Oranges.
177 Carl Sagan.
178 Neil Degrasse-Tyson.
179 Vinyl records.
180 Stoughton record sleeves.
181 Shrink-wrap stickers on a record.
182 Etching on a record.
183 The little notes etched in.
184 Record cover spines.
185 180-gram slabs of vinyl.
186 American-made hammers.
187 Anvils.
188 Beating Nakamoto at dice.
189 Gramma Josie's big pancakes.
190 Cholula hot sauce.
191 Sriracha hot sauce.
192 Going backstage at a show.
193 A nicely detailed car cockpit.
194 Chip clips.
195 Chips.
196 Pretzels.
197 Peanuts.
198 Thick lines.
199 How big the universe is.
200 Our insignificance in the universe.

Things We Hate

001 Kid Rock.
002 The farce Presidency of George Bush.
003 Southern California.
004 Hollywood and all its trimmings.
005 Pop Culture Performers.
006 Pop Culture Parasites.
007 Pop Culture Profiteers.
008 Pop Culture Paparazzi.
009 Nü Metal.
010 Sitcoms.
011 Gridlock.
012 Summer heat.
013 Cop stance.
014 Turbulence at 30,000 feet.
015 Taking off in a big-ass jet plane in a storm.
016 Air traffic control delays.
017 Missing a flight.
018 That middle seat, anywhere, really.
019 Missing the upgrade by one person.
020 Dropped cell phone calls.
021 Loud fucks on a cell phone.
022 Tsunamis.
023 The Iraq War.
024 Charley horse wake-up calls.
025 Flat tires.
026 Grooms wearing sandals.
027 Anything with a "Beach Theme."
028 Disciplining little Gary.
029 Opportunistic, bloodsucking mechanics.
030 Sock and sandal combos.
031 The random mall "Princes of Dorkness."
032 Hot Topic bondage pants
033 Malls.
034 People who say "Woo-Hoo."
035 Dust bunnies.
036 Spiders.
037 Halitosis.
038 Bills.
039 "Detuned guitars" by visiting "musicians."
040 New and mysterious guitar neck dings.
041 Lost remote controls.
042 Paper cuts.
043 Bad kerning.
044 "Clicking" hard drives.
045 Sore throats.
046 Missing home.
047 Fanny packs.
048 Kitchen humor.
049 Sushi.
050 Tribal tattoos.
051 Ambercrombie + Fitch bullshit.
052 The 405 from Los Angeles down to Irvine.
053 Surfer lore.
054 The word, "Dude."
055 Fucks who do the "Yah, yah, yah…" quip.
056 Happy hikers.
057 Milk with dinner.
058 Getting yer car towed.
059 Encores.
060 Artichoke hearts.
061 Republican NeoCons.
062 Creed.
063 Flight attendant attitude.
064 Aqua Socks.
065 "Uncle" Vans shoes.
066 Golf sweatshirts.
067 Faux "worn" hats. Motherfuckers.
068 Faux "worn" anything.
069 Bitch Devil Wife Complex.
070 Toby Keith.
071 Toby Keith's nose.
072 Toby Keith's facial hair.
073 Jock patriot anthems.
074 Country singers in the Bahamas.
075 Snowboarding Scene Claustrophobia.
076 Contemporary roadside signage.
077 Recounting previous night's drink list.
078 Poorly-kerned anything.
079 Predictable encores.
080 Mark "Marky Mark" Wahlberg's "acting."
081 Rascal Flatts.
082 Hollywood, Nashville.
083 Country music clichés.
084 "American Chopper" design sense.
085 Overactive bass players. Settle down.
086 Painful band publicity shots.
087 DIY disc/record packaging.
088 "My Little Brother Did It" record design.
089 Artichokes.
090 Olives.
091 Capers.
092 Beets.
093 Honey mustard.
094 Dancehall music.
095 WalMart.
096 Dollar General.
097 The strangling of small business America.
098 Drivers who don't use their turn signals.
099 Cigarettes.
100 Cigarette butts.
101 Cigarette smoke.
102 Cigarette ashtrays.
103 Cigarette diseases.
104 Cigarette deaths.
105 Vurps. (Vomit Burps).
106 Tom DeLay and his shit-eating grin.
107 Rush Limbaugh anything.
108 Fish bowl smell in a glass of water.
109 Infomercials.
110 Ted "Pastor Ted" Haggard.
111 Cute bands with nominal talent.
112 Tools made in China.
113 A dull blade.
114 Utah style wars.
115 Warren Jeffs and his malicious ways.
116 Subdivision signage. i.e.: Whispering Dicks
117 Nike logos on a truck cab window.
118 Cellphones with obnoxious ringtones.
119 The "strip malling" of America.
120 PBR aftertaste.
121 Foundation makeup.
122 The Tea Party.
123 Guy Fieri.
124 Michele Bachmann, that hateful beast.
125 Karl Rove's snide smile.
126 Anything Rick Santorum.
127 Whiteout conditions while driving.
128 Stacked food.
129 Prime mark abuse.
130 Cab drivers who just don't give a fuck.
131 Airport luggage handler tarmac dudes.
132 Red-eye flights.
133 First class passengers, eyeballing you.
134 Anything and everything Ted Cruz.
135 Soul patch facial formations.
136 Trolls.
137 Traffic on Sandy Blvd. in the morning.
138 People on bikes running stoplights.
139 Gratuitous public displays of affection.
140 Slap bass of any sort.
141 Loggins + Messina.
142 Stacked food.
143 Uncomfortable elevator rides.
144 Dust on your camera's photo sensor.
145 Vaping.
146 Vaping hardware.
147 Vaping stores.
148 Vaping client referrals.
149 Period. To. Make. A. Point. Bull. Shit.
150 Cat memes.
151 Mosquitoes.
152 Mosquito bites.
153 Saying goodbye to Dad.
154 Confusion over where Dad went.
155 Folky certitude from people after Dad died.
156 Fret buzz.
157 Guitar store clerks.
158 That distinct "Tough Guy" East Coast attitude.
159 Cats.
160 Cat litter boxes.
161 That fun "cat piss" smell in a house.
162 Needles.
163 Getting your blood drawn.
164 E-mail attachments bigger than 5mb.
165 Cheerleaders.
166 Cheerleader moms.
167 Overly-manicured dinner situations.
168 Overly-manicured dinner photoshoots.
169 Pictures of coffee.
170 Pictures of coffee with cream leaves.
171 Reckless cab drivers.
172 Baggage fees.
173 "Rock Crowds" in a movie. Never right.
174 Donald Trump.
175 Donald Trump's hair.
176 Donald Trump's voice.
177 Donald Trump anything.
178 Pompous, wheezing graduate students.
179 Dinged corners on a stack of posters.
180 Tight seatbelts.
181 Ingrown hairs.
182 Elbow warts.
183 Skin tags that just keep coming back.
184 Plastic surgery lips.
185 Plastic surgery noses.
186 Plastic surgery breasts.
187 Plastic surgery eyes.
188 Losing to Nakamoto at dice.
189 Poorly-labled computer files.
190 Days over 75 degrees.
191 Drivers hogging the highway's left lane.
192 Loud Sky Club business guy phone calls.
193 Bouncer attitude and stunted intellect.
194 Things growing in the garbage disposal.
195 Packing peanuts.
196 Crooked horizons in photographs.
197 California drivers on mellow Oregon streets.
198 The "service" in Portland restaurants.
199 "Spirited" fucks yelling in a restaurant.
200 The day we lost Dad.

File Hand-Off Checklist

It's a good feeling to get to the end of a project. I always feel accomplished and excited to make a living in design. Thankful. But before you go and celebrate, you have to make sure you are firing off that file as tight as possible. Here's our somewhat fail-safe way of readying files to ship,

01 "Save" yer file wherever it is at. In the current version you own. Make triple sure you've got it in a logical place, and, backed up for 1,000 years.

02 "Save As" the file, saving it to the desktop. This is the file you'll send off to the client/operator/vendor once everything checks out. I add a special extension to my files. I go with "_mech" as in "mechanical." So when you see that special file called, "GARY_BREATH_mech.ai." you know that sucker is ready to hand off.

03 Unlock Everything. Sometimes people will grab shit, missing the locked stuff. (Option-Command-2) unlocks everything on the page! Zoom out to check the art board.

04 Check yer colors. If the file calls for spot colors, make sure everything is colored properly throughout the document. Be it PMS colors or CMYK global builds, make sure everything is consistent.

05 Check those blacks. 100% K or Rich Black? I do a mix of "C:35 M:35 Y:35 K:100" as my trusted "Rich Black" build.

06 Check overprinted colors. Select everything, then check the "Attributes" palette. If the "Overprint Fill" box has a minus character in it, that means some of yer stuff is overprinting. That could complicate stuff down the line, and/or effect richness/colors when printing. Sometimes I'll drag stuff from another document that was "checked overprint" and it'll mess up the new document.

07 Clean out any unused color swatches. Get 'em out of there. Better safe than sorry. In the upper right corner of the "Swatches" palette, click on the little drop down menu, and go to "Select All Unused" and then click on the trash icon in the palette window. Bye bye incorrigible color swatches.

08 Get rid of any logos/goodies you aren't using in yer "symbol" palette. I keep mine loaded with DDC logos, client logos and shapes I hate having to redraw. Clean 'em out of there! Same deal as those unwanted colors. In the upper right corner of the "Symbol" palette, click on the little dropdown menu, and go to "Select All Unused" and then click on the trash icon in the palette window. Sayonara, suckers!

09 Check the spelling of everything. I do it twice, just cuz I get all cocky and click through the dialogue boxes a little too fast.

10 Outline the fonts: Might as well outline those fonts, too, unless the client needs to edit stuff. I always outline them, just to cut down on possible font problems after the hand-off. One less complication for some frustrated turd to invent when they start messing around with yer file.

11 "Expand" everything. You know, all the rounded edges and shit that might be "United" in the "Pathfinder" palette, but still needing to become one shape. A compound shape is always safer than a grouped chunk of pieces, but that only applies to when you hand the stuff off. Otherwise, keep it all "live."

12 Extra layers can complicate shit. Might as well just get it all on to one layer. Easier to deal with later on.

13 Check all placed images. Placed or embedded? Make sure the shit you have linked as efficiently as possible too. Embedding stuff can make files giant, so weigh the options before leaving them in.

14 Flatten all linked images. Just so people aren't messing up the Photoshop layers. Then, relink just to be triple sure.

15 Check the area surrounding the artboard. There might be some embarrassing stuff in there, hidden from view or whatever. Zoom way out, go to "Outline Preview" (Command-Y) and see if there is any stray shit in the outlying regions. Get rid of all that shit.

16 And for the final step, "Save" the thing down a couple versions. Nothing sucks more than having whatever "professional source" calling back crying about not having the latest version to open the file. And unclick "Create PDF Compatible File." That cuts down on file size something fierce. Also, just for extra protection, add the software version number to the file name.

17 Put the file in the original folder, alongside yer original file. Then you have yer original file with all the fixins, and, the file you handed off.

DDC FILE HAND-OFF CHECKLIST
"Regarding Adobe Illustrator"

CHECK ALL THAT APPLY	REQUIRED STEPS
☐	01. "Save" yer file wherever it is at.
☐	02. "Save As" the file, saving it to the desktop.
☐	03. Unlock everything.
☐	04. Check yer colors.
☐	05. Check those blacks.
☐	06. Check overprinted colors.
☐	07. Clean out any unused color swatches.
☐	08. Get rid of any logos/goodies you aren't using in yer "symbol" palette.
☐	09. Check the spelling of everything.
☐	10. Might as well outline those fonts, too.
☐	11. "Expand" everything.
☐	12. Extra layers can complicate shit.
☐	13. Check all placed images.
☐	14. And flatten all linked images, just so people aren't messing up the Photoshop layers.
☐	15. Check the area surrounding the artboard.
☐	16. And for the final step, "Save" the thing down a couple versions.
☐	17. Put the file in the original folder, alongside yer original file.

Checklist complete!

DDC-73   DRAPLIN.COM

DRAPLIN DESIGN CO., NORTH AMERICA

PROUDLY PRINTED IN THE U.S.A.   DDC FORM "ADOBE-IL-CHECKLIST"

Printer Prowess Test Section

When selecting a printer for the book, the decision was out of my hands. But of course, I trust them with my life. To the right here, you'll see me knocking a spirited affirmation out of the color or image behind it. Tricky stuff, getting those dots to line up. Let's put 'em to the test!

01 Rich Black   02 Creepy Photo   03 Process "Orange 021"   04 Blown Out Halftone

DDC Book File Naming Convention

In order to promote an efficent file management structure for this book projects, I adhered to a simple, effective file naming convention the whole way through. Here's what it looks like:

Year	Project	Section	File Name		File Type

DDC15_BOOK_MERCH_go_make_an_order_now.psd

I'd wager that it's one thing to make beautiful, effective designs, but just as important—*how* you build the stuff. That needs just as much attention. How you name the files and folders. And then, how you store the data. When the stuff is tight and right? That's the mark of a true craftsperson. Slow down a hair and get that shit dialed in.

Small Type Reference Guide

No.	Size	Helvetica Neue LT Std 65 Medium
01	6 pt	"You got a voice like the last day of catholic school." –Paul Westerberg
02	5.5 pt	"You got a voice like the last day of catholic school." –Paul Westerberg
03	5 pt	"You got a voice like the last day of catholic school." –Paul Westerberg
04	4.5 pt	"You got a voice like the last day of catholic school." –Paul Westerberg
05	4 pt	"You got a voice like the last day of catholic school." –Paul Westerberg
06	3.5 pt	"You got a voice like the last day of catholic school." –Paul Westerberg
07	3 pt	"You got a voice like the last day of catholic school." –Paul Westerberg
08	2.5 pt	"You got a voice like the last day of catholic school." –Paul Westerberg
09	2 pt	"You got a voice like the last day of catholic school." –Paul Westerberg
10	1.5 pt	"You got a voice like the last day of catholic school." –Paul Westerberg
11	1 pt	"You got a voice like the last day of catholic school." –Paul Westerberg

STERN WORDS: The Draplin Design Co. cannot be held responsible when you "tried to set the whole page in "5.5 pt Whatever" and failed miserably," we're just feeling showing you what things look like this small. Okay?

LOUDER THE CALL, THE RESULTS.

SERIOUS BUSINESS! Be on loud calls in loud airport clubs. Blurt out terms like "It Is What It Is" and "Pivot" and "Circle The Wagons" **AND THEN** instantly badmouth the guy you just finished that "big call" with, to whatever turd you are sucking down drinks next to. Talk about golf, timeshares properties and children named, "Mikaylee." Wear pleated pants. Talk loud.

Dept. D-B   S.S.C.S. — Society for Sky Club Silence   Cleveland, Oh.

CAN'T QUITE *MAKE IT* IN DESIGN?

Consider a big-time graduate degree to alleviate those woes. **INSTANTLY ELEVATE** your big brain up above the rest. Great opportunity. Go into deep, relentless debt. Design boring cultural calendars. Become a "teacher" without so much as a shred of "real world" experience. **DRINK HEAVILY.** Criticize whatever isn't nailed down. Utilize advanced skillset on Twitter and Facewhizz, trolling people who actually work for a living. Talk down to people. Hate your life. **QUICK WAY OUT** of actually having to invent something for yourself. You deserve an easier path. Let us help you.

DINGLEBERRY ART INSTITUTE, DEPT. 73, NEW YORK, N.Y.

AMPERSAND EPIDEMIC SWEEPS NATION!

Starting a new business and in need of a rustic, artisanal name? We can help.

"&"
- ☐ Drown & Perish
- ☐ Fart & Waft
- ☐ Chafe & Scratch
- ☐ Ball & Dangle
- ☐ Pick & Flick
- ☐ Blah & Meh
- ☐ Grunt & Push
- ☐ Puke & Choke
- ☐ Butt & Munch

Restaurants — Menswear Boutiques — Ice Cream Hustles — Coffee

Serious inquiries only.   Price............ WRITE FOR DETAILS

THAT BITTER TASTE

WASHED UP? So what if you "peaked" back in the early '90s? Out of work? Bored and not afraid to go after the throat of those still doing something with their lives? We know the feeling. Age range of 51-55 recommended. Strong predilection for dated, "post-modern" design. Learn how to leave comments that live forever on websites, detailing just how lost, mean and near death you are. Still time left!

IN JUST 140 CHARACTERS!

FIND YOUR VOICE: Trouble with spelling? Miniscule attention span? Limited, prickly communication skills? Are you exhibiting predictable thought patterns with nasty, unnecessary outbursts? Nursing lackluster tastes in bands, movies, podcasts and books? Susceptible to trends and other bullshit memes? Open a Twitter account and tell us about it. Use hashtag "#FART" and ruin the Internet with your output. Incessant.

VANITY SHOTS

Elevate your company and/or personality with a vanity shot. Look pensive. Look sultry. Look serious. Look the part. Fold your arms. Tilt your head at odd angles. Sell yourself! Instant results and better-paying clients. Write for details.

Carl Melanoma, Photographer, Boca Raton, Flor.

START YOUR OWN PODCAST

ACT LIKE YOU ARE IRA GLASS! Waste people's time with way too many emails trying to set up a time to talk. Fumble through technical difficulties and bore your guests with those same, canned witty starts and endings. Say stupid things. Tweet excessively and make people avoid that sixty minutes like the plague. Fun.

Deadwaves Broadcasting School, DEPT. "23", Gary, Ind.

Learning Can Be Fun.

STUDENTS! PUPILS! YOUNGSTERS! Instructions for writing that designer you look up to can be found here. We offer a long list of boring questions to pick from like, "What inspires you?" and "Any advice for an up-and-coming designer entering the workforce." Why get creative? Shave time off that useless degree you just financed with these time-tested inquiries. Use these exciting questions and keep that tradition of "cut-n-paste" shortcuts going. **MUCH TO LEARN.** Write for details.

DDC STUDENT SERVICES   Dept. "43", Portland, Ore.

FREE LOGO IDEAS:
- LIGHT BULBS
- BRAINS
- FACTORIES
- BRAIN FACTORIES
- LIGHT BULB BRAINS
- ANCHORS
- ARROWS
- GEARS
- EYEBALLS
- LIGHTNING
- LEAVES
- ARCS
- SWOOSHES
- SWIRLS
- KOKOPELLI

43 MB

LOOK HERE! **FREE PORTFOLIO TIP:** **PURE HATE:**

HERE'S THAT SUREFIRE WAY to never get a call back: Send a 43 MB e-mail attachment! And for extra impact, add that age-old quip about how your website is "in shambles and not to hold that against you." Works every time. Taco Bell is always hiring, so breathe easy. Please punch yourself in the face.

Schmee-El Communications, DEPT. "P", Paw Paw, Mich.

HOP ON THE LECTURE CIRCUIT

DO NOT WAIT ANY LONGER:

Develop a monotone delivery. **SAY SMART THINGS.** Talk about the same tired bullshit the last five yahoos did. Cry yourself to sleep in overpriced hotel rooms. Demand expensive flights. Bore that excited crowd to death. Make jokes about not having enough coffee. Act now.

Fleckman Speaker Training, DEPT. "D-5", Kansas City, Mo.

ALWAYS: Treat yer UPS guy, Mail lady and FedEx dropper-offer like they are gold. They are under the gun, all day long. have a little compassion, you impatient hunk of shit.

UP IN SMOKE: Taking inquiries for successful vaping francise. No idea what is in the stuff, but people still inhale it. Peculiar, futuristic hardware. Got Vape, 126 E. Breckinridge, Louisville, Kent.

THIS SPACE FOR RENT →

"Influence"
"Multiple Impressions"
"Quality Real Estate"

Reach out to us:
DDC ADVERTISING OPPORTUNITIES
Good luck getting a call back!

RETIRE AND BE HAPPY

Why are we working so much? And why the hell are we working with people we hate? We've asked these hardball questions a couple times in our life, made the right arrangements, and then split. Our solution: Do whatever it takes to save a shitwhack, and then up and quit. Self-starters only.

DDC FINANCIAL PLANNING DEPT.

AMERICAN-MADE MEMO BOOKS!

FIELD NOTES

Set of Three
48 Pages Per Book
Graph/Ruled/Plain

fieldnotesbrand.com

COMPUTER EQUIPMENT: Odd lot. Remnants from failed Internet "Cloud" business. Must go. Shitwich Liquidators, 34 Market, San Francisco, Calif.

COOL OFFICE: Marketing Guru needed to fill void and empty office with outdoor clothing company. Must be hip to the needs of 13-25-year-old youth demographic. Here's another excuse to "be down" even though you're probably an aging hag. Be the individual responsible for "Think Tank Atmosphere." Fluff job. Piece of cake. Company credit card. Dank Outerwear, 56 Cascade Drive, Beaverton, Oregon.

FREE LOGOS: Come into our offices and cry your eyes out. Claim economic hardships. Promise a list of shit that never comes to life. Put us in a position where we think that your life depends on us helping you with a logo design. Demand top-level service. Hem & haw. Settle on something. And then we never hear from you again. We still sleep at night, though. DDC Identity Solutions, Stark Street, Portland, Ore.

MIX-N-MATCH DECALS

DURABLE ADHESIVES   YOU CHOOSE

(DEC-01 through DEC-28)

CUT OUT AND MAIL NOW!

CIRCLE DECALS YOU WANT $1.00 PER DECAL

(Cash Only – Do Not Tape Coins)

DDC DECAL DIV.

CUT HERE

FOR THE TAKING: HALF-ASS IDENTITIES

TIRED OF THAT LACKLUSTER LIFE you built for yourself? Here's an easy one for you: *Simply become someone else!* Act like them. Talk like them. Imitate their already-imitated "design style" and schtick. And then, act frustrated and surprised when someone shows how you ripped off "whatever pathetic thing they built on their own accord." **GET CALLED OUT.** Will haunt you forever. Send name and address.

Shapeshifter Identity Institute   Dept. "F-U", Albuquerque, New Mex.

DON'T SEE IT HERE? *Like we care. Why are you reading this shit, anyway?*

COMPLAINTS?

TELL US WHAT YOU THINK We provide space.

01. ....
02. ....
03. ....
04. ....
05. ....

Get Cosmic. And Stay That Way.

Right now, right this very second, we are on a rock, floating in space, revolving around a star, our sun, whose warmth and distance make the conditions on earth possible for life.

And that sun, it's one little lightning bug's ass among some two hundred to four hundred billion stars just in the Milky Way galaxy. And that galaxy, when you pull back, it's just a tiny cluster among other billions of other clusters...

The insignificance is staggering.

We are a speck within a speck within a speck within a speck within a speck.

And what I love most about this stuff: What I'm talking about here is real.

And yet, it blows my mind that people don't have more anxiety about this. I don't fear it as much as I let the unfathomable size and paradoxical realities inspire me.

When I was a little kid, I had a hard time with the concept of eternity. I first learned about it in Sunday school catechism, and it never quite sat right with me. The teacher's odd sense of certitude about heaven, and how you'll go there when you die. Almost clerical in the telling of such a fantastical belief. And yet, the idea of infinite time and consciousness was terrifying. This horrific, haunting idea that, on whatever metaphysical or supernatural plane we were on, we'd go on and on and on ... forever? Enough to make you go mad.

Does the universe have an "edge?" If the universe is expanding since the big bang, what is it expanding into? What's outside of where it's expanding? Maybe it just goes on and on forever? And, whoa, stop for a second and think about this: If it goes on and on forever, that's pretty scary. But what if it just sort of stops? Which one is scarier? Here I go again, and I feel that deafening realization sneaking back up on me: This kind of thinking is shuddersome. And beautiful.

All these years later, I find these mind-bending explorations oddly soothing. At night, falling asleep, I'll read about this kind of stuff. I tried reading Stephen Hawking's *A Brief History of Time* and was lost by the theoretical certainty. My favorite stuff breaks space's mysteries down into simpler abstractions. The simplest math always blows me away the most.

Like this one: Look at a star. The light you see emanated a long, long time ago. It took all that time to get to us, and then back to where it started. The star might've died a long time before we ever saw its light. That kind of stuff. That's *real*.

Chances are, right now, this very second, somewhere in the universe, someone or something is thinking about us, too.

Or maybe it's just us? Some weird little itch inside me thinks that sounds pretty fuckin' pompous. Our little brains concluding we're the only ones? C'mon, humankind, open that thinker and let a little stardust in.

During my presentation when I get to this section, I sort of ask the audience for a show of hands regarding whether or not this reality freaks them out. Oddly enough, maybe a tenth of the hands will go up. That always freaks me out. People just don't think about it? Or they ignore it? Or have bigger fish to fry? Yeah, maybe they do have some grasp on the staggering size and conundrum of the universe but just don't care about it. I mean, mathematically, it's not like we'll ever really know. If it takes us 80,000 years just to travel to the next star at 37,000 mph, well, that's 79,958 more years than I've got to see it happen. Fucking awesome, scary and absolutely mind-blowing.

Since Dad died October 2013, I've found myself digging in deeper and deeper to the idea of mortality. And some idea of an afterlife. Realms unknowable.

Where'd Dad go? Is he still with us? Dust in the wind? Is he out in the ether "somewhere?" Up in heaven with Grandpa Joe, Gramma Josie, Grandpa Ted, Gramma Leo and little Gary? I hope so! At least, that's what I'm trained to hope for.

Or, do bugs have souls? For any of them that I've smashed out of existence, where did that little guy go? My nephew Oliver is five, and has some beautiful theories about spirits and souls. A couple months back, during breakfast, Oliver get's my sister Leah's attention and says, "Your spirit carries your happiness, madness and sadness. And if your spirit leaves when you die, they go inside other people." So Leah asks him, "Who has spirits?" And he doesn't miss a beat, "People, dogs, animals ... anything like that. Even spiders have souls." She stops him and asks, "What is a soul?" And he wraps it up and say this, "Souls are like

little things that carry your spirit. it's just how the truth works in stuff." All of this, coming from a five-year-old. I'll go with his telling. Someday I'll post the movie she took of it. It still chokes me up when he talks about "Papa," which was what he called Dad instead of "Grandpa." My dad LOVED that little boy.

I'm betting that all living things have souls. Hell, all things. I've played a couple of weird guitars that had minds of their own, that's for sure.

I think, on some level, that I'm okay with whatever scenario. If you just die, and that's it? All the more reason to live a good life down here on earth and be a good person. Make good use of your time. I sure as hell am trying.

It's the superstitions that are fear-based that freak me out the most. That's the best way of controlling each other that we can come up with? So harsh and exploitive. Televangelists with jet planes and mansions? Politicians speaking with God one-on-one? In a universe so vast and big, no wonder this bullshit exists. We have no idea, and it's so easy to latch on to some turkey with some charisma, selling your soul to Jesus for easy, monthly payments of $19.99.

I like to think something bigger is at play. If we are just some weird coincidence of the basic elements that mixed together to make life on earth, well, isn't that just incredible? But what if that's also going on in the next galaxy to us? And in all the galaxies out there? Right now, right this very second?

Lots of questions, I know.

Get cosmic.

DDC

Draplin
Design Co.

Pretty Much
Everything

Aaron James
Draplin

File Under:
Staggering Insignificance

246
247

GET COSMIC

The Greatest Dad in the World

Sure is tough writing this one. If I think about it too hard, I lose it and start crying. Dad died on October 13, 2013. We all miss him ferociously. And the idea of how I might never see him again? That's too much for me to accept. I don't like the constructs we've got to pick from. Heaven? Divine rule books? They all feel phony and contrived. Superstition. Folklore. Soothing mechanisms, with such pompous certitude: We'll meet again on the other side. Whatever the deal, I just hope I get to be with Dad again, wherever it is.

It's weird when people write in and tell me that they think they would've liked my dad. The sad part is this: I know they would've LOVED him. He had so much joy to give. Everyone needs a Jim Draplin in their life. That's the kind of guy he was. I shared him the best I could—at my talks, around the shop and on big road trips.

It's been tough disassembling his empire. Dad always used to say, "I just want one of everything!" We used to mess with Dad about being a hoarder. In his defense, he kept all those treasures with big plans. And acted on a good chunk of them. He saw so much potential in all types of stuff and always had cool projects going. He passed that frugal, creative quality on to my sisters and me. We grew up in a home outfitted with oak furniture that Dad rescued from the past. The smell of paint stripper is something I grew up around, constantly. That's where I got my love for the dead stuff out there. You ought to see my dad's sign collection!

What Dad Taught Me
First and foremost, Dad taught me how to laugh, and how to seek out humor in every situation. That's what I miss the most. Years and years of laughter. I'd call home, update Mom on the latest news and she'd say, "Jim, you want to talk to Aaron?" And Dad would reply, "Who?"

Dad taught me to pack a car. One of his finest laments was, "All I do is rub and pack." To clarify, that was rubbing the backs of all us kids, and then packing the car. Family vacation shit. Dad knew how to pack a car. How to consolidate things, then refine the whole mess. Or how to fix a car: "If something is wrong with my car, the first thing I check is to see if the license plate is on tight."

Or how to do things right the first time. Be it checking the oil, building a shelf or cutting the grass a certain way, Dad had an expert opinion and wouldn't stand for half-assed work. Plus, he showed me the benefits of using way too much wood glue on stuff. And finally, how to stand up for one's self. My dad didn't take any shit. One time, we were at the Grand Traverse Mall looking for a parking spot. Dad noticed a guy getting into his car as we rolled by him. Dad pulled ahead, and as the guy was backing out, another guy turned into the lane at the other end and raced up as Dad was backing up to grab the spot. Dad pulled in, and as we jumped out, the guy said, "Hey, that's my spot!" And Dad said, "We were waiting for the guy to pull out. It's ours." The guy then said something about how we shouldn't be surprised if something has happened to our car when we come back out. Dad didn't miss a beat: "I know you. You go to my church. You so much as touch my car? I'll kill ya." The guy just sped off, swearing and we laughed and made our way in to do some "Christmas shoplifting." Oh, Dad.

Bend the Rules, Man
Once the ceremony was over for my high school graduation, they had a party for the class at the school. There was food, photo booths and gambling tables to win prizes. Dad waved my group of buddies over and we saddled up to a blackjack table. "Okay, guys, just shut the fuck up and don't make any commotion." Each kid had a little baggie with a couple chips in it to start with. Before any cards were dealt, Dad reached into his bank of chips and gave each of us a stack. "Winners! All of you!" he exclaimed, and we proceeded to clean out the table. Every now and again, another volunteer parent would come by to check on the bank. And Dad would shake his head. "These guys are cleaning me out!" For a bunch of years after that night, I'd have random classmates come up to me and say stuff like "Your Dad. Wow. He got me a microwave oven that night!" That was my dad.

His Nightly Tingle
Dad used to brush his hair each night. He had quite the mane. He'd pontificate about something his barber Ron Damer from Bellaire told him years earlier. "You gotta stimulate the follicles," he'd say as he was pulling the comb back. "You gotta do one hundred brushes a night. It's good for the scalp." He'd freely administer this technique to all of us. I'd sit up against the couch between his knees and he'd brush my scalp and it would hurt like hell! I'd be grimacing in pain and he'd inquire, "See, it tingles, right?"

Dad Caught Me a Ball
It's a rare thing to catch a ball at a major league baseball game. It's another thing when you tell your kid you are going to. This is Dad's "Babe Ruth moment" of sorts.

I was lucky enough to record a couple conversations with Dad before he bit the dust, and here's my very favorite one, as told by Dad: "Okay, uh, it was Polish American Night and my brother Tom and I took all you kids to a Tigers game. During the whole course of the game, I kept telling you, 'Aaron, I'm gonna catch you a ball.' And I was drinking. The more beers I had, well, I still didn't catch you a ball. And you kept saying, 'Dad, when are you gonna catch me a ball?' And I'd say, 'I'm gonna catch you a ball, don't worry about it.' I believe they were playing the Cleveland Indians. It's the sixth or seventh inning, and we're sitting there, and all of the sudden, this foul ball tipped back, and a ball came over my head, hit the girders at Tiger Stadium, bounced on the cement, I stood up, grabbed the ball and a guy behind me grabbed my hands…no, cupped my hands! And I ripped it out of his hands and go, 'Here you go, Aaron.' That's the way it ended. I later found out that guy was really upset. We got to talking, you know, and I found out he was a doctor. I guess I was supposed to give in. I don't think so. It was one shot in a million and I handed it right to you. That's it. And I didn't…I don't think I had a beer in my hand. Maybe I let go of the beer and caught the ball? It's kind of vague. The beers, have, uh, 'clouded the memory' over the years."

On His Way to Sainthood
Jim Draplin knew how to ferret out a good deal; junked the finest of secondhand stores; cut his "killer pizza" with gigantic scissors; rooted for the Wings, Wolverines, Tigers and even the Lions; shared an EXTENSIVE catalog of jokes; gave out free beer chips at the Cedar Polka Fest; loved his old cars; always had a hundred beers in the fridge; decorated cakes; made birdhouses; loved his wife, children and grandchild, Oliver. Oh: He hated paying for taxes, parking, gas and ice.

My dad played Santa for thirty years, for everything from family appearances to corporate events to proud municipal gigs. And he'd donate all the funds to charities. Even in tough times. Dad would help out guys at the tool shops he sold to who were having a hard go. Just quick $10 and $20 spots. My dad taught us how to be thankful for the health and abundance in our lives and how to give to those in need. A contagious compassion.

I had my dad for 39.9 years, and that little fact alone is enough to make things okay. Instead of being sad that Dad's gone, I'd rather spend the time remembering how fuckin' awesome he was. The latter is just so big. Come back, Dad.

DDC

Draplin
Design Co.

Pretty Much
Everything

Aaron James
Draplin

File Under:
One Cool Dad

248
249

Fall Portrait 2005

So we head into Target or wherever. There's miffed moms holding cute babies in communion dresses in line with us. Dad and I wait patiently for our turn, request a "wooded scene," and sit down for the big shot. The lady photographer stops, looks at us and she's visibly pissed. She grumbles a bit and goes digging into a toolbox, pulling out an Allen wrench set. Turns out Dad and I didn't fit in the "vertical format" she was on such a roll with that fine morning.

SANTA JIM

"Santa Jim" card of business. 2009.

I MET
"Santa Jim"
Traverse City, Mich.

CERTIFIED HELPER OF
Santa Claus, North Pole

"Certified Helper" card of business. 2009.

"SHITCHYAH!"

The infamous portrait of Dad. Shows up on toolboxes and dusty rear view windows from Boyne City to Bend. 2001.

THIS MOMENT OF SPIRIT BROUGHT TO YOU BY THE DRAPLIN DESIGN CO.

"SHITCHYAH!"

—JIM DRAPLIN, MICHIGAN, U.S.A.

PROUDLY PRINTED IN THE U.S.A. – DRAPLIN DESIGN CO., NORTH AMERICA

BUMPER STICKER
LUGGAGE, DEN, GARAGE, LEAN-TO, RV
BEND BACK AND PEEL OFF

"DAD" BY
NATE UTESCH

Shitchyah!" bumper sticker of spirit. The idea is to take a stack into some roadside tricket shop, put them on the rack with everything else and walk out. 2015.

Dad was a good sport with all the stuff I'd make with his face on it. Truth is, he loved the coverage. He would pass out stickers, cards and buttons to his customers on his sales route, buddies at his morning coffee spot and wide-eyed kids questioning his loose affiliations with the North Pole.

I loved celebrating Dad on the site and in my talks. Hell, Dad loved to celebrate Dad. He was a good target to bring levity to an otherwise potential stuffy design climate. Dad always kept things fun, and I loved that part of him. I've tried to apply that same lighthearted spirit to the way

I work and the atmosphere in the shop. Dad made sure guests were comfortable. He was quick on his toes to make sandwiches, crack open beers or whip up a Vegan pizza for visiting scooterist P.J. Chmiel. A true champion of hospitality and humanity, Jim Draplin forever!

The Greatest Mom in the World

Dad was always a bit of a ball hog with the limelight. Mom all too often took the backseat, but know this much: She ran the show. Mom was the boss and kept us rug rats in line. Someone had to!

A Girl from Livonia, Michigan

Mom grew up quick. The oldest child of seven, she helped her mom and dad with the raising of her siblings. By the time she was on her own, her littlest brothers, Kevin and Terry, were five and seven. When she met my dad in 1968, he was brought into the mix and instantly became a de facto big brother in the family. She had so much responsibility at a young age that certain sacrifices were made with her schooling and free time. When I was making my first college decisions, Mom's guidance sealed the deal. She didn't have the same opportunities.

How Dad Met Mom

If this story doesn't illustrate what an animal my dad was, then I don't know what the hell to tell you. The tale of how my parents met starts like this: They were in line at an Oktoberfest in the Detroit area. You know how we've got the hoppy artisanal beer craze sweeping the nation these days? Back in the late '60s, it was Oktoberfest stuff. Dad being Dad, he cut the beer line right in front of her. Mom being Mom, she told him to take a hike, and he sweet-talked her enough in order to stay in line. They then chatted a bit, and he said, "See this Löwenbräu mug? This is my last one from the brewery tour I went on there. I want you to have it." Dad had gone to Munich the year before, and came back with big tales about exploits at the Hofbräuhaus and of a big Porsche purchase. So he gives her the little plastic mug off his lapel. Mom is touched by this sweet exchange, and before they know it, they are traveling, married and then figuring out what to do with my arrival. A couple years go by, and one day Mom is digging through some stuff and finds a big bag of the little plastic mugs.

The peace offering that got it all going. Actual size.

What Mom Taught Me

Mom taught me not to walk away from things. I was way behind on schoolwork and had to read *To Kill a Mockingbird* for a class discussion that coming Monday. Of course, I put it off for weeks, and the Sunday morning before the big day, I let it slip just how much I still had to read. Mom mobilized, and I wasn't allowed to skateboard or watch any TV that day. I hunkered down and read the whole book in one sitting. For a peckerhead fourteen-year-old with all the distractions in the world, that was an accomplishment. She'd check in on me every couple hours, and we'd talk about commitments and responsibilities and "working smart." That's one of the first times I can remember when I had to really dig deep and make it happen for myself. A little thing, sure, but I attribute the determination she fostered in me as a crucial skill set I'd call upon to stick out the carny pizza jobs, mean-spirited tree trimming bosses, brutal Alaskan summers and, ultimately, some tricky design jobs. I had taken the jobs, and it was up to me to finish them.

Mom and Dad had some tough years financially in the early '80s, and I never really understood the severity of it. I had a loving mom and dad, in a safe, structured, creative environment and had more than enough Lego, *Star Wars* toys and Adventure People to keep me busy. My sisters and I never felt it. I'm still impressed by that, all these years later.

Mom's a careful, wise decision maker. You have to understand, my dad's antics were so explosive and outlandish, someone had to balance things out. With every big decision I've made, I've always sought my mom's guidance to help me along.

That Kind of Mom

It was tough at first when we moved to Traverse City. I missed my life in Central Lake and felt a bit isolated in our new subdivision on Deerfield Lane. That early summer of 1988, I was always on my Haro FST freestyle bike, learning tricks in the driveway. One morning, Mom shows me an ad in the newspaper: The Haro trick team was coming to Traverse City! And the demo started in a couple hours! So excited. Mom drove me down to Brick Wheels on 14th Street and dropped me off. It's threatening rain and there's the team, setting up two quarter pipes and a couple bank ramps. Big California pros Dennis McCoy and Mat Hoffman are ripping the place up. Local ripper Adam Brown was there holding his own, too! That was my first sticker toss and I came home with a stack. The coolest.

That summer, Mom bought me my first real skateboard. I broke my Variflex one afternoon and was devastated, calculating the time until the next birthday or holiday. She saw how much time I was spending with it, and surprised me and said, "C'mon, let's go get you a new one!" So we whipped down to City Bike Shop and I got a Brand-X "X-Con." Just like that. One of the coolest moments of my life. It wasn't just the Haro demo or skateboard stuff. It's that she was looking out for us, and championing our interests. And this was the first time I recognized it. This is where Mom won me over to our new life in Traverse City, and I started to understand and love our big move.

Kick Out the Jams

My favorite thing Mom gave to me was her love of music. Growing up in Detroit, Mom saw the MC5, the Stooges, Mitch Ryder and a young upstart called Bobby Seger. Fascinating stories about Hash Bash in Ann Arbor, the Grande Ballroom in Detroit and seeing the Stones in '72 just add to the lore of being one of the lucky ones to have a "cool mom." We grew up with records playing. Neil Young, Joni Mitchell and Crosby, Stills & Nash. I remember Mom explaining the lyrics to Billy Joel's "Goodnight Saigon" to me. Such a heavy song. I was just nine and getting my first grasp of the horrors of war. Mom took me to see Bob Dylan in Portland in the fall of 2014. Couldn't recognize any of the songs, but to go see Dylan with your mom? The best. As the book went to print, Mom was out seeing Jackson Browne for a string of dates. Not bad for a seventy-year-old grandma— with one hell of a record collection!

Thank you, Lauren Draplin

I'm one of the lucky ones to have cool parents. That's the simplest way to put it. Good, caring, laughing, loving people who provided so much for our family and others around us. What a privilege. I have worked hard to be able to help those around me. One year, I bought Dad a big television. The next, it was helping Mom with new carpet. As this book goes to print, I'm planning a bit of a coup to pay off their house in Traverse City. That's my proudest achievement, being able to help out Mom and Dad over the years. Just like they did for my sisters and me. And I did it with graphic design, on my own terms.

No matter how rough things are in Portland or wherever I am, one call to Mom and everything gets better. I've had that my whole life with my mom. I don't know what I'd do without her. Here we go. Here come the waterworks. Love you, Mom.

Blowin' raspberries with Mom. Check out her killer Keith Richards hair. Summer 1974.

Mom keeping Chrysler together in the mid-'60s.

Summer of love! 1969!

Mom forever! 2015.

The World's Largest Appreciation List

This book is dedicated to Mom and Dad.

My Very Top Tier Human Beings: To Lauren Draplin for giving birth to me, sound advice, caring, MC5 records, incomparable spaghetti sauce and being the greatest mom in the world to Leah, Sarah and I, and so many others. To Dad for being the animal you were/are/will forever be, care packages sent out west, loose advice, endless laughter, going to bat for me in ninth grade and rubbing my back all those times. To Sarah Draplin for fitting me with audiologist grade ear plugs, enduring my brotherly love and taking great care of Mom and Dad. To Leah Draplin for moving out to Oregon, watching Gary, smuggling slices into the shop and mending my orange windbreaker. To Leah Draplin & Jacob Ashley for doing such an incredible job with the light of our lives, little Oliver James Ashley. To Oliver James Ashley for making me see the cosmos a little different way and making me slow down a bit to play more Lego. To Leigh McKolay for patience, grace, the thoroughest of questioning, square meals, airline middle seat sacrifices, giving a shit, roadtrip planning, the greatest birthday days ever and for putting up with me. To Ewan Martin for being the coolest teenager I know. *Squad.* To Christine Steele for being my coolest cousin, hands down. To John "Goo" Phemister and David Nakamoto for partnering with me at Wilderness, listening to my brand-building bullshit, doing lunch runs and allowing us to have the mellowest shop in Portland. Obie, Mia and Smokey, too. Wish Gary was here.

My Buddies: Eric Campbell, Derek Denoyer, Bry Aleshire, Chad Smith, Johnny White, Evan Rose, Dale Alan Dixon, Ryan "Ryno" Simonson, P.J. Chmiel, David Nakamoto, John "Goo" Phemister, Eric Lovejoy, Cameron Barrett, Damien Barrett, Jim Coudal, Jess Gibson, Mark Phillips, Mike Buckmaster, Eric Hillerns, Arlie John Carstens, Fasil Debeb, Fred Green, Pat "the eYe" Bridges, Jeff Baker, Larry Nuñez, Mike "Chief" Nusenow, Mark Sullivan, Jay Floyd, Matt Cooley, Ben Cooley, Travis Yamada, Jared Eberhardt, Brad Scheuffele, George Kleckner, Martino Fumagalli, Sean McMahon, Mike Whitehead, Vince Lavecchia, Roger Cameron, Josh Higgins, Hugh Weber and Matt Kass.

Beginnings in Detroit: The Steele side of the family: Gramma Leo, to Uncle Terry for taking great care of my mom, John Bell, Diana Fournier, to Uncle Kevin for teaching me guitar riffs, Auntie Kym, Jeff & Brandi Steele, to Uncle Pat for turning me on to the Smithereens, Aunt Judy, Scott, Shelley & Brian Steele, to Aunt Mary for those dumplings, Melodie Younce, to Uncle Mike for buying me a Powell Peralta "Bones" sweatshirt in 1989, Auntie Lisa, Jacqui, Kelsey & Mike Steele, Cousin Jeanie & Calvin Arrend ("Coolest Hair" award!), Mike, Matt & Julie Sadler, Uncle Jess Watson & Aunt Jean Watson, Phil & Suzanne, T.J., Tim & Stephanie Steele, Uncle Larry & Aunt Joan, Sue, Jerry, John, Kelly & Colleen Cane. The Draplin side of the family: Grandma Josie, to Uncle Tom for squeezing generations of children's feet, to Auntie Barbara for millions of kisses, to Tom Draplin in New York for being the first artist I looked up to, to Patrick Draplin for taking me to Northland and stacks of magazines, Tracey Draplin, Tim Draplin, Michael Draplin, Chico Shuda, Uncle Bob, David, Judy, Derek & Hannah Draplin, Brian Draplin, Jeff Trudell, Loanne Trudell, Gary Olson, Mike McQuade and Sybil Wilson.

Growing Up in Central Lake: John Prote, Tom Prote, Denny, Diane, Drew & Kellen Youngedyke, Gary, Susie, Stephie & Ronnie Mortensen, Brent & Janine Coaster, Bill & Ella Coaster, Jennifer McDowell, Robbie Dow, Jesse & Tara Denherder, Will, Linda, Dahna, Shana & Damian Lockhart, Dick, Lana, Tara & Zack Stoneburner, Randy, Mel, Chad & Erin Miller, John Miller, Nathan Miller, Alicia, Collin, Jackson & Henry Swanson, Deb Pickren Zerafa, Alan, Stewart & Emily Hickman, Brad Glasgow, Betty Glasgow, Andy Montgomery, Mary & Dani Spence (can still hear your dad's awesome laugh all the way up our street), Ann Westlund, Dennis, Dean & Mike Richardson, Bill Sutherland, Eric Sutherland, Sunshine Rowley, Christy Parker, Juliette Thiel, Wayne Rascon, Harry, Sharon, Angel & Chad Pletcher, Andy Hinz, Thomas Hinz, Tim Buffman, Wally Disbrow, Mary Bowden, Young's Party Store, Bachmann's General Store, Brownwood, Oscar Feliu, Marty the drummer, Ryan Newton, Corbin Newton, Second Chance Shoot (brass rat, Summer 1985), Andy Davis, Matt Davis, David Ryan, Rusty & Sherry, Jennifer Velding, Otto Beebe, Treeter Johnson, Gary Johnson, Roger Barnes, Bill Truscott, Bill Kemnitzer, Kyle Fredrickson, Chip Ames, Dennis Windish, Keith Malkowski, Jason Grafenauer, Robbie Bachmann and Dan Lorenz.

Formative Years in Traverse City: Eric, Megan & Hannah Campbell, Derek, Alexis, Olivia, Jude, Noah & Norah Denoyer, Bob & Helen Denoyer, Bry, Tracey, Eva, Lachlan & Baron Aleshire, Leon & Linda Lichty, Chad Smith, Mike & Paulette Smith, Johnny & Kate White, Harry Brumer, Mike Buckmaster, Brian, Barbara, Casey & Robbin Moore, Dan & Ruth Goldsmith, Mark, Deb, Jordan, Shelby & Jake Newhouse, Rene & Jackie Hoenshied, Ron & Teri Kraft, Hedy, Steve, Celia, Ray, Lauren, Will, Norah, Max, Evan, Shaun, Sarah, Tess, Cash, Kristin & Mitchell McKolay, J.K. Egloff, Lisa Hemming, Courtney Kelley, Barbara Saxton, Elon & Jenn Cameron,Mike, Mia & Arlo Lombrana, Amy Lyons, Brian Johnsen, Travis White, Travis Harrett, Kevin McIntosh, Matt Miner, Matt Hale, Ben Oswald, Jeremy Oswald, Steve Brydges, Tad Lautner, Jason Thompson, Scott Shumsky, Travis Thompson, Toby Thompson, Chad Waller, Jeremy "Bug" Belanger, Jeremy Bannon, Chad Jordan, Cal, Laura & Thor Steinorth, Jeremiah Goike, John Galnares, L.J. Gannon, Jon Dayton, Jim Arnold, Jim Alef, Jim Bellar, Jeff Jennings, Julie Jennings, Ryan Selby, Justin Selby, Don Buckmaster, Matt Hathaway, Julie Niehardt, Dave Bloxsom, Scott Casey, Nick Raffaele, various Crusted Creations peoples, Tim Burch, Scott Bendickson, Matt Bendickson, Jason Bendickson, J.T. Kroupa, Chris Williams, Jane Durga, Christy Holder & Brian Joynt, Julie Soloman, Emma Rosi, Brett Sipperly, Chuck Sipperly, Mark Shaub, Joel, Nikie, Brock & Maddie Sanderson, Katie Snell, Joel Pollock, Jason Lile, Steve Terry, Chad Brigham, Andy Powers, Nicole Nolan, Mark Gardner, Chad Whipp, Rick Harker, Sarah Tutlis, Megg Carney, Jeff, Natalie, Maren & Hazel Bryne, Becky Saxton, Aerin Madeline Sweeny, Abigail Phillips, Emily Walter, Michele Macintosh, Matt McGuire, Sam McGuire, The Barn Ramp, Corey Hooper, Darrin Smith, Ian Doten, Aron Doten, Pete Richards, Northwestern Michigan College peoples, Norm Averill, Jill Hinds, Doug Domine, Ken Marek, Steve Ballance, Carey Baribeau, Jay Harrington, Dave Marek, C.J. Girard, Mark Steinorth, Duncan, Shannon & Daphne White, Gary Howe, T.J. Carroll, Cory Luna, Nick Fisher, Jay Moncel, Shane Jackson, Ben Shaub, Eric DeCaire, Chris Timm, Mike, Sarah & Rowan Albaugh, Shawn Lichty, Nels Veliquette, Pat Montgomery, Nic Fisher, Jennifer Plamondon, C.J. Weber, Michael Poehlman, Jake Bright, Ralph Schultz, Bob Galoci, Jeff Dunlop, Jeremy Carter, Dana Venhuizen, Matt Donner, Tom Shumar, Michael Lloyd, New Moon Records, Alfie Crocker, Erick Darrow, Edgar Barlan, Bryan Hodge, Brian Klaft, Brandon Woods, Deron Holzschu, Brian Fawcett, David Vanocker from Union Street, Travis Laug, Ben Ludka, Dan McCormick, Cary Paton, Tony Peltier, Phil Detloff, Mark Anderson, Jeff Swan, Matt Hedlund, Branden Bearinger, Lisa St. John, Amy Mayville, Mark Forton, Laurie Powers, Mary Sabin, Christine Zoutendyk, Paul Zoutendyk, Alison Weise, Cher Charest, Ron Boyle, Phil Leiffers, Aaron Oleson, Greg Jakoski, Chris Kogelman, Jim Pearson, Chris Town, Scott Gordon, Gordo Snowboards, Jason Nagy, Deanna Ziemba, Sylvia Dana, Angela, Lydia, Reyna & Mischa O'Hearn, Sean & Stacy O'Keefe, Nate Griswald, Amy Appelhof, Mike King and all those dogs, Misha Corbin, Lane Corbin, Jesse Den Herder, Mike Forester, Samuel Valenti, Peter, Michelle & Phoebe Baker, Troy Deschano, Liz Gelfusa, Nick Kostandinos, Tony Wolski, Andy & Kristy Maniotes, Nick Panagakos, David Dodde, Greg Fugate, Melissa Misekow, Bill Sirl, Michael Moore and Autoworld.

Moving Out West to Bend: Travis Yamada, Chris Fink, Paul "Pablo" Peterson, Aaron Mallory, Scott Elliott, Lovie Bucknell, Cary Wright, Liz Boiseneau, Joey Boiseneau, Dan & Jackie Vance, Jason Knight, Allison Fauver, Jay Floyd, Aaron Loewe, Ross Wordhouse, Scotty Gramer, Tyler Fradet, Robbie Benson, Kevin, Angie, Avery & Taylor Porterfield, Jason Lilly, Barfly, Katie Duckett, Mary Burnham, Tucker Fransen, Bryan Haglan, Mike Yannoni, Bryan Ballantyne, Rob "Turtle" Hamilton, Suddy & Nicole Helzer, Debbie Gorman, Chris Metcalf, Nick Shuder, Jeff Mollencop, Allie Plute, Louie Fountain, Cory Rudishauer, Sean Donnell, Jamie Donatuto, Mark Rudin, Aimee Rudin-Brown, Rob Brown, Chris Laws, Matt & Pam Leonard, Pat & Vic Malendoski, Angela Jolly, Lael Gregory, Neill Duggan, Markie Wirges, Josh Dirksen, Jason McAlister, Marcus Egge, Chris Owen, Kale Gray, Jason Shurtz, Andrew Crawford, Jeff Lopez, David Sypniewski, Frankie Bilello, Dulce Frommer, Kristin Chadwick, Andy Tullis, Chris Hasler, Gary & Georell Bracelin, Tyler Dewilde, John Peterson, Dave Harrison, Smoked Monkeys snowboard shop, Clark Shelk, Winter Wave Bill, Matty Cloniger, Kris Jamieson, Shaun Little, Eric Todd Keeney, *Volcano Magazine*, Matt Baker, Dana Mackenzie, Leslie Blok, Rising Star Futons, Jim Ratzman, John Stewart, Carey Christman, J.D. Platt, Jess Smith, Hillary Neun, Jenny Bowden, Lorre Jones, Adam Haynes, Travis Carter, Little Scotty, Sparky, Ricky Batts, Karen Cheatham, Cersten Cheatham, Evil Sister Saloon, Kyle Phillips, Trevor Phillips, Robbie Morrow, Shon Peterson, Pete "Coolshit" Ingraham, Jake & Missy Hauswirth, Exit Real World, Robin Reinbold, Kiersten Sorensen, Miki Keller, Dirk Gragert, Tait Roeloffs, Quinn Shields, Chris "Bagler" Cunningham, Jessie "Chewy" Graham, Jubal Reynolds, Obadiah Sweitzer, John Musch, Bailer, Quality Snowboards, Joe Beebe, Mike Pugh, Allister Schultz, Peter Butsch, Rio Davidson, Phelan Curry and Witt Wear peoples.

That One Mt. Hood Summer: Eric Jahnz, Fran Russo, Joe Beebe, Christine Sperber, The Dirties, Chris Coyle, Matt Collins, Marc Derego, Ahmon Stamps, Rich McKay, Chuck Pearce, Todd Richards, Brian Besold, Jason Lilly, Athena, Ross Wordhouse, Carey Wright, Lael Gregory, tons of Bozeman dudes and Dave Rogers.

Alaskan Summers: Fred Green, Matt Leonard, David Brust, Latouche house roommates, Tyler Fanning, John Crews, Matt Adelizzi, Woody Hummel, Wes in the living room, Pam-Pam, Raven Mosher, Amber Peterson, Ian Kingston, Dan Vance, John Marshall, Priscilla Hensley, Mike & Kara Kirkpatrick, Kira Protasel, Ian Geroux, Chris Tower, Robert Kineen, Brown Sugar Bill, Gary, Hannah Kohler-Kelly, Rayette Martin, Seth Wilson, Jesse Syverson, Cameron Gay-Webster, Monte Wornath, Steven Martz, Shannon Rose, Philippe & Natalie Janicka, Karla Scarlatti, Burton Hill and Tressa Lynn James.

My Time in Minneapolis: Ryan "Ryno" Simonson, Jon, Amy, Jack & George Baugh, Michael Gaughan, Jason Miller, Charles Spencer Anderson, Laurie DeMartino, Todd Piper-Hauswith, Kurt Frederiksen, Bill Thorburn, Dan Black, Michael Godfrey, Matt Rezac, Aaron & Katie Dimmel, Becky Haas, Jerry Allan, Santiago Piedrafita, Jan Jancourt, Pam Arnold, Ben Clemence, Colette Gaiter, Sean McKay, Isaac Berenson, Bryan Haker, Greg Lang, Kym Macfarlane, Mickey's Diner in St. Paul, Lauren Nicole Pierce, Susan Seeley Roe, Josh Journey-Heinz, Will Staehle, Andrew Jenkins, Ryan Vulk, Karen Oh, Chad Kloepfer, Sab Chuyangheu, Anastasia Faunce, Helena Keeffe, Miki Araki-Daly, Teko Ralokwae, Jon & Alyssa Thomas, Caitlin Hurd, Jamie Pulley, Justin Braehm, Jovaney Hollingsworth, Sheraton Green, Erik T. Johnson, Karen Heineck, Haley Drab, Susan Anderson, CSA Design peoples, Todd Piper-Hauswirth, Kyle J. Hames, Andrew Blauvelt, Emmet Byrne, Walker Art Center peoples, Derek Schille, Joe Kral, Aaron Horkey, Jim, Mary, Melissa, Kris, Matt & Angela Okins, Justin Bakse, Kevin Wideman, Kevin at the Ideal Diner, Geoff Schley, Ted Halbur, Target peoples, Emmet Klocker, Tommy Kronquist, Dan Madsen, Mike Davis, Malichansouk Kouanchao, Jodi Milbert, Wes Winship, Ben Lafond, Joseph Belk, Burlesque North America peoples, Dan Ibarra, Michael Byzweski, Aesthetic Apparatus peoples, Greg Lang, Scott from Cal Surf, Steve Lastavich, Rama Hoffpauir, Derek Schille, Joseph Fickle, Greg Hubacek, Gip Matthews, Ivan Stegic, Ten7 peoples, Deb Littlejohn, Charlie Ross, Sally Ginsburg, Justin Israels, Dan Brisse, Oarfolkjokeopus Records, Eric & Nicole Olson, Process Type Foundry, Ben Levitz, Chank Diesel, Geoffrey Warner, Jackie Meisel, Alchemy Architects, Cory Loven, Sam Anderson, Eric Hamline, Sharon Werner, Tommy, Bob Chris, Slim and Paul.

San Juan Capistrano: Pat "The eYe" Bridges, Jeff, Lilly, Mika & Milo Baker, Mike "Chief" Nusenow, James Sullivan, Cody Felter, Dutch & Karen Schultz, Scott Howard, Justin Frost, Norb Garrett, Chris Smith, Steve Metcalf, Kevin Meehan, Lance Dalgart, Kim Stravers, Will Pennartz, Ruth Hosea, Randy Ward, Marty Ward, Kevin Back, Dave Reddick, Porter Fox, Chris Smith, Lauralyn Loynes, Inna Cazares, Ricky Irons, Jeff Canham, *Snowboarder Magazine* peoples, Gus Buckner, George Covalla, Travis Wood, Ryan Runke, Nate Christenson, Dave Appel, Cindy Lum, Bryan Knox, Ricky Melnik, Brandon Parrish, John Dewey, Kevin Keller and Chris Hotell. There's no one to really thank from Laguna Niguel. I didn't talk to one person there. That dick who lived next to me? Barely acknowledged me the 22 months I was there. So weird. Wait, there was a cool lady at the Target across the street. That's one person, I guess. So yeah, her.

Making Portland My Home: John "Goo", Fran & Remy Phemister, David Nakamoto, Fred Green, Mark Phillips, Dale, Betty, Moses & Otis Dixon, Eric & Carolina Lovejoy, Rod & Katie Snell, Jay & Heather Floyd, Jess Gibson & Kariena Ertsgaard, Chris Coyle, Maureen Pandos, Cory Grove, Mike Whitehead, Shawna Bilicic, Benjamin Holm, FINEX Cast Iron Cookware Co. peoples, Ben Cooley, Nancy Knutson, Lou Bank, Eric & Lisa Hillerns, Chuck, Kendra & Lillie Pearce, Ryan Coulter, Neil Dacosta & Sara Phillips, Shelby Menzel, Scotty Wittlake, Fasil Debeb & Melissa Henderson, Jennifer Sherowski, Kelly Stoecklin, Sierra Domaille, Willy Vlautin & Lee Posey, Sean Oldham, Dave Harding, Dan Eccles, Paul Brainard, Richmond Fontaine, Tyler & Melissa Ashcraft, Archie Mort, Michael Godfrey, Rick Gould, Bob & Marta Scales, Robby, Kim, Jack & Leo Hottois, Piney Kahn, Dean Gross, Chris Soli, Ben & Julie Munson, Josh Nelson, Sunny Burch, Edgar Morales, Kirk, Katie, Sophie & Hayley James, Matt Montagne, Gary Vossenkemper, Susan Sheldon, Cinco Design Office peoples, Kevin Nimick, Jeremy Matherly, Jason, Sarah & Archer Sturgill, Andy Forgash, Mark, Eulalie, Leila & Virginia Welsh, Mitch Morse, Greg Hennes, Kale Grey, Kate Bingaman-Burt & Clifton Burt, Will Bryant, Ben Vickery, Tina Snow Le, Martie Flores, Michael Buchino, Sunny Burch, Lee Burns, Andy Blumberg, Fro Waters, Scotty Conerly, Dan Connor, Jen Davidson, Jennifer Armbrust, Jason Resch, Thor Drake, SeeSee Motorcycles, Vin, Megan & Owen LaVecchia, Justin Lewis, J.D. Hooge, Instrument peoples, Bill Deyak, Benji Wetherley, Kharma Vella, Poler peoples, Chlöe Eudaly, Reading Frenzy, Orion Landau, Matt Jacobson, Mikey McKennedy, Greg Meleney, Danava, Jonathan Felix-Lund, Matt Brown, MiniMini, Sizzle Pie peoples, Relapse Records peoples, Scott Flaster, David Schriber, Greg & Robin Schmitt, Aaron Lee, Noah Lee, Matt, Leigh, Sophia & Lily Capozzi, Chad DeWilde, Brian "Gonzo" Gonzales, Matt Eller, Bill Morrison, Feel Good Anyway, Robin Reinbold, Seth Neefus, Casey Neefus, Red Clouds Collective peoples, Taylor Brubaker, Tim Karpinski, Jason Bayne, Dave Shiff, Shane Flood, Pox, Mark Warren-Jacques, Carey Quinton Haider, Cole Cooper, Jesse House, Molly Katzman, Jim Felt, Jody Hills, Griffin Felt, David Wien, Austin Will, Ryan Lynn, Kurt Foster, Jeremy Dietz, Danny Faccinetti, Jim Golden, Ray Gordon, Jesse Grandkoski, Paul Miller, Chris Reed, Jordan Hufnagel, Margi Getzloff, Chris Dunn, Danger Ehren McGhehey, James Rexroad, John Sherman, David Sullivan, Aaron Beam, Bryan Giles, Red Fang, Whitey McConnaughy, T.G. Firestone, Bobcat Taylor, Eric Olson, Lord Dying, Steve Carder, Kevin Garrison, The Lloyd Winter Family Awesomeness Explosion, Caleb Yarian, Casey Neill, Peter Yue, Craig Thompson, Topher Sinkingson, Mary Kysar, Tara Shirriff, MakeLike peoples, Josh Barrett of Create Legal, the world's most-patient accountant Will Price, Kisar Dhillon and his Pain Cave, Liz Dhillon, Yvonne Perez-Emerson, Chris, Gretchen & Eero Hotz, Jeff Bartel, Trevor Graves, Mark "Lew" Lewman, Nick Sherman, Morgan, Carey Garland, Eugene Good, Genna Osbourne, Adam Bagerski, Gerrit Creps, Joel & Leticia Kleinberg, Nemo Design peoples, Jason Chmielewski, Dave, Jessica & Sebastian Seaone, Brandon Shoessler & Deanna Rizzo, Leo Battersby, Amen Teter, Kirsten Blair, Steve Hoskins Jr., Wille & Rebekah Yli-Luoma, Heart Roasters peoples, Jak Green, Jake Schimpke, Adam Garcia, Duane King, Ian Coyle, Tyler & Elsa Lang, Abby Larsen & Caton Gates, Jeremy Pelley, Fritz Mesenbrink, Ben Parsons, OMFGCO peoples, Cabel Sasser, Neven Mrgan, Panic peoples, Tony Secolo & Kelly Coller, Tom Sessa, Roberta Lavadour, Jill Bliss, Jered Bogli, Louis & Molly Carlton, Dave Allen, Dennis Kegler, Elissa Kevrekian, Scott Leveranz, A.J. Lightfoot, Ellen McFadden, Andy Morris, Evan Kinkel, Graham Mueller, Sally Murdoch, Britta Nelson, Tsilli Pines, Joe Preston, Mike Scherba, Marcus Swanson, Elisabeth Charman, Ethan Allen Smith, Paul Anthony Troiano, Molly King, Rumblefish peoples, Jennifer Armbrust, Stacy Barber, Kristin DeVries, Chris Streger, Jason Murray, Ami Voutilainen, David Rae, Allen Hardin, Sam Baker, TEDxPortland peoples, K Mikey Merrill, Jona Bechtolt, Claire L. Evans, Yacht, Andy McMillan, Andy Baio, XOXO Festival peoples, Eric Mortensen Aeronautics and Space Administration, Richard Perez, Jennifer DeRosa, Eric & Melanie Samsel, Bob Fuckin' Smith, Ben Fee, Mark Perusich, Chris Erickson, Johnathan Eggiman, Julie Beeler, Chris McCoy, John Bohls, Isaac Brock, Modest Mouse, Ryan Baldoze, Glacial Pace Records, Andy Bollock, Aaron James, Josh Kenyon, Colby Nichols, Steven Kasprzyk, Brett Stenson, Jolby Partners peoples, Ben Pruess, Matthew Carroll, Dan Cronin, Andria Robbins, Chris Owen, Kevin Lee Florence, Jim & Shanta Prescott, Chris Prosser, Erik Railton, Preston Strout, Brian Reed, Bryan Fox, Stephen Fox, Drink Water peoples, Brad Simon, Sarah Hollowood, J.P. Devries, Sean Donnell, David Beauvais, Janet Freeman, Jessica Funaro & Ralf Youtz, Jeevan Singh, Kevin English, High Cascade Snowboard Camp peoples, Tim Windell, Sam Huff, Tanner Goods, Chelsea McLagan, Anthony Lakes Ski Area, Brooke Geery & Jared Souney, Chris Brunkhart, Matt Donahue, Matt Patton, Tactics, Saul Koll, Koll Guitars, April Cottini, Matt Drenik & Sorenne Gottlieb, David Burn, Tim Wiesch & Carly Davidson, Chris Gunderson, Nic Isfeld, Leslie Contreras, Chris Gunderson, Loren Hall, OSI Screenprinting peoples, Greg Newland, Rindi Davodsky, Jeff Miller, Travel Portland peoples, Ben Farver, Argonaut Cycles, Pam Hill, Julie Kahn, Kevin & Amy Eichner, Steven Macdonald, Jackie Mathys, Pete McCracken, Scott Vandehey, Burnside Digital, John Martin, Rachel Cotton, Emily Olivia, Daniel Clancey, Annie Regnier, Vince Sliworksi, Corey Smith, Lisa Frisch, Cori Jacobs, Trevor Solomon, Amy Ruppel, Dan Sorcinelli, Tijani Stewart, Kristin Johnson-Waggoner, Dave Shaley, Kevin Steigerwald, Crowd Compass, Bud Fawcett, Hand Eye Supply peoples, Bobby Meeks, Thomas Morris, Nate Bedortha, Kyle Beck, Truen Pence, Zaech Bard, Brian & Jess Craighill, Mark Hegarty, Damion Triplett, Michael Hernandez, Pascal Fritz, Scott Vandehey, Nick Parish, Lee Foltin, Kelly Halliburton and Fred & Toody Cole.

The Gang at Field Notes: Jim & Heidi Coudal, Michele Seiler, Bryan Bedell, Joe Dawson, Matt Jorgensen, Steve Delahoyde, Shea Cahill and Joe Blanski, Tyler Culligan, Skyler Wankel, Daniel Zarick, Darren Marshall, Amy Rowan and Jen Schuetz, Scott Foresman, Shelley Knight, Edwin Morris, Hannah Hague, Spencer Coudal, Travis Coudal, Brody Coudal, Girard Sweeney, Alex Rumsey, Jeremy Anderson, Fiona Bradley, Liam Bradley, Raegan Fingerman, Jenna Fingerman, Grace Coudal, Isabelle Coudal, Max Norris, Jarek Moorman, Christoph Szpunar, Caitlyn Verduzco, Matthew Miele, Bogdan Sipic, Alex Gilbert and Chelsey Van Naarden.

Alabama: Matt & Melissa Harris, Cary Norton, Scott Peek, Brian Scott Teasley, Roy Burns III, Reed Watson, Matthew Reed and Belle Adair. **Arizona:** Mike Sadler, Joey Burns, the entire Calexico discography, Ryan Trayte for putting together one boss Tucson breakfast, Karen Zimmermann, Angel Delgadillo for that hot towel shave I got while Dad watched, Dennis, Cindy & Felix Fesenmyer and Paul Howalt. **Northern California:** Alex Birch, Josh, Ramona & Leo Higgins, Justin, Elizabeth & Henry Pervorse, Eli Atkins, Jez Burrows, Nick Wilson, Facebook Analog Research Laboratory, Eric Richter, Chuck Platt, Greg Shapleigh, Casey Potter, Brendan Murphey, Giro peoples, Chad Hilton, Jason Schulte, Hatch, Jessica Hische & Russ Maschmeyer, Maria Kaiser, Jordi Sanchez, Kevin, Brooke & Maizy Ashley, Nic Kaiser, Marlee Kaiser, Ali Kaiser, Noah Stokes, Bold Development, Chuck & Stephanie Prophet, Justin Hostynek, VJ Varoon Jain, Amanda Marsalis, Jason Munn, Kenny Likitprakong, Eric Powers, Hobo Wine, Ben Zotto, Trevor "Big T" Martin, Upper Playground SF, Chris Wilmoth, Sean Walling, Soulcraft, Geoff Wagner, Bill Zindel and Benny Gold. **Southern California:** Arlie John Carstens, Jared Eberhardt, Milo Ventimiglia, Russ Cundiff, Chad Dinenna, Andy Laats, Nikki at Nixon, Mark Cruz, Dan Mac, Yolanda, Noah & Naomi Rosen, Mark, Tevis & Miles Michaylira, Jardine Hammond, Patrick Keeler, Embry III, Leslie, Embry IV & Ennis Rucker, Todd & Lindsy, Camden & Reef Richards, Ben Oswald, Lee & Leah Crane, Sinuhe Xavier, Jason Filipow, Shepherd Fairey, Paul Brown, David Yow, Mikey Leblanc, Scotty Zergebel, Chris "Coop" Cooper, Dave Benton, Nate Mendel of the Sunny Day Real Estate and Foo Fighters, Brett Wiley, Dave England, Ben Fee, Dave Benton, Jamie Muehlhausen, Beau Colburn and that tour of Capitol Records, Woo, Chris Fairbanks, Jim & Jane Hutchins, Hutcho Technologies, Mark Gardner, Wahoo's fish tacos #2 Chicken Bowl, Wylie Gelber, Dawes, Kevin Zacher, Nate Deschenes, Tawnya Schultz, Brad Alband, Rob Campbell, Kyle Clancy, Ryan Clemens, Dave Cuzner, Matt Ogens, John Jackson, Eric Jackson, Mike Bagnuolo, Dawn De La Fuente, Kyle Dewitt, Dustin Ortiz, Chris Engelsman, DiAnne Epperson, Noreen Morioka, Annie Fast, P.J. Fidler, Brian, Stacie & Oona Foote, Brian Garofalow, Ari Evan Gold, Scott Hultgren, Nicole Jackson, Dave Lee, Mark Wierenga, Cory Lorenzen, Andrew Gibbs, Jessica & Michael Deseo, Grant Wenzlau, Celina Pereira, Rebecca Bedrossian, Aaron Okayama, Peter McBride, Ricky Melnik, John Melotti, Travis Millard, Moses Aipa, Christopher Dooley, Michael Dooley, Clayton Summers, The Other Fudge, Mel Kadel, Joel Muzzey, Michele Rozo, Chris Teig, Joanne Stafman, Otis "O" Bartholomew, Dale Rehberg, Randy Ronquillo, Matt Swanson, Tim Swart, Tracy Thielman, Abe Vizcarra, Alissa Walker, Tom Montessaro, Ryan Hughes and Joe Westerlund. **Canada:** Allan Lorde, Steve St. Pierre, Janine Vangool, *Uppercase Magazine*, Dano Pendygrasse, Craig Medwyduk, Ian Gillies of Telegramme, T.J. Schneider, Chris Bayer, Cam Hoff, Harley Finkelstein, Christopher Lobay, Shopify, Alex Warburton, Ronn Dunnett, Shaun Hughes, Colin Whyte, T.J. Schneider, Shawn Pucknell, Jacqueline Poole, Cory Bayers, Riley Cran, Lost Type and Harley Finkelstein. **Chicago:** Christen Carter, Busy Beaver peoples, Justin Peddycoart, Matthew Stiffler, Mig Reyes, Max Tempkin, Justin Ahrens, Brooks Ruyle, Mode Project peoples, Ben Arditti, Don Guss, Cody Hudson, Steve Juras, Jason Kunesh, Aaron Salmon, Public Good Software, James Hughes, Jay Ryan, Ben Schneider, Carlos Segura, David L. Kinney, Max Wastler, *Made Right Here*, Steve Albini and Shellac. **Colorado:** George & Jackie Kleckner, Mike, Charlene, Holden & Hudson Basher, Marcy, Jason & Merrick Corcoran-Neerhof, Gary & Shelley Aleshire, Jeff, Hallie, Jack & Chloe Wastell, Scott Shumsky, Jason "Genghis Kern" Wedekind, Dave Amirault, Brad Fayfield, Matt Harvey, *Freeskier* peoples, Dave Graves, Paul Miller, Trent Bush, Elysia Syriac, Mike Daniel, Nic Drago, Cody Goldsmith, Brian Goldsmith and Susie Floros. **Delaware:** Andy Cruz, Rich Roat, Ken Barber, Brian Awitan, Allen Mercer, Luong Nguyen, Adam Cruz, Jeremy Dean, Ben Kiel (who doesn't know how close to death he was, messing with me that one time), House Industries peoples. **Georgia:** Henry, Sarah & Scarlett, Bun-E Carlos, & David Lee Roth Owings, Travis White, Jessica Brennan, Jonathan Lawrence, David Sizemore, Jason Craig, Bill Green, Russ Pate, Weir + Stewart peoples and Mike Jones. **Florida:** Charlie Trefry, Nick Sambrato, Hogan Birney, Mama's Sauce peoples, Josh "Hydro" Smith, Levi Ratliff, Kendrick Kidd, Diego Guevara, Carl Smith, Karen Kurycki, Clark Orr, Jenica Cox, Mark & Janeen Piotrowski and Neil Rankin. **Idaho:** Bart Kline, Jeremy & April Lanningham, Greg Goulet, Paul Whitworth, Matt Whitlock, Mark, Liz, Sascha & Roger Sullivan, Dannii McLin and all members, past and present of Built To Spill and Caustic Resin. **Indiana:** Nate Utesch, Brandon Roosa and Zombie Yeti. **Iowa:** Dana, Vanessa, Emiline & Zeke Lechtenberg, Chrissy Jensen, Bradley & Cate Dicharry, Mitch Putnam and Jerry Roberts. **Kansas:** Dominic Flask, Derek Helms, Tad Carpenter, Nick Naparstek and Junk Boys. **Kentucky:** Adam Hedgepeth and Will Oldham. **Massachussets:** Roger & Sarah Cameron, Marc Derego, John McCormack, Christopher Michon, River Brandon, James Fox, Fritz Klaetke, Tricia Byrnes, Darryl Norsen and Darryl Norsen's record collection. **Maryland:** Robert Generette III and Jeff Givens, Southern Skies Coffee. **Missouri:** Dan Padavic, Tad Carpenter and Doug Wilson. **Montana:** The Chris, Julia & Sid La Tray Experience. **Nebraska:** Nick Evans. **New York:** Tom, Ella & Owen Draplin, Cameron, Bonnie & Olivia Barrett, Damien, Katie, Casey & Maggie Barrett, Larry Nuñez, Dan, Niamh & Huck Cassaro, Matt, Karen & Fox Cooley, Eric Baker and his daily blasts, Debbie Millman, Gary Hustwit, Jeff Lopez, Tina Roth Eisenberg, Tattly peoples, Frank Chimero, Jessi Arrington, Studio Mates peoples, John Gall, Gabriel Levinson, Sarah Massey, Abrams Books peoples, Chip Kidd, James Victore, Tim Hoover, Jessica Karle, Ben Pieratt, Graham Clifford, Michael Beirut, Ian Smile, Jesse Kaczmarek, Christa Skinner, Billy Bacon, Ethan Bodnar, Elliott Curtis, Skillshare peoples, Rob Botsford, Brant Weil, Chris Bray, Krik Bray, Billykirk, Shawn Liu, Jason Santa-Maria, Mandy Brown, Peter Buchanan-Smith, Robin Hendrickson, ATO Records, Joseph X. Burke, Mick Collins, Billy Fowks, Scott Dadich, Billy Sorrentino, Paula Scher, Michael Perry, David Schwarz, Erik Karasyk, HUSH Studios, Mark Kohlman, McKee Floyd, Tim Lahan, Sue Lee, Ted & Jodi Leo, Jessica Kaplan, Adam Michaels, Prem Krishnamurthy, Patrick Miller, David Rees, John Hodgman, Chad Riley, Paul Safsel, Pete Scheira,

Mark Dudlik, Debbie Millman, Beth Venn, Pierre Stravinski, *Esquire*, Sarah Shallbetter, Scott, Shelley & Brian Steele, Madeline Sweeny, Brant Weil, Art Jones, Great Jones, Michael Williams, A Continuous Lean, Mark Weaver, Jason Noto, Doug Cunningham, Morning Breath Inc. and Lynn Gadson. **New Mexico:** Brad Gobdel, Andrew Campo, Walter, Jesse, Hank and Saul. **Nevada:** Chris Carnel, Mr. Moto, Collin Martin, Rusty Johnson, Amanda & Matt Lofink, Robbie Sell, Terry Mulvihill, George Butorac and Clarissa Begay Alesevich. **North Carolina:** Lenny Terenzi, Phil, Heather & Ellis Cook, Brad & Stella Cook, Merge Records, Josh Oakhurst, Skookum Digital Works, Greg Howard and Josh Leutz. **South Dakota:** Hugh, Amy, Emerson & Finn Weber, Jason Alley and Joe Shaeffer. **South Carolina:** Gil Shuler, Gene Crawford, Giovanni DiFeterici and Jay Barry. **Ohio:** Jason Snell, Ohio Knife, Chris Glass, Scott Moore of Moore Wood Type, L.C. Angell, Craig Heimbuch, Grace Dobush, Amy Conover, *HOW* magazine peoples, Don Pendleton, Aaron Sechrist and Joseph Hughes. **Oklahoma:** John Moreland, Bob "Dale", Lauren & Henry Fraser, George Salisbury, Wayne Coyne, Michael Ivins, Steven Drozd, Scott Booker, Flaming Lips peoples, Sandip Patel, Bit Confused, Cage App and John Hammer. **Pennsylvania:** Steve & Adrian DeCusatis, Jay Fanelli, Andy Beach, Mikey Burton, Carli Dottore, Ryan "Ryco" Connelly, Nik Greenblaat, Steven Fuller, Woolrich, Melissa Laine Scotton and Chuck & Tara White. **Tennessee:** Jody Collins, Kurt Wagner & Mary Mancini, Lambchop, Kyle Norwood, A. Micah Smith and Terrence Chouinard. **Texas:** Bart Kibbe, Josh Kramer, Geoff Peveto & Kristine Pauls, Rocketsauce, Decoder Ring, Design Ranch, Marc English, DJ Stout, Russell Toynes, Industry Print Shop, Tim Kerr (That one time I got a handshake in the doorway of Emo's), Juan in a Million, Christian Helms, Helms Workshop peoples, Chris Bilheimer, Jay Sauceda, Justin David Cox, Bobby Dixon, Office peoples, Noah Marion and his bad-ass goods, Chris Brown, John Tullis, David & Marcellina Kampa, Ben Jenkins family unit, Eric Lawhorn, Josh Leutz, Bryony Gomez-Palacio & Armin Vit. **Vermont:** Evan & Maja Novovic-Rose, Cris, Alison & Francesco Dabica, Lance, Vanessa, Xavier, Oscar & Isadore Violette, Mike Ponte, Seth Butler, Cristin Denight, Zach Nigro, Dave Cory, John Cavan, Seth Neary, Mike Gratz, Jesse Huffman, Lukas Huffman, Mike Paddock, Michelle Ollie, Randy Torcom, Luis Calderin, Shem & Rebecca Roose, Eli Lesser-Goldsmith, Cory McDonald, Bobby Hackney Jr., Julian Hackney, Urian Hackney, Paul Comegno, Steve Williams, Rough Francis, Death, Scott Lenhardt, Jake Burton, Bernie Sanders and Luis Guzman. **Virginia:** Brad Puck, Caleb Harris and Work. **Utah:** Dan, Jillian & Grey Christofferson, Tonino & Liz Copene, Dave Doman, Rob Marthis, Ethan Stone, Tech Nine, Nate & Andrea Silverstein, Jason "J2" Rasmus and Stan Evans. **Washington:** Brad & Bailee Schueffele, Jenn Long & Erik Nelson, Joe Florence, Bob "Gumby", Kayse & P.J. Gundram, Blue & Jackie Montgomery, even Johan, Lisa, Mac & Milo Malkoski, Mat & Stephanie Savage, Kyle Lunneborg, Scott "Sweaty" Downing, Joel Fraser, Mike "Styk" Styskal, Mark "Fank" Fankhauser, Jynn Hintz-Romano, Trevor Bradley who used to break dishes over his head in Alaska, Gabe Carter, Jason Guyer, Juno guys, Don Clark, Invisible Creature, Jimmy Clarke, Ian Doten, Adam Gerken, Woody Hummel, Jesse Ladoux, Jeff Kleinsmith, Sub Pop Records, Jeff Galbraith, Jessica Lu Lovett, Pete Saari, Mike Olson, LibTech peoples, Ken Birge, Assembly, *Frequency Magazine*, Sean Tedore, Scott Mavis, Norm & Myla Nelson, Mark Noterman, Kyle Phillips, Andrius & Akane Simutis, Adam Zacks, Kellie Talbot, Jon Schlect, Scott & Natalie Sullivan, Russell Winfield, Annette Viehelmann, Hunter & Al Waldron, Taylor Haynes, Doug Foss, Gary Winberg, Ephraim, Chui, Chris Hanis, Tim & Jenn Zimmerman, Chase Gallagher, Kyle Phillips, Matt Gormley, John Bowles, Art Chantry, Mark Arm and Tad Doyle. **Wisconsin:** Jeremy Oswald, Daniel Holter, License Labs, Justin Vernon, Kyle Frenette, Chris Messina, Thomas Wincek, Andrew Fitzpatrick, Ben Derickson, Matthew Skemp, Jon Mueller, Damien Strigens, Field Report, Matt Rohloff, Dylan Wells, Nate Garn, Jim Moran, Bill Moran, Stephanie Carpenter, Tootsie Marie Sommers, Mari Dawson, Light House Inn, Edward Haydin, Ryan Thacker, Jim Van Lanen Sr. and Hamilton Wood Type Museum. **Wyoming:** Willy from Bluebird, Travis Rice and Gary Hansen. **International Situations:** Martino, Claudia & Giulietta Fumagalli, Rhonnie, G.P., Darin Bendall, Brendan Dawes, Trey Cook, Jane Durga, Carmela Fleury, Jur Anepool, Hans Vershooten, Rob Hosieth, Brian, Evelyn & Natalie Johnsen, Angela Jolly, Fredrik Öst, Magnus Berg, Ged Palmer, Andrew Sekora and David Benedek.

Around the Shop: Miguel "Mike" Ortega the UPS guy, John Dombroski the mailman, Josh Bartlemay the mailman and Kamal at the UPS store on Sandy. **Merch People:** Sean McMahon, Rich Graham at Big Promotions, Nic Isfeld, Chris Gunderson, Leslie Contreras, Loren Hall, O.S.I. Screenprinting peoples. **Screen Printers:** Sara Thomas, Nick Wilson, Courtney Phillips, Thomas Jennings, Nate Puza and Ben Gunter from the Half and Half, Columbia, SC. Mike Davis, Jodi Milbert, Wes Winship, Ben Lafond from Burlesque of North America, Minneapolis, MN. Nick & Fran Bittakis, Kevin Abell, Ben Miller and Eric Zamarripa from Seizure Palace, Portland, OR. Dan Padavic from Vahalla, Kansas City, MO. Tony Diaz, Bart Kibbe and Bobby Dixon from Industry Print Shop, Austin, TX. Mama's Sauce, Brown Printing, Graphic Arts Center, Premier Press, Field Notes printers in Chicago **Printers:** Tyler Ashcraft, Anne Frank, Mike Scherba, Bob Wisner, Studio On Fire, Keegan & Meegan and Andy Stern from Diesel Fuel Prints. **Paper:** Jerry, Brian and Kim, and all the generations of the French Paper Company. Meeting Jerry: Me: "How many people work here?" Jerry: "About half." Jamie Saunders from Neenah Paper. **Adobe:** Annemarie Ballard, Terry Hemphill, Laurel D'Angelo, Anubhav Rohatgi, Dan Cowles, Paul Lundahl, Elissa Dunn and Adobe peoples.

Artists: Robert Williams, Coop, Evan Hecox, Barron Storey, Drew Struzan, Bob Peak, Paul Brown, Travis Millard, The Other Fudge, Ralph Steadman, Aaron Horkey, Pushead, John Baizley, Raymond Pettibon, Jay Ryan, Dan Black and Tim Lahan. **Skateboarding Artists:** Jim Phillips, Jimbo Phillips, Vernon Courtlandt Johnson, Todd Bratrud, Andy Jenkins, Marc McKee, Sean Cliver, Drew Friedman, Don Pendleton, Joe Castrucci, Andy Howell, Ron Cameron, Mark Gonzalez, Chris Pastras, Thomas Campbell, Ed Templeton, Lance Mountain, Garry Scott Davis, Neil Blender, Wes Humpston, C.R. Stecyk III and Tod Swank. **Photographers:** Birney Imes, Ansel Adams, Mary Ellen Mark, Bill Owens, Walker Evans, Glen E. Freidman and Charles Peterson. **Designers:** Saul Bass, Paul Rand, Lance Wyman, Verner Panton, Art Chantry, Richard Danne, Bruce Blackburn, Ivan Chermayeff, Tom Geismar, Millton Glaser, Seymour Chwast, Massimo Vignelli, Max Huber, Eliot Noyes, Herb Lubalin, Lester Beall, Louise Fili, April Greiman, Joseph Müller-Brockman, Chip Kidd, James Victore, Burton Kramer, Jim Ward-Morris, everything from Joe Castrucci and Jason Munn. **Record Stores:** Jackpot Records, Music Millenium, Everyday Music, Crossroads, Missisippi Records, Green Noise, 2nd Avenue Records The Record Exchange, Shake It Records, Electric Fetus and Reckless Records.

A Gigantic Thank You To: Everyone who interviewed me for magazines, blogs, student reports or whathaveyou. Everyone who put me in a magazine. *HOW Magazine* the first time, *HOW Magazine* the second time, *Creativity, Uppercase, Entrepreneur, Smith Journal, Print, Refueled, Uncrate, The Great Discontent* and *Juxtapoz*. All the podcasters who put me on their podcast! Way too many to list! Everyone who put me on their radio show: Sean Cannon from FPK Louisville, Jay Allen from Saskatoon Community Radio, CBC in Saskatoon and April Baer from Oregon Public Broadcasting's *State of Wonder*.

Fine Retail Establishments Who Carry DDC Merch: 2nd Level Goods, Alpine Modern, Anthology Madison, Brew City Online, Brooklyn Frame Works, Canary Collective, Canoe, Cross Timbers, Dos Manos, Frog and Toad, Hinterlands, Landshark, Loyal Supply Co., Lushdive, Midcoast Modern, Nash Frame, Neighborly, Nofo, Notegeist, Poler, Reading Frenzy, Shibe Sports, Shop The Fox, Telegramme, Touch of Modern, Jason Sajko, Upper Playground Portland, Trevor "Big T" Martin, Upper Playground San Francisco, Volume One, Why Louisville, Wuxtry Records and Yardsale.

DDC Merch: Everyone who bought some DDC merch! There's no way I can list all you animals here! But I will say, Kyle Caird takes the cake.

Everyone Who Let Come Tell My Story:

2007 001. Andrew Campo from Santa Fe Design Week, Santa Fe, NM.

2008 002. Mark Notermann from AIGA Seattle "Hills Have Eyes", Seattle, WA.

2009 003. Jason Resch from PNCA, Portland, OR. 004. Piney Kahn and Jason Resch from Cut & Paste, Portland, OR. 005. Seth Engman from AIGA Minnesota Design Camp, Nisswa, MN. 006. Charlie Trefry from Geekend, Savannah, GA. 007. Brandon Deloach and Brandi Lafleur from Dallas Society of Visual Communications, Dallas, TX. 008. Eric Hillerns from Designspeaks speaker series, Portland, OR.

2010 009. Kate Bingaman-Burt from Show and Tell, PSU, Portland, OR. 010. Kristin Munson, Maresa Thompson and Ari Savedra from AAF New Mexico, Albuquerque, NM. 011. Karol Tompkins from Richmond Ad Club, Richmond, VA. 012. Lee Waters, Kristy Pennino and Jason Ellison from Valencia Community College, Orlando, FL. 013. Conor Lawrence, Alice Ross and Veronica March from AAF Minnesota, St. Paul, MN. 014. Reilly Brennan, Liz Gelfusa and India Cleveland from AIGA Detroit, Detroit, MI. 015. Harlan Bloomer, Matthew Willemson and David T. Rogers from Minnesota State University Mankato, Mankato, MN.

2011 016. Erin Hamilton, Vered Mares, Mike Kirkpatrick and Sini Salminen from AIGA Alaska, Anchorage, AK. 017. Bryan Butler, Katie Sheahan, Nick Evans from AIGA Mizzou, Columbia, MO. 018. Kelsey Tyler from Portland Center Stage, Portland, OR. 019. Ryan Skinner, Terri Mitchell, Greg Laubach, Mark Robillard, Svante Nilson, Kathy Stevenson, Justin Skeesuck, Summer Jackson, Petrula Vrontikis, Petra Ives and Bobby Buchanan from AIGA San Diego Y16 Design Conference. 020. Joshua Kramer, Bart Kibbe, Meredith Phillips from Creative Workers Union, Austin, TX. 021. & 022. Lisa Kruse from AIGA Kansas City, Kansas City, MO. 023. Nick Evans from AAF Lincoln, Lincoln, NB. 024. Jeff Finley, Joseph Hughes and Go Media from Weapons of Mass Creation Conference, Cleveland, OH. 025. Samantha Hackett from Art Director's Association of Iowa, Des Moines, IA. 026. Jon Baugh, Jason Miller and Michaela Weir from Target Spark speaker series, Minneapolis, MN. 027. Steve DeCusatis from "Draplin Lectures In Philly", Philadelphia, PA. 028. Patrick Carter and Karen Kurycki from AIGA Jacksonville, Jacksonville, FL. 029. Eric Hillerns, Don Clark, from "Spit Swap" Seattle & Portland, Portland, OR. 030. Keri Newman from when I spoke in London, London, UK. 031. Brendan Dawes, Kate Towey, Gina Hewitt from when I spoke in Manchester, Manchester, UK.

2012 032. Mark Dudlik, Andy Cruz from AIGA Arizona, Phoenix, AZ. 033. Jillian Cole, Linda Orcelletto, Ted Taylor, John Dempsey from the Bend AAF, Bend, OR. 034. Letica Kleinberg from Pacific Northwest College of Art, Portland, OR. 035. Elysia Syriac, Kate Weright from AIGA Colorado, Denver, CO. 036. Andrew Blauvelt, Emmet Byrne and Dylan Cole from the Walker Art Center Insights speaker series, Minneapolis, MN. 037. & 038. Tsilli Pines, Paul Searle and Tina Roth Eisenberg from Portland Creative Mornings, Portland, OR. 039. & 040. Gene Crawford, Gil Shuler and David Griffiths from AIGA South Carolina, Columbia, SC. 041. Amie Beausoleil, Steve St. Pierre and Jeevan Singh from Create Ottawa, Ottawa, ON. 042. & 043. Shawn Pucknell, Lindsay Munro, Lisa Walters from FITC Toronto, ON. 044. Jon Johnson and Princess Twin Cinema, Waterloo, ON. 045. Mike Cober, Marga Lopez, Mark Busse from the Society of Graphic Designers of Canada, Vancouver, BC. 046. Evan Rose, Rough Francis, Alex Lalli and the crew at Signal Kitchen, Burlington, VT. 047. Ryan Stemkoski and Sean Finley from the Spokane Advertising Federation, Spokane, WA. 048. Matt Dobson, Kayla Mount, Elizabeth Spalding and Jaclyn Mullin from the Louisville Graphic Design Association, Louisville, KY. 049. Jessica Kuhn, Bryn Mooth, Matthew Porter, Von Glitschka, Heather Griffin, Lyn Menke and Megan Patrick from the HOW Design Conference, Boston, MA. Jamie Saunders from Neenah Paper when I got to sign all those posters at the HOW Design Conference, Boston, MA. 050. James Fox from the Somerville Library, Somerville, MA. 051. Patty Mar Simmons, Joslynn Anderson, John Condemi, Rick Tomich and Val Lehnerd from the Las Vegas AIGA, Las Vegas, NV. 052. Cam Hoff and Adam Goetz from the Calgary Inter-Agency Coalition, Calgary, AB. 053. Rick Turoczy, Joshua Reich, Mark Zusman and Matt Manza from the Portland Digital eXperience, Portland, OR. Trevor Solomon from MusicFestNorthwest, Portland, OR. 054. Armin Vit & Bryony Gomez-Palacio from the Brand New Conference, New York, NY. 055. Tim Lee from AIGA Salt Lake City, Salt Lake City, UT. 056. & 057. Andrea Lisle from the Memphis Brooks Museum of Art, Memphis, TN. 058. Matt Allison from Think Tank Conference, AIGA Nashville, Nashville, TN. 059. Bradley Dicharry from the University of Iowa, Iowa City, IA. 060. LeeAnn Eddins, Cedar Rapids-Iowa City AAF, Cedar Rapids, IA. 061. Dana Lechtenberg from Cedar Valley AAF, Cedar Falls, IA. 062. Shannon Murphy and Greg Dietzenbach from Dubuque AAF, Dubuque, IA. 063. Cameron Koczon from Brooklyn Beta, Brooklyn, NY. 064. Jonathan Hughes and Kim Panthers from the Ad Club of Buffalo, Buffalo, NY. 065. Yvonne Perez-Emerson from SketchXChange, Portland, OR. 066. Noah Rothschild, Darren Marshall and Kelsey Kreiling from Doejo, Chicago, IL. 067. Matthew Jacobson from Digitas, Chicago, IL. 068. Andy McMillan from Build Conference, Belfast, IRE. 069. Fredrik Öst from Yay Festival, Stockholm, Sweden. 070. Jason Alley and Lane Shull from AAF Black Hills, Rapid City, SD. 071. Rob Duncan from AIGA San Francisco at the California College of Art, San Francisco, CA. 072. Eric Powers, Brian Moose and Anna Prokhorova of the Citrix Design Summit, San Jose, CA. 073. Jamie Sexton of the Portland Advertising Federation, Portland, OR. 074. Rhajer Cameron, Jennifer Dziekan and William Decoteau from the Christmas party at LEGO Systems Inc., Enfield, CT.

2013 075. Carolyn Sewell, Ashleigh Smith from AIGA DC, Washington, DC. 076. & 077. Carol Whaler, Sean King, Graham Clifford from Type Director's Club, New York, NY. 078. Sean Rodham and Jeremy "Jerms" Lanningham from AIGA Boise, Boise, ID. 079. Adam Johnson, Maggie Kantor from Savannah College of Art and Design. 080. Christopher Schmitt, Kristi Peters and Ari Style from InControl Conference, Orlando, FL. 081. Philip Thepkaysone and Josue Olivas from UT Arlington Student Group, Arlington, TX. 082. Stephanie Newman and Meta Newhouse from Montana State University, Bozeman, MT. 083. Hugh Weber from OTA Sessions, Sioux Falls, SD. 084. Brad Clemonson from from Fargo AAF, Fargo, ND. 085. Chris Lewman and Butch Rigby from Brand Lab, Kansas City, KS. 086. Brian Johnson, Colin Robertson from AIGA Reno/Tahoe, Reno, NV. 087. Lisa Apolinski, Sean Selvey and Anna Cearley from NewSchool of Architecture + Design, San Diego, CA. 088. Noreen Morioka, Aaron Gleen, Diane Grajeda, Eric Martinez, Jason Adam and Brittney Backos from AIGA Los Angeles, Los Angeles, CA. 089. Lori Shields and Teri Hamburger from AAF Omaha, Omaha, NB. 090. Nicholas Burroughs from AIGA Nebraska, Omaha, NB. 091. Eric Raasch and Ruth Ann Scott from South Dakota Advertising Federation, Sioux Falls, SD. 092. Shawn Pucknell, Lisa Walters and Andrew Fraser from FITC Toronto, Toronto, ON. 093. Adam Smith from Rochester Institute of Technology, Rochester, NY. 094. Gene Crawford, Giovanni DiFeterici and Jay Barry from Converge SE, Columbia, SC. 095. Mike Jones and Simeon Hendrix from Creative South, Columbus, GA. 096. Sean Wilkinson and Chris Avantaggio from AIGA Maine, Portland, ME. 097. Alton Lowry from Made By Few Conference, Little Rock, AR. 098. Terry Hemphill, A.J. Joseph, Cari Knowlton, Annemarie Bellard, Sarah Eaton, Brenda Sutherland and Ken Mortara from AbobeMAX, Los Angeles, CA. 099. Cordelia Norris from AIGA Knoxvile, Knoxville, TN. 100. Adam Martin from AAF Lexington, Lexington, KY. 101. Kevin Brindley, Kimberly Diedrich and Benjamin Gelnett from AIGA Charlotte, Josh Oakhurst from Skookum Digital Works, Giovanni Ulloa from Ally Bank, Charlotte, NC. 102. Sharon Teng and Justin Pervose from MailChimp, Atlanta, GA. 103. Dominic Flask, Ben Redington, Doug Stucky, Melissa Carduff and Tammy Cox from Wichita AIGA, Wichita, KS. 104. Shawn Johnston and Shannon Fisher from Interlink Conference, Vancouver, BC. 105. Tobias Berblinger from the Curiosity Club of Hand-Eye Supply, Portland, Ore. 106. Jennifer Remsik and Jim Remsik from MakeShit Conference, Madison, WI. 107. Jeremy Taylor from Vans, Cypress, CA. 108. John Godwin from Great Falls Advertising Federation, Great Falls, MT. 109. Ellie Kemery from Makerhaus, Seattle, WA. 110. Ali Palmerson from AIGA San Antonio, San Antonio, TX. 111. Andy Rich, Tyler Swanner and John Luu from AIGA Houston, Daniel Atkinson from Contemporary Arts Museum Houston, Houston, TX. 112. Bart Kibbe and Josh Kramer from AIGA Austin, David Kampa, Marcillina Kampa and John Tullis from McGarrah-Jessee, Austin, TX. 113. Matthew Flick from the School of Advertising Art, Kettering, OH. 114. LeAnne Wagner, Brad Plastid from AIGA Cincinnati, Jason Snell and warmongers from Ohio Knife, Cincinnati, OH. 115. Katie Sczublewski and Sandra K. Theis from the AAF Central Minnesota, Mary Bruno from Bruno Press, St. Cloud, MN. 116. Jan Jancourt, Kerry Morgan, Katrin Loss and Deeno A. Golding from Minneapolis College of Art and Design, Minneapolis, MN. 117. Bonnie Siegler, Armin Vit, Kathleen Budny, Lucy Andersen, Andrew Blauvelt, Rick Valicenti, Laurie DeMartino, Charles S. Anderson, Marian Bantjes, Jessica Hische, Mike Perry, Laurs Beckwith, Emmet Bryne, Josh Silverman, Aidan O'Connor, Elaine Bowen, AIGA100 Chairs from AIGA National, Minneapolis, MN. 119. Kate Bingaman-Burt from Show & Tell, Portland State University, Portland, OR. 120. Had to cancel the Honolulu show due to dad kicking the bucket. 121. Val Head and Jason Head from Web Design Day, Pittsburgh, PA. 122. Nick Turner from TopCon, Chattanooga, TN. 123. Ron Myers, Josh Tuck from Ron Myers Design Events, Fort Wayne, IN. 124. Douglas Brand, Steve Quinn, Charlene Smith from Seek Conference, Northern Illinois University, Dekalb, IL. 125. Sandip Patel and Rukmini Ravikumar from AIGA Oklahoma, Oklahoma City, OK.

2014 126. Chris Muñoz and Amy Gawronski from Symantec, Cupertino, CA. 127. Josh Higgins, Kelly Tran, Hannah Fletcher and Maria Giudice from Facebook, Menlo Park, CA. 128. Suzzane Powney, Jude Landry from Mississippi State in Starkville, MS. 129. Karen Zimmerman, Kelly Leslie, Seandean K. Anderson and Carrie M. Scharf from the University of Arizona School of Art, Tucson, AZ. 130. Porter Haney, Mark Johnson from, Mollie Andrade, John DiMarco, Joe Mahon and Justin Thorpe from Tech Cocktail in Las Vegas, NV. 131. Mihali Stavlas, Silke Eze, Evan Carroll, Rick Satcher, Stan Phelps from High Five Conference, Raleigh, NC. 132. Rosario Martinez-Cañas, from the New World School of the Arts, Miami, FL. 133. Mackenzie King, Jack Storey from CCAD Mind-Market at the Columbus College of Art and Design, Columbus, OH. 134. Jennah Lear and Jamie Windebrenner from AIGA Cleveland, Cleveland, OH. 135. Jacqueline Woods, Harley Rivét, Jarita Greyeyes and Kelsie Fraser from FUZE Conference, Saskastoon, SK. 136. Randy Hergott, Ryan Schmidt, Jay Allen, Debra Marshall and Chris Morin from Saskatchewan Design Week, Saskatoon, SK. 137. Chris Provins, Ken Bautista, Seth Hardie and Kane Tchir from Hunt & Gather, Edmonton, AB. 138. Meghan Arnold, Sadie Short, Kali Nikitas, Erik Spiekermann from TYPO SF, San Francisco, CA. 139. David Rae, Vin LaVecchia, Sam Baker from TEDx Portland, Portland, OR. 140. Krystal Hinckley, Jared Schafer and Jean Dahlgren from Sage College, Albany, NY. 141. Doug Cheever, Jill Orsburn, Katie McCormack, Erin Maddox from AIGA Milwaukee, Milwaukee, WI. 142. Gene Crawford, Giovanni DiFeterici and Jay Barry from ConvergeSE, Columbia, SC. 143. Karli Petrovic, Bridgid Agricola, Amy Conover, Gary Lynch, Alicia Capetillo from the HOW Live Conference, Boston, MA. 144. Scott Harris from Columbia AAF, Columbia, SC. 145. Joey Herzberg from AAF Augusta, Augusta, GA. 146. Cameron Duthie, Christopher Slevin of the Meat Conference, Aberdeen, SCT. 147. Steven Kasprzyk and all the kids who listened to me ramble over at Portland State University, Portland, OR. 148. Anthony "Ant" Sanders, Christian Manzella and Joel Kilby from GIANT Conference, Charleston, SC. 149. Jim Moran, Bill Moran, Stephanie Carpenter and volunteers from the Hamilton Woodtype Museum, Two Rivers, WI. 150 Jason Shults, Nikia Reveal, Ed Maceyko, Jeanine Crossmon and Corey Favor from the University Communications Brand and Marketing at the University of Ohio, Columbus, OH. 151. Lisa Lewis of Des Moines AAF, Des Moines, IA. 152. Stephanie Parrish, Betsy Konop from the Artists Talks/Portland Art Museum, Portland, OR. 153. Mike Stone and Mark Bollman from American Field, Boston, MA. 154. Tara Nesbitt and all the good people of Atomicdust from St. Louis Design Week, Missouri, St. Louis, MO. 155. Janice Kmetz, Sandy Zimmer and Eun-Kyung Suh from the Department of Art & Design, University of Minnesota, Duluth, MN. 156. Joshua Buckwalter and Adam DelMarcelle from AIGA Central Pennsylvania, Lancaster, PA. 157. Josh Horton from Creative Works Conference, Memphis, TN. 158. Annemarie Ballard, Laurel D'Angelo, Elissa Dunn, Cari Knowlton, Ken Mortara, Russell Preston Brown, Amanda Trevino, Sandra Dyas from Adobe MAX, Los Angeles, CA. 159. Eric Hillerns, Ashley Forrette and Tsilli Pines from Designspeaks, Portland, OR. 160. Shannon Harris, Matt Harris from Big Communications, Jared Ragland from University of Alabama at Birmingham, Cary Norton and all the good people Design Week Birmingham, Birmingham, AL. 161. Rebecca Tegtmeyer, Michelle Word, Jacquelynn Sullivan from the Design Guest Lecture Series at Michigan State University, East Lansing, MI. 162. Richard Zeid, Meg Duguid and Meimei Yu of Columbia College Chicago, Chicago, IL. 163. Gwen O'Brien, Spencer High and Terra Muckenthaler of AIGA West Michigan, Kyle G. Austin of Kendall College of Art and Design, Grand Rapids, MI. 164. Hillary Ashworth, Mark Scheibmayr, Michelle Pereira, Lauren Nisbet, Allan Haley, Erik Spiekermann of the DesignThinkers Conference, Toronto, ON. 165. Gene Crawford, Giovanni DiFeterici, Jay Barry and Carl Smith of ConvergeFL in Jacksonville, FL. 166. Riley Carroll and Daryl Stevens of O'More College of Design, Franklin, TN. (Riley saved the day that morning, getting my ass to the airport, realizing I left my wallet in the room, racing back to grab it, and then racing back to the airport to get it to me. Command performance!) 167. Brigid Agricola, Amy Conover and Samantha Toombs from How Interactive Design Conference, San Francisco, CA.

2015 168. Jeff VanKleeck, Charmaine Martinez and Albert Wagner from California Polytechnic University, San Luis Obispo, CA. 169. Nick Hafner, Carolyn Jentner and Abigail Forman from University of Akron, Akron, OH. 170. Mihali Stavlas, Silke Eze, Evan Carroll, Rick Satcher, Stan Phelps from High Five Conference, Raleigh, NC. 171. Steve St. Pierre, Michael Zavacky and Meg Findlay from McMillan Advertising, Ottawa, ON. 172. Tom Futrell from Louisiana Tech, Ruston, LA. 173. John Hammer, Katie Livingston, Ruth Mudroch and Dan VanBuskirk from Art Director's Club of Tulsa, Tulsa, OK. 174. Josh Sullivan, Charlie Rosenbury and Chad Spencer from Springfield Creatives, Springfield, MO. 175. Jeremy Lanningham from Boise, ID. 176. Guenet Abraham, Michael Muccoli and Gary Rozanc from University of Maryland, Baltimore County, Baltimore, MD. 177. Geoff Peveto, Courtney Ryan, Cody Haltom and Sherri Dollar-Muñoz from Austin Design Ranch, Hunt, TX. 178. Ed Roberts and Rachael McGuffin from Triangle AdFed Clients, Creatives & Crafts, Raleigh, NC. 179. Vitaly Friedman, Nadja Völker from SmashingConf LA, Santa Monica, CA. 180. Gene Crawford, Giovanni DiFeterici and Jay Barry from GROK, Greenville, SC. 181. Greg Newland, Rindi Davodsky, Jeff Miller at Travel Portland, Portland, OR. 182. Amy Conover, Bridgid Agricola and Barb Klus from HOW Design Live 2015, Chicago, IL. 183. Franziska Parschau, Benno Rudolf, Erik Spiekermann, Jürgen Siebert and Friederike Brundiers from TYPO Berlin, Berlin, DE. 184. Ellie Robinson, Sarah Robinson and Damo Cross from Future Live Insights, Las Vegas, NV. 185. Ben Nelson from Starbucks, Seattle, Washington. 186. Matt Anderson from Struck, Portland, OR. 187. Josh Higgins, Hannah Fletcher, Ritchie Cruzado and Katie Ryan from Facebook, Menlo Park, CA. 188. Brittany Schade, Kent Smith, Kate Blizzard, Christine DeBondt from Western Washington University, Bellingham, WA. 189. Anthony "Ant" Sanders, Christian Manzella and Joel Kilby from GIANT Conference, Charleston, SC. 190. Eric Campbell, Jason Dake, Terry Tarnow from Dennos Museum, Traverse City, MI. 191., 192. & 193. Peter Moses from JMC Academy, Sydney, AU. 194. Zach Inglis and Laura Sanders from Hybrid Conference, Dublin, Ireland. 195. Shawn Pucknell, Jacqueline Poole from CAMP Festival, FITC, Calgary, AB. 196. Michele Bersani and Tommy Lincoln from AIGA Upstate NY Design Week, Syracuse, NY. 197. Arlton Lowry from Made By Few, Little Rock, AR. 198. Mitch Putnam, Justin Ishmael, Justin Brookhart, Mary Rose Wiley, David Rancatore from MondoCon, Austin, TX. 199. Laurel D'Angelo, Amanda Trevino, Velammal Lakshmanan, Judd Rogers, from Adobe MAX 2015, Los Angeles, CA. 200. Bonnie Siegler and Kathleen Budny from Command X, AIGA National Conference, New Orleans, LA. 201. Adam Wester and Kassie Scribner from Salt Lake City Design Week, Salt Lake City, UT. 202. Shawn Pucknell, Jacqueline Poole from Collide Halifax, FITC, Halifax, NS. 203. Jeffrey Zeldman and Toby Melina from An Event Apart, San Francisco, CA. 204. Andrew Boardman from GDC Manitoba, Winnipeg, MB. 205. Barbara Spanton from CanUX, Ottawa, Ontario. 206. Bradley Dicharry from the University of Iowa, Iowa City, IA. 207. & 208. Kolby McElvain and Josh Miles from AAF Indianapolis/AIGA Indianapolis and Bob Ewing and Element Three from Fuse Workshops, Indianapolis, IN.

2016 209. Samuel Romero from Florida Southern College, Lakeland, FL. 210. Lynne Allen and Evan Smith from Boston University, Boston, MA. 211. Amanda Garcia, Nicholas McMillan, Sarah Gamez and Tina Marie Lentz from Texas A&M University-Corpus Christi, Corpus Christi, TX. 212. Mike Jones from Creative South, Columbus, GA. 213. Matt Dawson From Crop Conference, Baton Rouge, LA.

In Memorium: Always thinking about: James Draplin, Emily Draplin, Gramma Josie, Grandpa Joe, Gramma Leo, Grandpa Ted, Uncle Jess, Mike "Papa" Falcone, Grandma Mary Falcone, Kevin Draplin, Auntie Chris, Jane Olson, Jimmy Kroupa, Linda Richardson, Hedy McKolay, Griffin Felt, Jason Wathen, Claudia Hickman, Chance McDowell, Vicky Perkins, Kris Okins, Warren Brosch, Mike Vihon, Little Renvek, Katie Barrett, Eric Stutsman, Bill Roemer, Nathan Miller, Harry Pletcher, Matt Adelizzi and John Hughes.

Four-legged Friends: Gary, Toby, Zöe, Zack, Charlie, Bagel, Zen and Otto.

A Sad, Surreal Thank You to So Many: I got so many wonderful condolence letters when Dad died, and just didn't know how to reply. One part overwhelmed, and one part sad as hell. But please know, I appreciated every single one of them, and have them with all of Dad's materials from that sad October of 2013.

Apologies: And, damn, if we forgot you, well, chalk it up as, "just another example of me being the horrible person I am." Too many commas in that sentence.

And Finally, Those Who Can Suck It: The turd who ruined a cool part of Southeast Portland for me—the lowest of the low. The restaurant guy who will never be let in my corner of the shop again, ever. The pricks in that Indiana cornfield, that one time. The couple of scumbags who ripped me off. Various stubborn trade show union dicks who wouldn't lift a finger to let me use a cart or dolley, sitting there, on their smoke break. Mean-spirited post office clerks. A couple choice web developers. Anyone who gave me a dirty look while boarding a plane.

Colophon

Draplin Design Co.
Pretty Much Everything
Aaron James Draplin

Designed, Edited, Sweated-Over, Scanned-In, Tuned-Up, Tuned A Full Step Down, Schemed-Up, Paginated, Fretted Over, Backed Up, Kerned, Dug Out of Dark Corners, Color-Corrected and Lived by Aaron James Draplin, Draplin Design Co.

Guidance, goading and therapy from John Gall.

With assistance from a team of articulate, patient people at Abrams in New York City:
Editors: John Gall with Sarah Massey
Managing Editor: Gabriel Levinson
Production Manager: Denise LaCongo
Design Manager: Devin Grosz
Copy Editor: Rob Sternitzky
Proofreading: Angus Johnston
Around-the-Shop Photography Assistance: John "Goo" Phemister and David Nakamoto
August 2015 Design Assistant: Cory Loven

Photography Notes: Front Flyleaf: Portrait by Michael Poehlman. Page 002: Portrait by Derek Giltner. Page 005: Portrait by Aaron Okayama. Pages: 008-011: Photos courtesy of Draplin family archives. Page 019: Action photos by Chad Smith, except "Hitting Jumps on Cinder Cone" by Quinn Shields. Page 025: "Leaner, meaner..." photo by Eric Campbell. Page 032-033: Photo by Dave England. Page 038: Photo by David Nakamoto. Page 073: Photos courtesy of Cobra Dogs. Page 076: "What's Good For His Mouth is Good For Mine" photo by Tim Zimmerman. Pages 088-089 & 092-093: Product photography by Mark Welsh. Page 101: "Aaron & Jim" photo by Leigh McKolay. Pages 108-111: Product photography by Bryan Bedell/Field Notes archives. Page 147: "Aaron & Dad' photo by Leigh McKolay. Page 182-183: Photo by Jess Gibson. Page 186: "Aaron bending over" photo by Jared Eberhardt. Page 187: "Aaron looking up at Jared" photo by Leigh McKolay. Page 190: Inset photos by Jan Van Kleeck. Pages 194-195: Photo by Leigh McKolay. Page 203: Photos courtesy of Deckstarter. Page 205: Photo by Leigh McKolay. Page 206-211: Shop photography by Neil Dacosta. Page 215: Photos courtesy of Finex Cast Iron Cookware Co. Page 216: Photograph by Pete Souza. (From the White House: This photograph is provided by THE WHITE HOUSE as a courtesy and may be printed by the subject(s) in the photograph for personal use only. The photograph may not be manipulated in any way and may not otherwise be reproduced, disseminated or broadcast, without the written permission of the White House Photo Office. This photograph may not be used in any commercial or political materials, advertisements, emails, products, promotions that in any way suggests approval or endorsement of the President, the First Family, or the White House.) Page 219: Photography by Jess Gibson. Page 222-223: Photo by Nate Croft. Page 247: "Ultra-Deep Field" photo by the Hubble Telescope, courtesy of NASA. Page 249: Photo by Ryan "Ryno" Simonson. 252-254: Photos courtesy of Draplin family archives. Inside back cover: Portrait by Leah Nash.

Production Notes: The typefaces used in this book are "Lubalin Graph Bold" for the big stuff, and then "Helvetica Medium" and "Helvetica Bold" everywhere else. The decision to go with Lubalin Graph is a nod to Herb Lubalin and his brilliant, vibrant typefaces and body of work. Max Miedinger and Eduard Hoffmann's incomparable Helvetica has always offered a modern, orderly quality and still feels as fresh today, as it did when we first saw it in the late 1970s on that big Space Shuttle and on 1980s Legoland packaging. The so-called "design" of the book follows a simple grid, inspired by three-column Joseph Müller Brockman layouts. Sort of a "simple, orderly architecture, filled up with garbage" kind of thing. Remember all that bullshit post-modern, damaged, scritchity, scratchity bullshit from the mid-1990s? You don't? Precisely. The books within an arm's reach during the making of this book: *The Untold Stories Behind 29 Logos, 100 Years of Swiss Graphic Design, Josef Müller Brockman: Pioneer of Swiss Graphic Design, Herb Lubalin: American Graphic Designer, Saul Bass, Hello I Am Erik, Lester Beall: Trailblazer of American Graphic Design, Otl Aicher, Paul Rand, FHK Henrion, Some People Can't Surf: The Graphic Design of Art Chantry, Victore: or, Who Died and Made You Boss?, Manuals 1: Design & Identity Guidelines, Manuals 2: Design & Identity Guidelines, Trade Marks & Symbols 1, Trade Marks & Symbols 2, The Art of Coop: Devil's Advocate* and *Lance Wyman: The Monograph.* You'll notice a 5th-color hit of "Pantone Orange 021" spot color all the way through the book, in keeping with our "as orange as possible" over-arching DDC policy. 256 pages, filled up the best we could. But really, with the cover, back cover and end papers, that's like 262 pages, but who's counting? 8" x 10" in dimension. That's roughly 1,746 square feet of real estate. The innards are 157gsm Matte Art smooth, coated paper. The end pages are 140gsm W/F uncoated paper. We'd be baldfaced liars if we told you we didn't feel bad about the trees that were cut down to make this mess. The cover is "Wibalin over 3mm board" utilizing the thickest stuff we could get our hands on. Printed far away by specialists in China. We exhausted all options for printing, first starting with stateside quotes and were told "That's about the best we can do" and took it all overseas. We'd like to thank the good people who printed, collated and assembled this book, although you still remain a bit of a mystery to us. This book was written, designed and edited from the middle of May 2015 to the absolute, patience-tested, "no more favors" latest possible part of October 2015. No pants were worn in the making of this book.

What It's Like Making a Book: Getting rolling on this thing was challenging. With all projects—big, small, pretty or ugly—I pride myself on knowing how to plan my attack, and then execute. But here, I was second-guessing myself. That same old shit along the lines of "I can't believe I get to make a book," and "Am I even worthy of a book?" as well as the ever-haunting "Sure don't want to let anyone down" sentiments, were and still are nipping at my heels. John Gall was a name I already knew from the book-design world through his incredible collage work. When he first e-mailed me, I freaked out. On one hand, I knew I was in good company. But on the other, I was freaked out that I got the call up to the big leagues. My very first reaction was to sort of recoil and question if I was ready for something like this. Did I have enough work to show? Or enough perspective? I knew I had a mountain of stuff, but the scariest part still haunted me: Would people dig it? And, as I'm writing this—from Mom's dining room table in Michigan—hell, I've still got those jitters. I remember looking at who Abrams was after I got the big call. They did the Victore and Sagmeister books, and that blew me away! Those were big names... big personalities... and big careers! All big. From the get-go, it was hard to envision my book being out there among design heavies like those guys. Plus, "Draplin" would fall close to "Eames" on their roster. Not bad!

Self-Publishing Jitters: And of course, I got a little cocky. There's a big part of me that wanted to do this whole thing completely on my own. I mean, my buddy Frank Chimero did it beautifully—with his writing, design and promotion—so maybe I could, too? But then again, Frank said that when it was time to deliver the goods, things got a little weird. Being an indie band is a tough go; little things become big things, and quick. And hell, did I have enough space in the garage to store all those books? And, hell, I still don't really know what an ISBN number is. This was my shot. I wanted to enjoy the process of making a book. As you get it going, you freak out that a project of this magnitude will turn into "another client." You know: Where you have to scratch and claw to get back up to the keyboard to actually work on the stuff. If left up to my own devices, I would've stretched this thing out a couple years, hemming, hawing, whining, wheezing and so on. So thank you to John, Sarah and Gabriel at Abrams, for pushing me along.

What I Hope This Book Accomplishes: I hope a kid who reads it will be inspired to look at a life in design in a little bit different way than the schlock that's fed to us. You don't have to hate your job. You don't have to accept working for clients who push you around. You can build your own life. Let the last 256 pages be a big, meaty finger waved in the face of "How they told me it was gonna be."

Rig Specs: Apple Mac Pro 3.5 GHz 6-Core Intel Xeon E5, 32 GB RAM super tube with 1 TB Flash hard drive, running OS X El Capitan 10.11. Two flickering Apple Cinema HD Display 30-incher monitors, where the shit goes down the main one and on the second one, our palettes, iTunes, iChat and Twitter. A third Apple Thunderbolt Display 27-inch monitor for battling excessive e-mail threads and dinging notifications. An Apple 15.4-incher MacBook Pro, Retina Display, 2.8 GHz Intel Core i7, 16 GB RAM, 1 TB Flash Hard Drive for the road use, e-mail and hammering on shit while on planes. Apple 128 GB iPhone 6 that we can't seem to put down. Apple 32 GB iPad. Hewlett Packard 1200 Toner Printer. ("Old Faithful.") Epson V600 Flatbed Scanner. (Precariously on loan from Nakamoto.) 14-incher Wacom tablet, used maybe once a year. Pegasus 8 GB External Hard Drive (Client Archives.) G-Technology 500 GB High-Speed Portable Drive (Road Archives). Lacie 1TB External Hard Drive. (Backup for items 10 & 11.) Lacie 3TB External Hard Drive. (Backup for items 09-11.) Lacie 500GB Rugged Hard Disk. (For DDC Mobile Command Unit.) Eye One Display II Gretag color calibrator. 80 GB iPod for DDC Open Road missions. Fujifilm X100S 16.3 MP with 20mm Pancake Lens. Canon EOS 30d Digital SLR. Canon 7D Digital SLR with 24-70mm Zoom Lens, using natural Portland light that spilled in through our big windows. Canon Elan II E, 28/80mm, SLR Camera. (Automatic as shit.) Transcend USB 3.0 Super Speed Multi-Card Reader (Unknowingly on loan from Goo.) Apple World Travel Adapter Kit. (For when we "go global," y'know?) Apple Airport. Bose 40274 Companion 2 Series II MultiMedia Speakers. Apple Cordless Magic Mouse. Apple Wireless Keyboard. Bose Quiet-Comfort 25 Acoustic Noise Cancelling Headphones. Lots of cords all tangled to hell. Steelcase 30" x 72" Currency Founder Desk, 30" x 48" Currency author Desk and 30" x 72" Currency Editor Desk, all in "Virginia Walnut" colorway. 36 Flor "Working Class/Dark Grey" carpet tiles, Herman Miller Aeron "graphite frame/ graphite base" chair in the "Large" size. 2008 Martin D-35 acoustic guitar, 2013 Fender American Vintage '65 Reissue Jazzmaster Aztec Gold electric guitar, 2005 Koll Duo Glide electric guitar in "Maple", 1986 Fender Japanese Telecaster electric guitar in "Black/White", 1998 DeArmond Jet Star Guild S-200 Tribute electric guitar in "Green Machine Green", 2013 Thunderbird Non-Reverse bass guitar in "Pelham Blue", 1998 DeArmond Jet Star Guild tribute electric bass in "Death Black", 1954 Fender Champ 5C1 amp, 2010 Fender Bassman TV Fifteen Combo 350W 120V bass amp. Filson Briefcase Computer Bag in "Tan", Medium Duffle Bag in "Tan" and Extra Large Rolling Duffle in "Tan" for lugging gear around town and on the road. Carhartt Men's 3XL Tall Denim Jean Jacket in "Authentic Blue." Cabela's Roughneck 3XL Tall Nylon Packable Jacket in "Burnt Orange." Various Saucony Jazz, Shadow and Shadow 5000 kicks in an array of colors. One iron will.

You can find us on the web:
draplin.com
fieldnotesbrand.com
ddcbook.com

Library of Congress Control Number: 2015949569

ISBN: 978-1-4197-2017-8

Copyright © 2016 Aaron James Draplin, Draplin Design Co.

Published in 2016 by Abrams, an imprint of ABRAMS. All rights reserved. No portion of this book may be reproduced, stored in a retrieval system, or transmitted in any form or by any means, mechanical, electronic, photocopying, recording, or otherwise, without written permission from the publisher.

Printed and bound in China.

10

Abrams books are available at special discounts when purchased in quantity for premiums and promotions as well as fundraising or educational use. Special editions can also be created to specification.

For details, contact specialsales@abramsbooks.com or the address below.

ABRAMS The Art of Books
195 Broadway, New York, NY 10007
abramsbooks.com